REGENTS CRITICS SERIES

General Editor: Paul A. Olson

LITERARY CRITICISM OF
WILLIAM WORDSWORTH

Other volumes of the Regents Critics Series are:

Literary Criticism of William Wordsworth

Edited by

Paul M. Zall

UNIVERSITY OF NEBRASKA PRESS · LINCOLN

4 0 1 1

Regents Critics Series

The Regents Critics Series provides reading texts of significant literary critics in the Western tradition. The series treats criticism as a useful tool: an introduction to the critic's own poetry and prose if he is a poet or novelist, an introduction to other work in his day if he is more judge than creator. Nowhere is criticism regarded as an end in itself but as what it is—a means to the understanding of the language of art as it has existed and been understood in various periods and societies.

Each volume includes a scholarly introduction which describes how the work collected came to be written, and suggests its uses. All texts are edited in the most conservative fashion consonant with the production of a good reading text; and all translated texts observe the dictum that the letter gives life and the spirit kills when a technical or rigorous passage is being put into English. Other types of passages may be more freely treated. Footnoting and other scholarly paraphernalia are restricted to the essential minimum. Such features as a bibliographical checklist are carried where they are appropriate to the work in hand. If a volume is the first collection of the author's critical writing, this is noted in the bibliographical data.

PAUL A. OLSON

University of Nebraska

v

Contents

Introduction

Wordsworth was primarily a practicing critic. His critical essays synthesize a number of principles current in the eighteenth century and redirect the focus of criticism to the operations of the mind in creating and appreciating poetry. But he was less concerned with setting up a consistent aesthetic system than with explaining the practical powers of poetry to a practical-minded public. He believed that poetry had the power to medicine men's minds by providing the inner man release from the pressures of the outer world. In an age when social, political, and economic pressures mounted "almost hourly," men's need for poetry increased proportionally. Poetry could provide healing sensations that would exercise the imagination in creative activity and stimulate awareness of man's brotherhood in a universe bonded by love. Wordsworth believed, in short, that the ultimate aim of poetry was no less than the regeneration of society.

As a practicing poet, Wordsworth wrote about poetry in terms of his own work, explaining or defending his practice, especially when it conflicted with conventional ideas of what poetry ought to be. To Wordsworth, contemporary ideas about poetry were based on the practice of Alexander Pope, but Wordsworth found Pope overly concerned with "manners," his language incongruous with the feelings of men, his descriptions of nature inaccurate. Moreover, he thought Pope's antithetical mode of expression in the heroic couplet placed equal emphasis on agreeable and disagreeable passions. If poetry were to achieve its highest aim, Wordsworth insisted, it must emphasize agreeable passions only. Dissatisfied with Pope, then, he turned for his models to earlier poets—Chaucer, Spenser, Shakespeare, Milton. Their concerns were with morals rather than manners; their language was accurately expressive of recognizable passions; their descriptions had the fidelity of eye-witness reports; and their subjects were healthy, elemental passions. They were to provide the pattern for the resurrection of poetry.

Wordsworth's initial strategy was to let the poems in the *Lyrical Ballads* of 1798 speak for themselves, with only a brief note that they differed from contemporary poetry by way of experiment. Most of the practicing critics who reviewed the poems were sympathetic, since Wordsworth and his collaborator Coleridge were well enough schooled in eighteenth-century poetics that they conformed to requirements of decorum and verisimilitude: adjusting the form of the poem to the subject, the materials to the form, and the language to the materials. Wordsworth's additional requirement of psychological accuracy and preference for elemental passions meant that his subjects, materials, and language were on a level lower than usual in serious poetry; but so long as they were held in nice balance, the reviewers applauded his genius.[1] For the edition of 1800, however, Wordsworth acceded to Coleridge's urgings for a prefatory essay explaining what he was trying to do and why.[2] He emphasized the need to cleanse poetry of "false refinement" and "artificial devices" which, as everyone knew, derived from Pope. And, more, the title page now carried Wordsworth's name and also a motto that translates: "This is not for your taste, follower of Pope!" This arrogant contempt for conventional standards, not the poems in *Lyrical Ballads*, roused the wrath of the professional reviewers.

A new breed of professional reviewer appeared with the founding of the *Edinburgh Review* in October, 1802. Led by Francis Jeffrey, its reviewers composed expansive dissertations, in contrast to earlier reviews that were seldom more than notes connecting lengthy quotations. Further, the *Edinburgh* reviewers used the book under discussion merely as a springboard to talk about general principles, and frequently used scurrilous ridicule to dismiss a book swiftly, particularly when it displayed insufficient enthusiasm for conventional standards of taste or Whig politics. Wordsworth, of course, became Jeffrey's prime target from the outset, and the target of

1. E.g., *Monthly Mirror*, VI (October 1798): "The author has certainly accomplished his purpose . . . . If this style were more generally adopted, it would tend to correct that depraved taste, occasioned by an incessant *importation* from the press of *sonnets* and other poems, which has already made considerable inroads upon the judgment" (p. 224).

2. *Times Literary Supplement*, April 28, 1950, p. 261.

other reviewers aspiring to Jeffrey's popular success. He was accused of degrading the province and language of poetry, of debasing his talents out of sheer perversity. When *Poems in Two Volumes* appeared in 1807, Jeffrey ridiculed Wordsworth's "infantine simplicity" ("All the world laughs at Elegiac stanzas to a sucking-pig . . . or Pindarics on gooseberry pye . . . .") and raged at his "wrong-headedness" in continuing this vein after having been warned against it.[3] Swarms of satirists swooped in following Jeffrey's attack, and Wordsworth refrained from publishing books of poetry for seven years because of the "public outcry."[4]

Though he withheld the bulk of the poetry he continued to compose, Wordsworth did not hesitate to publish prose, especially in 1809–1810 when Coleridge issued his weekly journal, *The Friend*. Wordsworth wrote a long essay on epitaphs that introduced itself as the first in a series devoted to clarifying basic principles in poetry. Unfortunately, *The Friend* went out of business before the series could continue. Drafts of two other essays, however, show that they constituted a reply to Jeffrey, striking pointedly at Pope and Dr. Johnson and aiming to discredit the Popean standard.

Then, beginning in 1814, after years of withholding his poems, Wordsworth published three major poetical works within twelve months. The *Excursion* appeared first, and met Jeffrey's notorious review beginning "This will never do!"[5] But the publication of the book in a sumptuous, expensive edition marked Wordsworth's declaration of independence from Jeffrey and the public for which he stood. Asserting his independence more explicitly, he included a preface Miltonic in defiance and in dedication to an audience "fit though few." He declared that he was submitting to the judgment of time the contest between the validity of his imagination and the standards of Popean convention. Some months later, the preface to a completely new arrangement of his collected *Poems* explained schoolmasterly what he meant by validity of imagination, and its appendix showed historically that in poetry, popularity and immortality most often stand in inverse relationship. Jeffrey greeted

3. *Edinburgh Review*, XI (October 1807), 218.
4. See *Middle Years*, pp. 184–185, 419.
5. *Edinburgh Review*, XXIV (June 1815), 1–30.

the third major work, *The White Doe of Rylstone*, by suggesting that Wordsworth must now be a confirmed drunkard or a madman,[6] and the issue became one of personal rather than critical abuse. Wordsworth replied in kind, in his *Letter to a Friend of Robert Burns*, thereafter remaining silent in public about poets, poetry, and periodical reviewers.

The effects of Jeffrey's criticism were particularly harmful to a poet trying to earn a living with poetry. A sinecure and additional income contributed to Wordsworth's independence in 1814, but he was still faced with the problem of creating the taste by which he could be enjoyed and by which he could achieve the goal he had set for his poetry. Resigned to writing for posterity, he nevertheless complained in 1816: "The state of the public Mind is at present little adapted to relish any part of my poetical effusion. . . . There is . . . too much real distress, and above all too much imaginary depression, and downright party spirit."[7]

Ten years later, however, his poems were congenial to the public mind. Significantly, it was about this time that publishers refused to issue poetry as quite unsalable, and the quarterly reviews declined in the face of steady gains by magazines "for the people," dedicated to self-help and moral uplift rather than politics, poetics, or polemics. Wordsworth's poems conformed to requirements for utility: John Stuart Mill described their effect on him during a nervous breakdown as "medicine for my state of mind." "They seemed to be the very culture of the feelings, which I was in quest of. In them I seemed to draw from a source of inward joy, of sympathy and imaginative pleasure which could be shared in by all human beings . . . ."[8] Wordsworth would have replied: "Of course!"

Wordsworth had planned such reaction to his poems as Mill described. His theory and practice were both vindicated. It is well to keep in mind, however, that the theory developed out of the practice, in explanation of it, though the outlines of Wordsworth's plan were evident in the Preface of 1800. He said there that to

6. *Edinburgh Review*, XXV (October 1815), 335.

7. *Middle Years*, p. 721.

8. *Autobiography*, ed. J. J. Cass (New York: Columbia University Press, 1924), p. 104.

explain his poetry properly would require analyzing the health of national taste, but this would require showing how language and the mind interact and retracing revolutions in literature and society. He accomplished all this by 1816, but in no systematic fashion. Only at the risk, then, of making him appear more systematic than he was, can we piece together broad outlines of his principles.

Wordsworth's chief concern is with the capability of poetry to restore man's spiritual powers by bridging the gap between the world about him and the world within. Since John Locke's time, it had been generally accepted that the world and its perceiver were separate entities; that the "secondary qualities" of abstraction and the "primary qualities" of sensation were distinctly discrete; and that sensation was the only mode of perceiving the world, while subsequent reflection led to developing abstract ideas about it. The problem for Wordsworth is that man is now lost to the tranquillizing, uplifting sensations abounding in natural surroundings. Further, selfish pursuits have separated him from other men; neglect of reflection has blinded him to the connection between the natural and the moral worlds. Wordsworth's solution is poetry that will stimulate beneficent sensations, reawaken sympathy, and revivify the reflective powers of the mind. He tries to link the external and the internal worlds by recreating precise forms of nature with all the breath and spirit of associations inherent in them. As the forms of nature are symbols of some higher order, so Wordsworth displays them "not as they exist in themselves, but as they *seem* to exist to the *senses* and to the *passions*."[9] In this aspect, nothing in nature exists in absolute singleness, but in the context of all past experience and in relation to the present state of the mind perceiving it (as dramatically projected in "Tintern Abbey").

The real concerns of poetry, like those of religion, are with abstractions "too weighty for the mind to support them without relieving itself by resting a great part of the burthen upon words and symbols."[10] Thus Wordsworth employs language as a symbolic reflection of the mind in motion, reacting with its environment, which takes on the coloration of both primary qualities inherent

9. See p. 160
10. See p. 163

in natural forms and secondary qualities developed and developing in the mind. In this way his poetry conveys the spirit as well as the letter of what it is talking about, bridging the two worlds of man, internal and external, spiritual and material, subjective and objective.

This kind of poetry requires a high order of poetic skill. Wordsworth insists upon poetic language that is more than Pope's "dress of thought," but that is also an incarnation of the process that created it with impurities pruned by the poet's judgment. The poet had first to identify the experience he would describe, then analyze and reflect upon it, working it over in the crucible of his imagination. Then he would decide upon the fittest vehicle for its expression, and rigorously select his words for accuracy of connotation as well as denotation. Properly expressive language would be at once rhythmical and figuratively exact because it is associated with elemental feelings. Meter would provide added pleasure through recognizable regularity in constant change, similitude in dissimilitude. Prose might serve to convey the expression, but it would be less pleasurable; and pleasure was essential to the operations of the mind Wordsworth aimed to simulate and stimulate.

Obviously skill alone is not enough. The true poet is blessed, in addition, with a highly sensitized mind that rediscovers truths so common as to have been ignored and forgotten, yet laden with beneficent associations. To foster this sensitivity in the minds of less fortunate men, Wordsworth proposed to provide his imagination as surrogate for theirs, and thus concentrates on analyzing and demonstrating its operations. In a note to "The Thorn" in 1800, he calls imagination "the faculty which produces impressive effects out of simple elements."[11] In the Preface of 1815, he discriminates it from fancy, which depends more on recall and willful combinations of definite objects, by saying that imagination copes with the indefinite and the illimitable, analyzing, unifying, and evoking familiar objects in new illuminations.[12] One of the unpublished essays for *The Friend* had spoken of familiar sensations as "grounded upon the universal intellectual property of men," so

11. See p. 12.
12. See p. 153.

that when properly manipulated they could be used to express truths "in their whole compass with the freshness and clearness of an original intuition."[13] By focusing his attention on the role of the imagination in the interplay of mind and environment, Wordsworth rediscovered an endless vein of mental operations as a source and an end of poetry.

Wordsworth often uses "imagination" in a sense synonymous with earlier notions of "right reason." In this aspect, the faculty plays the crucial role in the creative process, actively striving to achieve mastery of both the internal and the external worlds, not satisfied with knowledge of either world alone. The poet may receive intense delight from his sensations, and an equal pleasure from realizing the imagination's dominance over his sense impressions, but it is this higher faculty that combines both kinds of pleasure for a higher pleasure still, such as is experienced when the "intimations" celebrated in the "Intimations Ode" are refined into "assurances." Even discursive reason plays a role in the poetic process, as the "recollecting" or organizing faculty that channels overflow of feeling and prunes expression of disagreeable elements. Applied in criticism, discursive reason, along with imagination in all its operations, engages the letter and the spirit of the text in a search for common sense and psychological accuracy, summed up as "truth to nature." Lacking this truth, a work cannot find a place in a healthy mind and fails in its fundamental aim.

The practical problem Wordsworth faced was to create the taste that would enable his poetry to achieve its aim, when it was much easier for people to appreciate the titillating sensations and facile abstractions of the followers of Pope. Yet he insisted upon doing it his way: "I have not written down to the level of superficial observers and unthinking minds. Every great Poet is a Teacher; I wish either to be considered as a Teacher, or as nothing."[14] He insisted on truth in the letter as well as the spirit. When a critic alluded to the poem "on Daffodils reflected in the water," Wordsworth exclaimed: "How is it possible for flowers to be *reflected* in water where there are *waves*?"[15] This passion for accuracy carried over into his criticism

13. See pp. 117–118.
14. *Middle Years*, p. 170.   15. *Ibid.*

also, and he read the texts of others as carefully as he composed his own. He had selected his language with care and expected readers to read it accordingly. But this, of course, put too much of a burden on readers who looked upon poetry as mere entertainment or memorable restatements of "what oft was thought." Wordsworth shifted the focus of poetry to "what oft was felt" and was forced to wait until people realigned their reading habits.

Rightly confident that he would eventually be appreciated, Wordsworth received fame, honors, and financial satisfaction in his later years. Yet his greatest personal satisfaction is found reflected in the Postscript to the 1835 edition of his *Poems*. It is concerned almost entirely with discussion of public morality and civic affairs, but he concluded with fifty-four lines from Book XII of the (then unpublished) *Prelude*, recapitulating his service to the people in medicining their minds. There was no longer need for explanation or defense of his poetic principles or his practice, for his way had been justified.

Note on the Text

This edition provides complete texts of Wordsworth's major critical essays, plus excerpts from letters and other material illustrating or expanding upon the major essays. Though often reprinted, the major essays have seldom been presented in their early versions, which more accurately reflect the movement of Wordsworth's ideas over twenty years. For this reason two early versions are given of the Preface to *Lyrical Ballads*, and the editorial practice departs from standard procedure in the Regents Critics Series in not modernizing the text. Typographical corrections and emendations have been introduced silently because justifying each correction would overload the notes. Wordsworth's own notes are placed in brackets in the footnotes, with the letter *W*.

The texts are based on first editions in the Wordsworth Collection of the Cornell University Library and in the Henry E. Huntington Library. Letters have been checked against manuscripts whenever possible. They have been published in a uniform edition with the poetical works by the Clarendon Press: *Letters of William and Dorothy Wordsworth*, ed. Ernest de Selincourt and Helen Darbishire

(6 vols.; Oxford: Clarendon Press, 1935–1939); *Early Letters* (1787–1805); *Middle Years* (1806–1820) in two volumes; and *Later Years* (1821–1850) in three volumes. Citations in the notes refer to these volumes. References to *Poetical Works* are to *Poetical Works of William Wordsworth*, ed. Ernest de Selincourt and Helen Darbishire (5 vols.; Oxford: Clarendon Press, 1940–1949, 1954). References to *The Prelude* are to *The Prelude*, ed. Ernest de Selincourt (Oxford: Oxford University Press, 1928).

PAUL M. ZALL

California State College at Los Angeles

LITERARY CRITICISM OF
WILLIAM WORDSWORTH

In the following selections, three asterisks (* * *) indicate that a portion of the original has been omitted.

Preface to "The Borderers" (1797)

Wordsworth composed "The Borderers" in the winter of 1795–1796 as a closet drama, to be read rather than staged. The Preface was prepared in the spring of 1797 when he revised the play for the stage. When the play was rejected, Wordsworth put it aside until 1842, when he revised it thoroughly, again as closet drama, and included it among his collected poems, but without the Preface. The play is pseudo-Shakespearean tragedy, imitative of Othello but with scenes of terror and sentimentality more like the Gothic novel: Set in the thirteenth century, the plot focuses on the villainous Rivers, who works Iago-like on Mortimer, the noble chief of a robber band on the Scotch border, to lead him along the path of degeneration he himself had traveled after having been deceived into killing the father of the woman he loved. Now he deceives Mortimer into doing away with the father of the woman Mortimer loves. After the crime, Rivers confesses to his treachery. Mortimer goes mad temporarily (as Rivers had done), but instead of following Rivers' path, he goes off to seek expiation for his sin, while Rivers meets death at the hands of Mortimer's troops. The Preface explaining the theory behind the play was not published until 1926.

Let us suppose a young man of great intellectual powers yet without any solid principles of genuine benevolence. His master passions are pride and the love of distinction. He has deeply imbibed a spirit of enterprise in a tumultuous age. He goes into the world and is betrayed into a great crime. That influence on which all his happiness is built immediately deserts him. His talents are robbed of their weight, his exertions are unavailing, and he quits the world in disgust, with strong misanthropic feelings. In his retirement he is impelled to examine the unreasonableness of established opinions; and the force of his mind exhausts itself in constant efforts to separate the elements of virtue and vice. It is his pleasure and his consolation to hunt out whatever is bad in actions usually esteemed virtuous, and to detect the good in actions which the universal sense of mankind teaches us to reprobate. While the general exertion of his intellect seduces him from the remembrance of his own crime, the particular conclusions to which he is led have a tendency to reconcile him to himself. His feelings are interested in making him a moral sceptic, and as his scepticism increases he is raised in his own esteem. After this process has been continued some time his natural energy and restlessness impel him again into the world. In this state, pressed by the recollection of his guilt, he seeks relief from two sources, action and meditation. Of actions those are most attractive which best exhibit his own powers, partly from the original pride of his own character, and still more because the loss of authority and influence which followed upon his crime was the first circumstance which impressed him with the magnitude of that crime, and brought along with it those tormenting sensations by which he is assailed. The recovery of his original importance and the exhibition of his own powers are, therefore, in his mind almost identified with the extinction of those powerful feelings which attend the recollection of his guilt. Perhaps there is no cause which has greater weight in preventing the return of bad men to virtue than that good actions being for the most part in their nature silent and regularly progressive, they do not present those sudden results which can afford a sufficient stimulus to a troubled mind. In processes of vice the effects are more frequently immediate, palpable and extensive. Power is much more easily manifested in destroying than in creating. A child, Rousseau has observed, will tear in pieces fifty toys before he will think of making one.[1] From these causes, assisted by disgust and misanthropic feeling, the character we are now contemplating will have a strong tendency to vice. His energies are most impressively manifest in works of devastation. He is the Orlando of Ariosto, the Cardenio of Cervantes, who lays waste the groves that should shelter him. He has rebelled against the world and the laws of the world, and he regards them as tyrannical masters; convinced that he is right in some of his conclusions, he nourishes a contempt for mankind the more dangerous because he has been led to it by reflection. Being in the habit of considering the world as a body

1. See *Emilius* (2 vols.; London, 1763), I, 57–58.

which is in some sort of war with him, he has a feeling borrowed from that habit which gives an additional zest to his hatred of those members of society whom he hates and to his own contempt of those whom he despises. Add to this, that a mind fond of nourishing sentiments of contempt will be prone to the admission of those feelings which are considered under any uncommon bond of relation (as must be the case with a man who has quarrelled with the world), and the feelings will mutually strengthen each other. In this morbid state of mind he cannot exist without occupation, he requires constant provocations, all his pleasures are prospective, he is perpetually invoking a phantom, he commits new crimes to drive away the memory of the past. But the lenitives of his pain are twofold, meditation as well as action. Accordingly, his reason is almost exclusively employed in justifying his past enormities and in enabling him to commit new ones. He is perpetually imposing upon himself, he has a sophism for every crime. The *mild* effusions of thought, the milk of human reason are unknown to him. His imagination is powerful, being strengthened by the habit of picturing possible forms of society where his crimes would be no longer crimes, and he would enjoy that estimation to which, from his intellectual attainments, he deems himself entitled. The nicer shades of manners he disregards; but whenever upon looking back upon past ages, or in surveying the practices of different countries in the age in which he lives, he finds such contrarieties as seem to affect the principles of *morals*, he exults over his discovery, and applies it to his heart as the dearest of consolations. Such a mind cannot but discover some truths, but he is unable to profit by them, and in his hands they become instruments of evil.

He presses truth and falsehood into the same service. He looks at society through an optical glass of a peculiar tint; something of the forms of objects he takes from objects, but their colour is exclusively what he gives them; it is one, and it is his own. Having indulged a habit, dangerous in a man who has fallen, of dallying with moral calculations, he becomes an empiric, and a daring and unfeeling empiric. He disguises from himself his own malignity by assuming the character of a speculator in morals, and one who has the hardihood to realize his speculations.

It will easily be perceived that to such a mind those enterprizes which are most extraordinary will in time appear the most inviting. His appetite from being exhausted becomes unnatural. Accordingly he will struggle so to characterize and to exalt actions little and contemptible in themselves by a forced greatness of *manner*, and will chequer and degrade enterprizes great in their atrocity by grotesque littleness of manner and fantastic obliquities. He is like a worn out voluptuary—he finds his temptation in strangeness, he is unable to suppress a low hankering after the double entendre in vice; yet his thirst after the extraordinary buoys him up, and supported by a habit of constant reflexion he frequently breaks out into what has the appearance of greatness; and in sudden emergencies, when he is called upon by surprize and thrown out of the path of his regular habits, or when dormant associations are awakened tracing the revolutions through which his character has passed, in painting his former self he really *is* great.

Benefits conferred on a man like this will be the seeds of a worse feeling than ingratitude. They will give birth to positive hatred. Let him be deprived of power, though by means which he despises, and he will never forgive. It will scarcely be denied that such a mind, by very slight external motives, may be led to the commission of the greatest enormities. Let its malignant feelings be fixed on a particular object, and the rest follows of itself.

Having shaken off the obligations of religion and morality in a dark and tempestuous age, it is probable that such a character will be infected with a tinge of superstition. The period in which he lives teems with great events which he feels he cannot control. That influence which his pride makes him unwilling to allow to his fellow-men he has no reluctance to ascribe to invisible agents: his pride impels him to superstition and shapes the nature of his belief: his creed is his own: it is made and not adopted.

A character like this, or some of its features at least, I have attempted to delineate in the following drama. I have introduced him deliberately prosecuting the destruction of an amiable young man by the most atrocious means, and with a pertinacity, as it should seem, not to be accounted for but on the supposition of the most malignant injuries. No such injuries however appear to have been sustained. What then are his motives? First it must be observed that to make the non-existence of a common motive itself a motive to action is a practice which we are never so prone to attribute exclusively to madmen as when we forget ourselves. Our love of the marvellous is not confined to external things. There is no object on which it settles with more delight than on our own minds. This habit is in the very essence of the habit which we are delineating.

But there are particles of that poisonous mineral of which Iago speaks gnawing his inwards;[2] his malevolent feelings are excited, and he hates the more deeply because he feels he ought not to hate.

We all know that the dissatisfaction accompanying the first impulses towards a criminal action, where the mind is familiar with guilt, acts as a stimulus to proceed in that action. Uneasiness must be driven away by fresh uneasiness, obstinacy, waywardness and wilful blindness are alternatives resorted to, till there is an universal insurrection of every depraved feeling of the heart.

Besides, in a course of criminal conduct every fresh step that we make appears a justification of the one which preceded it, it seems to bring again the moment of liberty and choice; it banishes the idea of repentance, and seems to set remorse at defiance. Every time we plan a fresh accumulation of our guilt we have restored to us something like that original state of mind, that perturbed pleasure, which first made the crime attractive.

If after these general remarks, I am asked what are Rivers's motives to the atrocity detailed in the drama, I answer they are founded chiefly on the very constitution of his character; in his pride which borders even upon madness; in his restless disposition; in his disturbed mind; in his superstition; in irresistible propensities to embody in practical experiments his worst and most extravagant speculations; in his thoughts and in his feelings; in his perverted reason justifying his perverted instincts. The general moral intended to be impressed by the delineation of such a character is obvious—it is to shew the dangerous use which may be made of reason when a man has committed a great crime.

There is a kind of superstition which makes us shudder when we find moral sentiments to which we attach a sacred importance applied to vicious purposes. In real life this is done every day, and

2. *Othello*, II.i.306.

we do not feel the disgust. The difference is here. In works of imagination we see the motive and the end. In real life we rarely see either the one or the other; and when the distress comes it prevents us from attending to the cause. This superstition of which I have spoken is not without its use; yet it appears to be one great source of our vices; it is our constant engine in seducing each other. We are lulled asleep by its agency, and betrayed before we know that an attempt is made to betray us.

I have endeavoured to shake this prejudice, persuaded that in so doing I was well employed. It has been a further object with me to shew that from abuses interwoven with the texture of society a bad man may be furnished with sophisms in support of his crimes which it would be difficult to answer.

One word more upon the subject of motives. In private life what is more common than when we hear of lawsuits prosecuted to the utter ruin of the parties, and the most deadly feuds in families, to find them attributed to trifling and apparently inadequate sources? But when our malignant passions operate the original causes which called them forth are soon supplanted, yet when we account for the effect we forget the immediate impulse, and the whole is attributed to the force from which the first motion was received. The vessel keeps sailing on, and we attribute her progress in the voyage to the ropes which first towed her out of harbour.

To this must be added that we are too apt to apply our own moral sentiments as a measure of the conduct of others. We insensibly suppose that a criminal action assumes the same form to the agent as to ourselves. We forget that his feelings and his reason are equally busy in contracting its dimensions and pleading for its necessity.

A TRAGEDY.
"Of human actions reason though you can,
It may be reason, but it is not man;
His principle of action once explore,
That instant 'tis his principle no more."
Pope.[3]

Ernest de Selincourt, *Oxford Lectures on Poetry* (Oxford: Clarendon Press, 1934), pp. 165–170; and *Poetical Works*, I, 345–349.

3. "Moral Essay I (Epistle to Cobham)," ll. 35–38.

Advertisement to *Lyrical Ballads,*
with a Few Other Poems (1798)

Lyrical Ballads, with a Few Other Poems *grew out of a collaborative effort by Wordsworth and Coleridge to help pay their expenses for a year in Germany. They had planned to publish the poem that eventually became* "The Ancient Mariner" *as a single work; but as completed by Coleridge, it was too short to satisfy their arrangements with the Bristol publisher Joseph Cottle, and they added twenty-two shorter poems. Scholars now think that the famous edition published by Cottle in Bristol consisted of only two dozen copies for Wordsworth's and Coleridge's personal use, and that he passed the work on to a London publisher, assuming it not worth the expense of printing.*[1] *The London edition appeared about October 4, 1798, only six or seven months after it was conceived. It appeared anonymously at Coleridge's insistence:* "Wordsworth's name is nothing—to a large number of persons mine stinks."[2] *He had been writing unpopular political pieces in the newspapers and pamphlets during the past three years, while Wordsworth had published practically nothing with his name on it since the innocuous* Evening Walk *and* Descriptive Sketches *of 1793. Coleridge contributed three blank verse poems besides* "The Ancient Mariner," *and Wordsworth contributed nineteen short poems. Less than half of the poems in the volume could conceivably be called ballads, and fewer than half of these again could be called* "lyrical" *ballads. That term, as generally understood, referred to such expressive poems as* "The Reverie of Poor Susan," *in contrast to narrative poems such as* "The Ancient Mariner." *Thus the* "Advertisement" *(which we would today call a foreword) is as applicable to the* "Other Poems" *listed in the title as to the* "Lyrical Ballads"*; e.g., Coleridge subtitled his* "Nightingale" *as a* "Conversational Poem," *connecting it with the* "Advertisement's" *statement about the language of conversation.*

1. See D. F. Foxon, "The Printing of the *Lyrical Ballads*," *Library*, IX (1954), 221–241.

2. *Collected Letters*, ed. E. L. Griggs (6 vols.; Oxford: Clarendon Press, 1956–1964), I, 412.

It is the honourable characteristic of Poetry that its materials are to be found in every subject which can interest the human mind. The evidence of this fact is to be sought, not in the writings of Critics, but in those of Poets themselves.

The majority of the following poems are to be considered as experiments. They were written chiefly with a view to ascertain how far the language of conversation in the middle and lower classes of society is adapted to the purposes of poetic pleasure. Readers accustomed to the gaudiness and inane phraseology of many modern writers,[3] if they persist in reading this book to its conclusion, will perhaps frequently have to struggle with feelings of strangeness and aukwardness: they will look round for poetry, and will be induced to enquire by what species of courtesy these attempts can be permitted to assume that title. It is desirable that such readers, for their own sakes, should not suffer the solitary word Poetry, a word of very disputed meaning, to stand in the way of their gratification; but that, while they are perusing this book, they should ask themselves if it contains a natural delineation of human passions, human characters, and human incidents; and if the answer be favorable to the author's wishes, that they should consent to be pleased in spite of that most dreadful enemy to our pleasures, our own pre-established codes of decision.

Readers of superior judgment may disapprove of the style in which many of these pieces are executed. It must be expected that many lines and phrases will not exactly suit their taste. It will perhaps appear to them, that wishing to avoid the prevalent fault of the day, the author has sometimes descended too low, and that many of his expressions are too familiar, and not of sufficient

---

3. Coleridge had parodied the "gaudiness and inane phraseology" of contemporary writers (including himself) in the *Monthly Magazine* of the previous November; e.g.:

> Pensive at eve, on the hard world I mus'd,
> And my poor heart was sad: so at the moon
> I gaz'd—and sigh'd, and sigh'd!—for, ah! how soon
> Eve darkens into night. Mine eye perus'd
> With tearful vacancy the *dampy* grass
> Which wept and glitter'd in the paly ray ....

See D. V. Erdman, "Coleridge as Nehemiah Higginbottom," *Modern Language Notes*, LXXIII (1958), 569–580.

dignity. It is apprehended, that the more conversant the reader is with our elder writers, and with those in modern times who have been the most successful in painting manners and passions,[4] the fewer complaints of this kind will he have to make.

An accurate taste in poetry, and in all the other arts, Sir Joshua Reynolds has observed, is an acquired talent, which can only be produced by severe thought, and a long continued intercourse with the best models of composition.[5] This is mentioned not with so ridiculous a purpose as to prevent the most inexperienced reader from judging for himself; but merely to temper the rashness of decision, and to suggest that if poetry be a subject on which much time has not been bestowed, the judgment may be erroneous, and that in many cases it necessarily will be so.

The tale of Goody Blake and Harry Gill is founded on a well-authenticated fact which happened in Warwickshire.[6] Of the other poems in the collection, it may be proper to say that they are either absolute inventions of the author, or facts which took place within his personal observation or that of his friends. The poem of The Thorn, as the reader will soon discover, is not supposed to be spoken in the author's own person: the character of the loquacious narrator will sufficiently shew itself in the course of the story. The Rime of the Ancyent Marinere was professedly written in imitation of the *style*, as well as of the spirit of the elder poets; but with a few exceptions, the Author believes that the language adopted in it has been equally intelligible for these three last centuries. The lines entitled Expostulation and Reply, and those which follow, arose out of conversation with a friend who was somewhat unreasonably attached to modern books of moral philosophy.[7]

Lyrical Ballads, with a Few Other Poems (London, 1798), pp. [i]–v.

4. Robert Burns is an example: "Everywhere you have the presence of human life. The communications that proceed from Burns come to the mind with the life and charm of recognitions. But Burns also is energetic solemn and sublime in sentiment" (*Early Letters*, p. 222).

5. Discourse XII, *Discourses*, ed. R. R. Wark (San Marino: Huntington Library Press, 1959), p. 219.

6. The source of the "fact" was Erasmus Darwin's *Zoonomia*. See *Poetical Works*, IV, 439.

7. The "friend" is traditionally assumed to have been William Hazlitt.

Note to "The Thorn" (1800)

Despite his explicit statement in the final paragraph of the 1798 "Advertisement" ("The Thorn, as the reader will soon discover is not supposed to be spoken in the author's own person . . . ."), Wordsworth must have received criticism about the poem and felt a stronger note necessary. The two objects discussed in the note—dramatic, objective representation and the appropriateness of tautological style—later came to be central in the disagreement between Wordsworth and Coleridge.

This Poem ought to have been preceded by an introductory Poem, which I have been prevented from writing by never having felt myself in a mood when it was probable that I should write it well.—The character which I have here introduced speaking is sufficiently common. The Reader will perhaps have a general notion of it, if he has ever known a man, a Captain of a small trading vessel for example, who being past the middle age of life, had retired upon an annuity or small independent income to some village or country town of which he was not a native, or in which he had not been accustomed to live. Such men having little to do become credulous and talkative from indolence; and from the same cause, and other predisposing causes by which it is probable that such men may have been affected, they are prone to superstition. On which account it appeared to me proper to select a character like this to exhibit some of the general laws by which superstition acts upon the mind. Superstitious men are almost always men of slow faculties and deep feelings; their minds are not loose but adhesive; they have a reasonable share of imagination, by which word I mean the faculty which produces impressive effects out of simple elements; but they are utterly destitute of fancy, the power by which pleasure and surprize are excited by sudden varieties of situation and by accumulated imagery.

It was my wish in this poem to shew the manner in which such men cleave to the same ideas; and to follow the turns of passion, always different, yet not palpably different, by which their conversation is swayed. I had two objects to attain; first, to represent a picture which should not be unimpressive yet consistent with the character that should describe it, secondly, while I adhered to the style in which such persons describe, to take care that words, which in their minds are impregnated with passion, should likewise convey passion to Readers who are not accustomed to sympathize with men feeling in that manner or using such language. It seemed to me that this might be done by calling in the assistance of Lyrical and rapid Metre. It was necessary that the Poem, to be natural, should in reality move slowly; yet I hoped, that, by the aid of the metre, to those who should at all enter into the spirit of the Poem, it would appear to move quickly. The Reader will have the kindness to excuse this note as I am sensible that an introductory Poem is necessary to give this Poem its full effect.

Upon this occasion I will request permission to add a few words closely connected with THE THORN and many other Poems in these Volumes. There is a numerous class of readers who imagine that the same words cannot be repeated without tautology: this is a great error: virtual tautology is much oftener produced by using different words when the meaning is exactly the same. Words, a Poet's words more particularly, ought to be weighed in the balance of feeling and not measured by the space which they occupy upon paper. For the Reader cannot be too often reminded that Poetry is passion: it is the history or science of feelings: now every man must know that an attempt is rarely made to communicate impassioned feelings without something of an accompanying consciousness of the inadequateness of our own powers, or the deficiencies of language. During such efforts there will be a craving in the mind, and as long as it is unsatisfied the Speaker will cling to the same words, or words of the same character. There are also various other reasons why repetition and apparent tautology are frequently beauties of the highest kind. Among the chief of these reasons is the interest which the mind attaches to words, not only as symbols of the passion, but as *things*, active and efficient, which are of themselves part of the passion. And further, from a spirit of fondness, exultation, and gratitude, the mind luxuriates in the repetition of words which appear successfully to communicate its feelings. The truth of these remarks might be shewn by innumerable passages from the Bible and from the impassioned poetry of every nation.

> "Awake, awake Deborah: awake, awake, utter a song:
> Arise Barak, and lead thy captivity captive, thou Son of Abinoam.
> At her feet he bowed, he fell, he lay down: at her feet he bowed,
>   he fell; where he bowed there he fell down dead.
> Why is his Chariot so long in coming? Why tarry the Wheels of
>   his Chariot?"
>
> Judges, Chap. 5th. Verses 12th, 27th, and part of 28th.

See also the whole of that tumultuous and wonderful Poem.

Lyrical Ballads, with Other Poems (2 vols.; London, 1800), I, [211–214].

Preface to *Lyrical Ballads, with Other Poems* (1800)

The second edition was titled Lyrical Ballads, with Other Poems (*in contrast to* Lyrical Ballads, with a Few Other Poems), *because there were now two volumes. Though dated 1800, the edition appeared early in January, 1801. The Preface was written during September and October, and was being revised as late as December 23. Wordsworth later maintained that he "never cared a straw about the theory, and the Preface was written at the request of Mr. Coleridge out of sheer good nature."*[1] *Coleridge supports this assertion: "Wordsworth's Preface is half a child of my own Brain, & so arose out of Conversations, so frequent, that with few exceptions we could scarcely either of us perhaps positively say, which first started any particular Thought."*[2] *Another preface was planned for the second volume also, but never materialized.*[3]

The first volume contained the poems published in the 1798 edition, substituting Coleridge's "Love" for his "Convict." The second volume contained Wordsworth's new poems, and his name now appeared on the title page. The title page included a motto: "Quam nihil ad genium, Papiniane, tuum!"—loosely translated, "This is not for your taste, follower of Pope!"—setting the tone for the Preface.

The First Volume of these Poems has already been submitted to general perusal. It was published, as an experiment which, I hoped, might be of some use to ascertain, how far, by fitting to

1. *Times Literary Supplement*, April 28, 1950, p. 261.
2. *Collected Letters*, ed. E. L. Griggs (6 vols.; Oxford: Clarendon Press, 1956–1964), II, 830.
3. *Early Letters*, p. 257.

metrical arrangement a selection of the real language[4] of men in a state of vivid sensation, that sort of pleasure and that quantity of pleasure may be imparted, which a Poet may rationally endeavour to impart.

I had formed no very inaccurate estimate of the probable effect of those Poems: I flattered myself that they who should be pleased with them would read them with more than common pleasure: and on the other hand I was well aware that by those who should dislike them they would be read with more than common dislike. The result has differed from my expectation in this only, that I have pleased a greater number, than I ventured to hope I should please.

For the sake of variety and from a consciousness of my own weakness I was induced to request the assistance of a Friend, who furnished me with the Poems of the ANCIENT MARINER, the FOSTER-MOTHER'S TALE, the NIGHTINGALE, the DUNGEON, and the Poem entitled LOVE. I should not, however, have requested this assistance, had I not believed that the poems of my Friend would in a great measure have the same tendency as my own, and that, though there would be found a difference, there would be found no discordance in the colours of our style; as our opinions on the subject of poetry do almost entirely coincide.

Several of my Friends are anxious for the success of these Poems from a belief, that if the views, with which they were composed, were indeed realized, a class of Poetry would be produced, well adapted to interest mankind permanently, and not unimportant in the multiplicity and in the quality of its moral relations: and on this account they have advised me to prefix a systematic defence of the theory, upon which the poems were written. But I was unwilling to undertake the task, because I knew that on this occasion the Reader would look coldly upon my arguments, since I might be suspected of having been principally influenced by the selfish and foolish hope of *reasoning* him into an approbation of these particular Poems: and I was still more unwilling to undertake the task, because adequately to display my opinions and fully to enforce my arguments would require a space wholly disproportionate to the nature of a preface.

4. In the prefaces generally, "language" means more than diction and word order, and refers to what we would call idiom or characteristic way of saying things.

For to treat the subject with the clearness and coherence, of which I believe it susceptible, it would be necessary to give a full account of the present state of the public taste in this country, and to determine how far this taste is healthy or depraved; which again could not be determined, without pointing out, in what manner language and the human mind act and react on each other, and without retracing the revolutions not of literature alone but likewise of society itself. I have therefore altogether declined to enter regularly upon this defence; yet I am sensible, that there would be some impropriety in abruptly obtruding upon the Public, without a few words of introduction, Poems so materially different from those, upon which general approbation is at present bestowed.

It is supposed, that by the act of writing in verse an Author makes a formal engagement that he will gratify certain known habits of association, that he not only thus apprizes the Reader that certain classes of ideas and expressions will be found in his book, but that others will be carefully excluded. This exponent or symbol held forth by metrical language must in different æras of literature have excited very different expectations: for example, in the age of Catullus Terence and Lucretia,[5] and that of Statius or Claudian, and in our own country, in the age of Shakespeare and Beaumont and Fletcher, and that of Donne and Cowley, or Dryden, or Pope. I will not take upon me to determine the exact import of the promise which by the act of writing in verse an Author in the present day makes to his Reader; but I am certain it will appear to many persons that I have not fulfilled the terms of an engagement thus voluntarily contracted. I hope therefore the Reader will not censure me, if I attempt to state what I have proposed to myself to perform, and also, (as far as the limits of a preface will permit) to explain some of the chief reasons which have determined me in the choice of my purpose: that at least he may be spared any unpleasant feeling of disappointment, and that I myself may be protected from the most dishonorable accusation which can be brought against an Author, namely, that of an indolence which prevents him from endeavouring to ascertain what is his duty, or, when his duty is ascertained prevents him from performing it.

5. Wordsworth pairs off Roman poets of the golden (early) and silver (late) ages.

The principal object then which I proposed to myself in these Poems was to make the incidents of common life interesting by tracing in them, truly though not ostentatiously, the primary laws of our nature: chiefly as far as regards the manner in which we associate ideas in a state of excitement. Low and rustic life was generally chosen because in that situation the essential passions of the heart find a better soil in which they can attain their maturity, are less under restraint, and speak a plainer and more emphatic language; because in that situation our elementary feelings exist in a state of greater simplicity and consequently may be more accurately contemplated and more forcibly communicated; because the manners of rural life germinate from those elementary feelings; and from the necessary character of rural occupations are more easily comprehended; and are more durable; and lastly, because in that situation the passions of men are incorporated with the beautiful and permanent forms of nature. The language too of these men is adopted (purified indeed from what appear to be its real defects, from all lasting and rational causes of dislike or disgust)[6] because such men hourly communicate with the best objects[7] from which the best part of language is originally derived; and because, from their rank in society and the sameness and narrow circle of their intercourse, being less under the action of social vanity they convey their feelings and notions in simple and unelaborated expressions. Accordingly such a language arising out of repeated experience and regular feelings is a more permanent and a far more philosophical[8] language than that which is frequently substituted for it by Poets, who think that they are conferring honour upon themselves and their art in proportion as they separate themselves from the sympathies of men, and indulge in arbitrary and capricious habits of expression in order to furnish food for fickle tastes and fickle appetites of their own creation.[9]

6. Ribaldry, blasphemy, and angry or drunken language.

7. Not simply physical objects, but more generally "the great and universal passions of men, the most general and interesting of their occupations, and the entire world of nature," as mentioned below, p. 25.

8. "Precise," "accurate," "unambiguous."

9. [It is worth while here to observe that the affecting parts of Chaucer are almost always expressed in language pure and universally intelligible even to this day.—W.]

I cannot be insensible of the present outcry against the triviality and meanness both of thought and language, which some of my contemporaries have occasionally introduced into their metrical compositions; and I acknowledge that this defect where it exists, is more dishonorable to the Writer's own character than false refinement or arbitrary innovation, though I should contend at the same time that it is far less pernicious in the sum of its consequences. From such verses the Poems in these volumes will be found distinguished at least by one mark of difference, that each of them has a worthy *purpose*. Not that I mean to say, that I always began to write with a distinct purpose formally conceived; but I believe that my habits of meditation have so formed my feelings, as that my descriptions of such objects as strongly excite those feelings, will be found to carry along with them a *purpose*. If in this opinion I am mistaken I can have little right to the name of a Poet. For all good poetry is the spontaneous overflow of powerful feelings; but though this be true, Poems to which any value can be attached, were never produced on any variety of subjects but by a man who being possessed of more than usual organic sensibility had also thought long and deeply. For our continued influxes of feeling are modified and directed by our thoughts, which are indeed the representatives of all our past feelings; and as by contemplating the relation of these general representatives to each other, we discover what is really important to men, so by the repetition and continuance of this act feelings connected with important subjects will be nourished, till at length, if we be originally possessed of much organic sensibility, such habits of mind will be produced that by obeying blindly and mechanically the impulses of those habits we shall describe objects and utter sentiments of such a nature and in such connection with each other, that the understanding of the being to whom we address ourselves, if he be in a healthful state of association, must necessarily be in some degree enlightened, his taste exalted, and his affections ameliorated.

I have said that each of these poems has a purpose. I have also informed my Reader what this purpose will be found principally to be: namely to illustrate the manner in which our feelings and ideas are associated in a state of excitement. But speaking in less general language, it is to follow the fluxes and refluxes of the mind when agitated by the great and simple affections of our nature.[10] This object I have endeavoured in these short essays to attain by various means; by tracing the maternal passion through many of its more subtle windings, as in the poems of the IDIOT BOY and the MAD MOTHER; by accompanying the last struggles of a human being at the approach of death, cleaving in solitude to life and society, as in the Poem of the FORSAKEN INDIAN; by shewing, as in the Stanzas entitled WE ARE SEVEN, the perplexity and obscurity which in childhood attend our notion of death, or rather our utter inability to admit that notion; or by displaying the strength of fraternal, or to speak more philosophically, of moral attachment when early associated with the great and beautiful objects of nature, as in THE BROTHERS; or, as in the Incident of SIMON LEE, by placing my Reader in the way of receiving from ordinary moral sensations another and more salutary impression than we are accustomed to receive from them. It has also been part of my general purpose to attempt to sketch characters under the influence of less impassioned feelings, as in the OLD MAN TRAVELLING, THE TWO THIEVES, &c. characters of which the elements are simple, belonging rather to nature than to manners,[11] such as exist now and will probably always exist, and which from their constitution may be distinctly and profitably contemplated. I will not abuse the indulgence of my Reader by dwelling longer upon this subject; but it is proper that I should mention one other circumstance which distinguishes these Poems from the popular Poetry of the day; it is this, that the feeling therein developed gives importance to the action and situation and not the action and situation to the feeling. My meaning will be rendered perfectly intelligible by referring my Reader to the Poems entitled POOR SUSAN and the CHILDLESS FATHER, particularly to the last Stanza of the latter Poem.

I will not suffer a sense of false modesty to prevent me from asserting, that I point my Reader's attention to this mark of dis-

10. Psychological drives as well as reactions to sense impressions.

11. "Nature" refers here to the general character or disposition inherent in mankind generally; "manners" refers to more specific traits in certain types of people, usually developing from the kind of life they lead.

tinction far less for the sake of these particular Poems than from the general importance of the subject. The subject is indeed important! For the human mind is capable of excitement without the application of gross and violent stimulants; and he must have a very faint perception of its beauty and dignity who does not know this, and who does not further know that one being is elevated above another in proportion as he possesses this capability. It has therefore appeared to me that to endeavour to produce or enlarge this capability is one of the best services in which, at any period, a Writer can be engaged; but this service, excellent at all times, is especially so at the present day. For a multitude of causes unknown to former times are now acting with a combined force to blunt the discriminating powers of the mind, and unfitting it for all voluntary exertion to reduce it to a state of almost savage torpor. The most effective of these causes are the great national events which are daily taking place, and the encreasing accumulation of men in cities, where the uniformity of their occupations produces a craving for extraordinary incident which the rapid communication of intelligence hourly gratifies.[12] To this tendency of life and manners the literature and theatrical exhibitions of the country have conformed themselves. The invaluable works of our elder writers, I had almost said the works of Shakespear and Milton, are driven into neglect by frantic novels, sickly and stupid German Tragedies, and deluges of idle and extravagant stories in verse.[13]—When I think upon this degrading thirst after outrageous stimulation I am almost ashamed to have spoken of the feeble effort with which I have endeavoured to counteract it; and reflecting upon the magnitude of the general evil, I should be oppressed with no dishonorable melancholy, had I not a deep impression of certain inherent and indestructible qualities of the human mind, and likewise of certain powers in the great and permanent objects that act upon it which are equally inherent and

12. One of the major national events was the war with France. Manchester is an example of a city whose population doubled between 1760 and 1790, and rapid communication was enhanced by invention of the telegraph.

13. Gothic novels (e.g., *The Monk*), German drama (Schiller's *Robbers*), and verse narratives (Joanna Baillie's *Night Scenes of Other Times*). See *Prelude*, VII, 675–721, for a full list of factors contributing to "torpor."

Who wanted a second edition?

Shift of power

indestructible; and did I not further add to this impression a belief that the time is approaching when the evil will be systematically opposed by men of greater powers and with far more distinguished success.

Having dwelt thus long on the subjects and aim of these Poems, I shall request the Reader's permission to apprize him of a few circumstances relating to their *style*, in order, among other reasons, that I may not be censured for not having performed what I never attempted. Except in a very few instances the Reader will find no personifications of abstract ideas in these volumes, not that I mean to censure such personifications: they may be well fitted for certain sorts of composition, but in these Poems I propose to myself to imitate, and, as far as possible, to adopt the very language of men, and I do not find that such personifications make any regular or natural part of that language. I wish to keep my Reader in the company of flesh and blood, persuaded that by so doing I shall interest him. Not but that I believe that others who pursue a different track may interest him likewise: I do not interfere with their claim, I only wish to prefer a different claim of my own. There will also be found in these volumes little of what is usually called poetic diction; I have taken as much pains to avoid it as others ordinarily take to produce it; this I have done for the reason already alleged, to bring my language near to the language of men, and further, because the pleasure which I have proposed to myself to impart is of a kind very different from that which is supposed by many persons to be the proper object of poetry. I do not know how without being culpably particular I can give my Reader a more exact notion of the style in which I wished these poems to be written than by informing him that I have at all times endeavoured to look steadily at my subject, consequently I hope it will be found that there is in these Poems little falsehood of description, and that my ideas are expressed in language fitted to their respective importance. Something I must have gained by this practice, as it is friendly to one property of all good poetry, namely good sense; but it has necessarily cut me off from a large portion of phrases and figures of speech which from father to son have long been regarded as the common inheritance of Poets. I have also thought it expedient

why was it "poetic diction" = improper

truth / look = important

Old language-cliche

to restrict myself still further, having abstained from the use of many expressions, in themselves proper and beautiful, but which have been foolishly repeated by bad Poets till such feelings of disgust are connected with them as it is scarcely possible by any art of association to overpower.

If in a Poem there should be found a series of lines, or even a single line, in which the language, though naturally arranged and according to the strict laws of metre, does not differ from that of prose, there is a numerous class of critics who, when they stumble upon these prosaisms as they call them, imagine that they have made a notable discovery, and exult over the Poet as over a man ignorant of his own profession. Now these men would establish a canon of criticism which the Reader will conclude he must utterly reject if he wishes to be pleased with these volumes. And it would be a most easy task to prove to him that not only the language of a large portion of every good poem, even of the most elevated character, must necessarily, except with reference to the metre, in no respect differ from that of good prose, but likewise that some of the most interesting parts of the best poems will be found to be strictly the language of prose when prose is well written. The truth of this assertion might be demonstrated by innumerable passages from almost all the poetical writings, even of Milton himself. I have not space for much quotation; but, to illustrate the subject in a general manner, I will here adduce a short composition of Gray, who was at the head of those who by their reasonings have attempted to widen the space of separation betwixt Prose and Metrical composition, and was more than any other man curiously elaborate in the structure of his own poetic diction.

uses prose in poem / idea of having structure?

> In vain to me the smiling mornings shine,
> And reddening Phoebus lifts his golden fire:
> The birds in vain their amorous descant join,
> Or chearful fields resume their green attire:
> These ears alas! for other notes repine;
> *A different object do these eyes require;*
> *My lonely anguish melts no heart but mine;*
> *And in my breast the imperfect joys expire;*
> Yet Morning smiles the busy race to cheer,

And new-born pleasure brings to happier men;
The fields to all their wonted tribute bear;
To warm their little loves the birds complain.
I fruitless mourn to him that cannot hear
And weep the more because I weep in vain.[14]

It will easily be perceived that the only part of this Sonnet which is of any value is the lines printed in Italics: it is equally obvious that except in the rhyme, and in the use of the single word "fruitless" for fruitlessly, which is so far a defect, the language of these lines does in no respect differ from that of prose.

Is there then, it will be asked, no essential difference between the language of prose and metrical composition? I answer that there neither is nor can be any essential difference. We are fond of tracing the resemblance between Poetry and Painting, and, accordingly, we call them Sisters: but where shall we find bonds of connection sufficiently strict to typify the affinity betwixt metrical and prose composition? They both speak by and to the same organs; the bodies in which both of them are clothed may be said to be of the same substance, their affections are kindred and almost identical, not necessarily differing even in degree; Poetry[15] sheds no tears "such as Angels weep,"[16] but natural and human tears; she can boast of no celestial Ichor that distinguishes her vital juices from those of prose; the same human blood circulates through the veins of them both.

If it be affirmed that rhyme and metrical arrangement of themselves constitute a distinction which overturns what I have been

14. "Sonnet on the Death of Richard West." For Gray's remarks on the language of poetry, see his *Correspondence*, ed. P. Toynbee and L. Whibley (3 vols.; Oxford: Clarendon Press, 1935), I, 192–193. Gray is arguing, however, for the propriety of using the language of Chaucer and Shakespeare.

15. [I here use the word "Poetry" (though against my own judgment) as opposed to the word Prose, and synonymous with metrical composition. But much confusion has been introduced into criticism by this contradistinction of Poetry and Prose, instead of the more philosophical one of Poetry and Science. The only strict antithesis to Prose is Metre.—W.] On this topic the Preface echoes an article in the *Monthly Magazine* for July, 1796. See W. J. B. Owen, "Wordsworth's Preface to Lyrical Ballads," *Anglistica*, IX (1957), 23–25.

16. *Paradise Lost*, I, 620.

saying on the strict affinity of metrical language with that of prose, and paves the way for other distinctions which the mind voluntarily admits, I answer that the distinction of rhyme and metre is regular and uniform, and not, like that which is produced by what is usually called poetic diction, arbitrary and subject to infinite caprices upon which no calculation whatever can be made. In the one case the Reader is utterly at the mercy of the Poet respecting what imagery or diction he may choose to connect with the passion, whereas in the other the metre obeys certain laws, to which the Poet and Reader both willingly submit because they are certain, and because no interference is made by them with the passion but such as the concurring testimony of ages has shewn to heighten and improve the pleasure which co-exists with it.

It will now be proper to answer an obvious question, namely, why, professing these opinions have I written in verse? To this in the first place I reply, because, however I may have restricted myself, there is still left open to me what confessedly constitutes the most valuable object of all writing whether in prose or verse, the great and universal passions of men, the most general and interesting of their occupations, and the entire world of nature, from which I am at liberty to supply myself with endless combinations of forms and imagery. Now, granting for a moment that whatever is interesting in these objects may be as vividly described in prose, why am I to be condemned if to such description I have endeavoured to superadd the charm which by the consent of all nations is acknowledged to exist in metrical language? To this it will be answered, that a very small part of the pleasure given by Poetry depends upon the metre, and that it is injudicious to write in metre unless it be accompanied with the other artificial distinctions of style with which metre is usually accompanied, and that by such deviation more will be lost from the shock which will be thereby given to the Reader's associations than will be counterbalanced by any pleasure which he can derive from the general power of numbers. In answer to those who thus contend for the necessity of accompanying metre with certain appropriate colours of style in order to the accomplishment of its appropriate end, and who also, in my opinion, greatly under-rate the power of metre in itself, it might perhaps be almost sufficient to observe that poems are extant, written upon more humble subjects, and in a more naked and simple style than what I have aimed at, which poems have continued to give pleasure from generation to generation. Now, if nakedness and simplicity be a defect, the fact here mentioned affords a strong presumption that poems somewhat less naked and simple are capable of affording pleasure at the present day; and all that I am now attempting is to justify myself for having written under the impression of this belief.

But I might point out various causes why, when the style is manly, and the subject of some importance, words metrically arranged will long continue to impart such a pleasure to mankind as he who is sensible of the extent of that pleasure will be desirous to impart. The end of Poetry is to produce excitement in co-existence with an over-balance of pleasure. Now, by the supposition, excitement is an unusual and irregular state of the mind; ideas and feelings do not in that state succeed each other in accustomed order. But if the words by which this excitement is produced are in themselves powerful, or the images and feelings have an undue proportion of pain connected with them, there is some danger that the excitement may be carried beyond its proper bounds. Now the co-presence of something regular, something to which the mind has been accustomed when in an unexcited or a less excited state, cannot but have great efficacy in tempering and restraining the passion by an intertexture of ordinary feeling. This may be illustrated by appealing to the Reader's own experience of the reluctance with which he comes to the re-perusal of the distressful parts of Clarissa Harlowe, or the Gamester.[17] While Shakespeare's writings, in the most pathetic scenes, never act upon us as pathetic beyond the bounds of pleasure—an effect which is in a great degree to be ascribed to small, but continual and regular impulses of pleasurable surprise from the metrical arrangement.—On the other hand (what it must be allowed will much more frequently happen) if the Poet's words should be incommensurate with the passion, and inadequate to raise the Reader to a height of desirable excitement, then, (unless

17. Samuel Richardson's *Clarissa* (1747–1748) and Edward Moore's popular domestic play in prose (1753).

the Poet's choice of his metre has been grossly injudicious) in the feelings of pleasure which the Reader has been accustomed to connect with metre in general, and in the feeling, whether chearful or melancholy, which he has been accustomed to connect with that particular movement of metre, there will be found something which will greatly contribute to impart passion to the words, and to effect the complex end which the Poet proposes to himself.

If I had undertaken a systematic defence of the theory upon which these poems are written, it would have been my duty to develope the various causes upon which the pleasure received from metrical language depends. Among the chief of these causes is to be reckoned a principle which must be well known to those who have made any of the Arts the object of accurate reflection; I mean the pleasure which the mind derives from the perception of similitude in dissimilitude. This principle is the great spring of the activity of our minds and their chief feeder. From this principle the direction of the sexual appetite, and all the passions connected with it take their origin: It is the life of our ordinary conversation; and upon the accuracy with which similitude in dissimilitude, and dissimilitude in similitude are perceived, depend our taste and our moral feelings. It would not have been a useless employment to have applied this principle to the consideration of metre, and to have shewn that metre is hence enabled to afford much pleasure, and to have pointed out in what manner that pleasure is produced. But my limits will not permit me to enter upon this subject, and I must content myself with a general summary.

I have said that Poetry is the spontaneous overflow of powerful feelings: it takes its origin from emotion recollected in tranquillity: the emotion is contemplated till by a species of reaction the tranquillity gradually disappears, and an emotion, similar to that which was before the subject of contemplation, is gradually produced, and does itself actually exist in the mind. In this mood successful composition generally begins, and in a mood similar to this it is carried on; but the emotion, of whatever kind and in whatever degree, from various causes is qualified by various pleasures, so that in describing any passions whatsoever, which are voluntarily described, the mind will upon the whole be in a state of enjoyment.

Now if Nature be thus cautious in preserving in a state of enjoyment a being thus employed, the Poet ought to profit by the lesson thus held forth to him, and ought especially to take care, that whatever passions he communicates to his Reader, those passions, if his Reader's mind be sound and vigorous, should always be accompanied with an overbalance of pleasure. Now the music of harmonious metrical language, the sense of difficulty overcome, and the blind association of pleasure which has been previously received from works of rhyme or metre of the same or similar construction, all these imperceptibly make up a complex feeling of delight, which is of the most important use in tempering the painful feeling which will always be found intermingled with powerful descriptions of the deeper passions. This effect is always produced in pathetic and impassioned poetry; while in lighter compositions the ease and gracefulness with which the Poet manages his numbers are themselves confessedly a principal source of the gratification of the Reader. I might perhaps include all which it is *necessary* to say upon this subject by affirming what few persons will deny, that of two descriptions either of passions, manners, or characters, each of them equally well executed, the one in prose and the other in verse, the verse will be read a hundred times where the prose is read once. We see that Pope by the power of verse alone, has contrived to render the plainest common sense interesting, and even frequently to invest it with the appearance of passion. In consequence of these convictions I related in metre the Tale of GOODY BLAKE and HARRY GILL, which is one of the rudest of this collection. I wished to draw attention to the truth that the power of the human imagination is sufficient to produce such changes even in our physical nature as might almost appear miraculous. The truth is an important one; the fact (for it is a *fact*) is a valuable illustration of it. And I have the satisfaction of knowing that it has been communicated to many hundreds of people who would never have heard of it, had it not been narrated as a Ballad, and in a more impressive metre than is usual in Ballads.

Having thus adverted to a few of the reasons why I have written in verse, and why I have chosen subjects from common life, and endeavoured to bring my language near to the real language of

Main pts

men, if I have been too minute in pleading my own cause, I have at the same time been treating a subject of general interest; and it is for this reason that I request the Reader's permission to add a few words with reference solely to these particular poems, and to some defects which will probably be found in them. I am sensible that my associations must have sometimes been particular instead of general, and that, consequently, giving to things a false importance, sometimes from diseased impulses I may have written upon unworthy subjects; but I am less apprehensive on this account, than that my language may frequently have suffered from those arbitrary connections of feelings and ideas with particular words, from which no man can altogether protect himself. Hence I have no doubt that in some instances feelings even of the ludicrous may be given to my Readers by expressions which appeared to me tender and pathetic. Such faulty expressions, were I convinced they were faulty at present, and that they must necessarily continue to be so, I would willingly take all reasonable pains to correct. But it is dangerous to make these alterations on the simple authority of a few individuals, or even of certain classes of men; for where the understanding of an Author is not convinced, or his feelings altered, this cannot be done without great injury to himself: for his own feelings are his stay and support, and if he sets them aside in one instance, he may be induced to repeat this act till his mind loses all confidence in itself and becomes utterly debilitated. To this it may be added, that the Reader ought never to forget that he is himself exposed to the same errors as the Poet, and perhaps in a much greater degree: for there can be no presumption in saying that it is not probable he will be so well acquainted with the various stages of meaning through which words have passed, or with the fickleness or stability of the relations of particular ideas to each other; and above all, since he is so much less interested in the subject, he may decide lightly and carelessly.

Long as I have detained my Reader, I hope he will permit me to caution him against a mode of false criticism which has been applied to Poetry in which the language closely resembles that of life and nature. Such verses have been triumphed over in parodies of which Dr. Johnson's Stanza is a fair specimen.

> "I put my hat upon my head,
> And walk'd into the Strand,
> And there I met another man
> Whose hat was in his hand."[18]

Immediately under these lines I will place one of the most justly admired stanzas of the "*Babes* in the Wood."

> "These pretty Babes with hand in hand
> Went wandering up and down;
> But never more they saw the Man
> Approaching from the Town."[19]

In both of these stanzas the words, and the order of the words, in no respect differ from the most unimpassioned conversation. There are words in both, for example, "the Strand," and "the Town," connected with none but the most familiar ideas; yet the one stanza we admit as admirable, and the other as a fair example of the superlatively contemptible. Whence arises this difference? Not from the metre, not from the language, not from the order of the words; but the *matter* expressed in Dr. Johnson's stanza is contemptible. The proper method of treating trivial and simple verses to which Dr. Johnson's stanza would be a fair parallelism is not to say this is a bad kind of poetry, or this is not poetry, but this wants sense; it is neither interesting in itself, nor can lead to any thing interesting; the images neither originate in that sane state of feeling which arises out of thought, nor can excite thought or feeling in the Reader. This is the only sensible manner of dealing with such verses: Why trouble yourself about the species till you have previously decided upon the genus? Why take pains to prove that an Ape is not a Newton when it is self-evident that he is not a man.

I have one request to make of my Reader, which is, that in judging these Poems he would decide by his own feelings genuinely,

---

18. Dr. Johnson's stanza had been published in the *London Magazine*, April, 1785. See *Poems of Samuel Johnson*, ed. D. Nichol Smith and E. L. McAdam (Oxford: Clarendon Press, 1941), pp. 157–158.

19. This version has been found elsewhere only in a street-ballad broadside. See F. W. Bateson, *Wordsworth: A Reinterpretation* (London: Longmans, 1954), p. 135. The version in Percy's *Reliques* (4th ed.; London, 1794), III, 176, has in the third line: "But never more could see the Man."

and not by reflection upon what will probably be the judgment of others. How common is it to hear a person say, "I myself do not object to this style of composition or this or that expression, but to such and such classes of people it will appear mean or ludicrous." This mode of criticism so destructive of all sound unadulterated judgment is almost universal: I have therefore to request that the Reader would abide independently by his own feelings, and that if he finds himself affected he would not suffer such conjectures to interfere with his pleasure.

If an Author by any single composition has impressed us with respect for his talents, it is useful to consider this as affording a presumption, that, on other occasions where we have been displeased, he nevertheless may not have written ill or absurdly; and, further, to give him so much credit for this one composition as may induce us to review what has displeased us with more care than we should otherwise have bestowed upon it. This is not only an act of justice, but in our decisions upon poetry especially, may conduce in a high degree to the improvement of our own taste: for an *accurate* taste in Poetry and in all the other arts, as Sir Joshua Reynolds has observed, is an *acquired* talent, which can only be produced by thought and a long continued intercourse with the best models of composition. This is mentioned not with so ridiculous a purpose as to prevent the most inexperienced Reader from judging for himself, (I have already said that I wish him to judge for himself;) but merely to temper the rashness of decision, and to suggest that if Poetry be a subject on which much time has not been bestowed, the judgment may be erroneous, and that in many cases it necessarily will be so.

I know that nothing would have so effectually contributed to further the end which I have in view as to have shewn of what kind the pleasure is, and how the pleasure is produced which is confessedly produced by metrical composition essentially different from what I have here endeavoured to recommend; for the Reader will say that he has been pleased by such composition and what can I do more for him? The power of any art is limited and he will suspect that if I propose to furnish him with new friends it is only upon condition of his abandoning his old friends. Besides, as I have said, the Reader is himself conscious of the pleasure which he has received from such composition, composition to which he has peculiarly attached the endearing name of Poetry; and all men feel an habitual gratitude, and something of an honorable bigotry for the objects which have long continued to please them: we not only wish to be pleased, but to be pleased in that particular way in which we have been accustomed to be pleased. There is a host of arguments in these feelings; and I should be the less able to combat them successfully, as I am willing to allow, that, in order entirely to enjoy the Poetry which I am recommending, it would be necessary to give up much of what is ordinarily enjoyed. But would my limits have permitted me to point out how this pleasure is produced, I might have removed many obstacles, and assisted my Reader in perceiving that the powers of language are not so limited as he may suppose; and that it is possible that poetry may give other enjoyments, of a purer, more lasting, and more exquisite nature. But this part of my subject I have been obliged altogether to omit: as it has been less my present aim to prove that the interest excited by some other kinds of poetry is less vivid, and less worthy of the nobler powers of the mind, than to offer reasons for presuming, that, if the object which I have proposed to myself were adequately attained, a species of poetry would be produced, which is genuine poetry; in its nature well adapted to interest mankind permanently, and likewise important in the multiplicity and quality of its moral relations.

From what has been said, and from a perusal of the Poems, the Reader will be able clearly to perceive the object which I have proposed to myself: he will determine how far I have attained this object; and, what is a much more important question, whether it be worth attaining; and upon the decision of these two questions will rest my claim to the approbation of the public.

Lyrical Ballads, with Other Poems (2 vols.; London, 1800), I, [v]–xlvi.

Letter to Charles James Fox
(January 14, 1801)

It was standard practice to send inscribed copies of new books to people in public life who might publicize them. Fox was leader of the opposition party in Parliament, long a hero of liberals because of his fights against the government's repressive measures associated with, first, the French Revolution, and then the war with France. Politics aside, Wordsworth admired Fox's humanitarianism, as the letter emphasizes. In his reply, about a year later, Fox said that the poems gave him great pleasure; that his favorites were "Goody Blake and Harry Gill," "We Are Seven," and "The Idiot Boy"; but that he could not share Wordsworth's enthusiasm for "The Brothers" and "Michael" because he felt blank verse inappropriate for such simple subjects.[1]

It is not without much difficulty, that I have summoned the courage to request your acceptance of these Volumes. Should I express my real feelings, I am sure that I should seem to make a parade of diffidence and humility.

Several of the poems contained in these Volumes are written upon subjects, which are the common property of all Poets, and which, at some period of your life, must have been interesting to a man of your sensibility, and perhaps may still continue to be so. It would be highly gratifying to me to suppose that even in a single instance the manner in which I have treated these general topics should afford you any pleasure; but such a hope does not influence me upon the present occasion; in truth I do not feel it. Besides, I am convinced

1. Mary Moorman, *William Wordsworth, The Early Years, 1770–1803* (Oxford: Clarendon Press, 1957), pp. 504–505.

that there must be many things in this collection, which may impress you with an unfavorable idea of my intellectual powers. I do not say this with a wish to degrade myself; but I am sensible that this must be the case, from the different circles in which we have moved, and the different objects with which we have been conversant.

Being utterly unknown to you as I am, I am well aware, that if I am justified in writing to you at all, it is necessary, my letter should be short; but I have feelings within me which I hope will so far shew themselves in this letter, as to excuse the trespass which I am afraid I shall make. In common with the whole of the English People I have observed in your public character a constant predominance of sensibility of heart. Necessitated as you have been from your public situation to have much to do with men in bodies, & in classes, and accordingly to contemplate them in that relation, it has been your praise that you have not thereby been prevented from looking upon them as individuals, and that you have habitually left your heart open to be influenced by them in that capacity. This habit cannot but have made you dear to Poets; and I am sure that, if since your first entrance into public life there has been a single true poet living in England, he must have loved you.

But were I assured that I myself had a just claim to the title of a Poet, all the dignity being attached to the word which belongs to it, I do not think that I should have ventured for that reason to offer these volumes to you: at present it is solely on account of two poems in the second volume, the one entitled "the Brothers," and the other "Michael" that I have been emboldened to take this liberty.

It appears to me that the most calamitous effect, which has followed the measures which have lately been pursued in this country, is a rapid decay of the domestic affections among the lower orders of society. This effect the present Rulers of this country are not conscious of, or they disregard it. For many years past, the tendency of society amongst almost all the nations of Europe has been to produce it. But recently by the spreading of manufactures through every part of the country, by the heavy taxes upon postage, by Workhouses, Houses of Industry, and the invention of Soup-shops &c &c[2] superadded to the encreasing disproportion between the price of labour and that of the necessaries of life, the bonds of domestic feeling among the poor, as far as the influence of these things has extended, have been weakened, & in innumerable instances entirely destroyed. The evil would be the less to be regretted, if these institutions were regarded only as palliatives to a disease; but the vanity and pride of their promoters are so subtly interwoven with them, that they are deemed great discoveries and blessings to humanity. In the mean time parents are separated from their children, & children from their parents; the wife no longer prepares with her own hands a meal for her husband, the produce of his labour; there is little doing in his house in which his affections can be interested, and but little left in it which he can love. I have two neighbours, a man and his wife, both upwards of eighty years of age; they live alone; the husband has been confined to his bed many months and has never had, nor till within these few weeks has ever needed, any body to attend to him but his wife. She has recently been seized with a lameness which has often prevented her from being able to carry him his food to his bed; the neighbours fetch water for her from the well, and do other kind offices for them both, but her infirmities encrease. She told my Servant two days ago that she was afraid they must both be boarded out among some other Poor of the parish (they have long been supported by the parish) but she said, it was hard, having kept house together so long, to come to this, and she was sure that "it would burst her heart." I mention this fact to shew how deeply the spirit of independence is, even yet, rooted in some parts of the country. These people could not express themselves in this way without an almost sublime conviction of the blessings of independent domestic life. If it is true, as I believe, that this spirit is rapidly disappearing, no greater curse can befal a land.

I earnestly entreat your pardon for having detained you so long.

2. Taxes had been trebled to support the war against France. "Workhouses," where the indigent did menial labor, differed from "Houses of Industry," where the poor worked at trades such as weaving or cabinet making. "Soup-shops" were the same as later soup kitchens where charitable groups provided free meals for the poor.

In the two Poems, "the Brothers" and "Michael" I have attempted
to draw a picture of the domestic affections as I know they exist
amongst a class of men who are now almost confined to the North
of England. They are small independent *proprietors* of land here
called Statesmen, men of respectable education who daily labour
on their own little properties. The domestic affections will always be
strong amongst men who live in a country not crowded with
population, if these men are placed above poverty. But if they are
proprietors of small estates which have descended to them from
their ancestors, the power which these affections will acquire amongst
such men is inconceivable by those who have only had an opportunity
of observing hired labourers, farmers, and the manufacturing Poor.
Their little tract of land serves as a kind of permanent rallying point
for their domestic feelings, as a tablet upon which they are written
which makes them objects of memory in a thousand instances when
they would otherwise be forgotten. It is a fountain fitted to the
nature of social man from which supplies of affection, as pure as
his heart was intended for, are daily drawn. This class of men is
rapidly disappearing. You, Sir, have a consciousness, upon which
every good man will congratulate you, that the whole of your
public conduct has in one way or other been directed to the
preservation of this class of men, and those who hold similar
situations. You have felt that the most sacred of all property is the
property of the Poor. The two poems which I have mentioned were
written with a view to shew that men who do not wear fine cloaths
can feel deeply. "Pectus enim est quod disertos facit, et vis mentis.
Ideoque imperitis quoque, si modo sint aliquo affectu concitati,
verba non desunt."[3] The poems are faithful copies from Nature; & I
hope, whatever effect they may have upon you, you will at least be
able to perceive that they may excite profitable sympathies in
many kind and good hearts, and may in some small degree enlarge
our feelings of reverence for our species, and our knowledge of
human nature, by shewing that our best qualities are possessed by

3. "For it is strength of feeling that makes eloquence, and energy of intellect.
And even to the illiterate, if only they be moved by deep passion, words are not
wanting" (Quintilian, *Institutes of Oratory*, X.vii.15). These lines also appear as
epigraph in the edition of 1802.

men whom we are too apt to consider, not with reference to the points in which they resemble us, but to those in which they manifestly differ from us. I thought, at a time when these feelings are sapped in so many ways that the two poems might co-operate, however feebly, with the illustrious efforts which you have made to stem this and other evils with which the country is labouring, and it is on this account alone that I have taken the liberty of thus addressing you.

Wishing earnestly that the time may come when the country may perceive what it has lost by neglecting your advice, and hoping that your latter days may be attended with health and comfort,

I remain, with the highest respect & admiration,
Your most obedient & humble Servt

W Wordsworth

Early Letters, pp. 259–263, with minor corrections from manuscript.

Preface to *Lyrical Ballads, with Pastoral and Other Poems* (1802)

The edition of 1800 sold so well that about six months after its appearance, the publisher, Thomas Longman, asked Wordsworth to prepare another. The new edition was published in April, 1802. Its title page now emphasized such poems as "Michael" and "The Brothers"; its Preface contained a large addition; and an Appendix expanded the Preface's discussion of "poetic diction." Wordsworth's additions to the Preface were apparently his own, independent of Coleridge. Though Coleridge admired the new version, certain of its remarks, coupled with the Appendix, led him to a reappraisal of their critical positions and in turn led to his remarks on Wordsworth in Biographia Literaria.

The first Volume of these Poems has already been submitted to general perusal. It was published, as an experiment, which, I hoped, might be of some use to ascertain, how far, by fitting to metrical arrangement a selection of the real language of men in a state of vivid sensation, that sort of pleasure and that quantity of pleasure may be imparted, which a Poet may rationally endeavour to impart.

I had formed no very inaccurate estimate of the probable effect of those Poems: I flattered myself that they who should be pleased with them would read them with more than common pleasure: and, on the other hand, I was well aware, that by those who should dislike them they would be read with more than common dislike. The result has differed from my expectation in this only, that I have pleased a greater number, than I ventured to hope I should please.

For the sake of variety, and from a consciousness of my own weakness, I was induced to request the assistance of a Friend, who

furnished me with the Poems of the ANCIENT MARINER, the FOSTER-
MOTHER'S TALE, the NIGHTINGALE, and the Poem entitled LOVE. I
should not, however, have requested this assistance, had I not
believed that the Poems of my Friend would in a great measure
have the same tendency as my own, and that, though there would
be found a difference, there would be found no discordance in the
colours of our style; as our opinions on the subject of poetry do
almost entirely coincide.

Several of my Friends are anxious for the success of these Poems
from a belief, that, if the views with which they were composed
were indeed realized, a class of Poetry would be produced, well
adapted to interest mankind permanently, and not unimportant in
the multiplicity, and in the quality of its moral relations: and on
this account they have advised me to prefix a systematic defence of
the theory upon which the poems were written. But I was unwilling
to undertake the task, because I knew that on this occasion the
Reader would look coldly upon my arguments, since I might be
suspected of having been principally influenced by the selfish and
foolish hope of *reasoning* him into an approbation of these particular
Poems: and I was still more unwilling to undertake the task,
because, adequately to display my opinions, and fully to enforce my
arguments, would require a space wholly disproportionate to the
nature of a preface. For to treat the subject with the clearness and
coherence, of which I believe it susceptible, it would be necessary
to give a full account of the present state of the public taste in this
country, and to determine how far this taste is healthy or depraved;
which, again, could not be determined, without pointing out, in
what manner language and the human mind act and re-act on each
other, and without retracing the revolutions, not of literature alone,
but likewise of society itself. I have therefore altogether declined to
enter regularly upon this defence; yet I am sensible, that there
would be some impropriety in abruptly obtruding upon the Public,
without a few words of introduction, Poems so materially different
from those, upon which general approbation is at present bestowed.

It is supposed, that by the act of writing in verse an Author makes
a formal engagement that he will gratify certain known habits of
association; that he not only thus apprizes the Reader that certain

classes of ideas and expressions will be found in his book, but that others will be carefully excluded. This exponent or symbol held forth by metrical language must in different æras of literature have excited very different expectations: for example, in the age of Catullus, Terence and Lucretius, and that of Statius or Claudian; and in our own country, in the age of Shakespeare and Beaumont and Fletcher, and that of Donne and Cowley, or Dryden, or Pope. I will not take upon me to determine the exact import of the promise which by the act of writing in verse an Author, in the present day, makes to his Reader; but I am certain, it will appear to many persons that I have not fulfilled the terms of an engagement thus voluntarily contracted. They who have been accustomed to the gaudiness and inane phraseology of many modern writers, if they persist in reading this book to its conclusion, will, no doubt, frequently have to struggle with feelings of strangeness and aukwardness: they will look round for poetry, and will be induced to inquire by what species of courtesy these attempts can be permitted to assume that title. I hope therefore the Reader will not censure me, if I attempt to state what I have proposed to myself to perform; and also, (as far as the limits of a preface will permit) to explain some of the chief reasons which have determined me in the choice of my purpose: that at least he may be spared any unpleasant feeling of disappointment, and that I myself may be protected from the most dishonourable accusation which can be brought against an Author, namely, that of an indolence which prevents him from endeavouring to ascertain what is his duty, or, when his duty is ascertained, prevents him from performing it.

The principal object, then, which I proposed to myself in these Poems was to choose incidents and situations from common life, and to relate or describe them, throughout, as far as was possible, in a selection of language really used by men; and, at the same time, to throw over them a certain colouring of imagination, whereby ordinary things should be presented to the mind in an unusual way; and, further, and above all, to make these incidents and situations interesting by tracing in them, truly though not ostentatiously, the primary laws of our nature: chiefly, as far as regards the manner in which we associate ideas in a state of excitement.

Low and rustic life was generally chosen, because in that condition, the essential passions of the heart find a better soil in which they can attain their maturity, are less under restraint, and speak a plainer and more emphatic language; because in that condition of life our elementary feelings co-exist in a state of greater simplicity, and, consequently, may be more accurately contemplated, and more forcibly communicated; because the manners of rural life germinate from those elementary feelings; and, from the necessary character of rural occupations, are more easily comprehended; and are more durable; and lastly, because in that condition the passions of men are incorporated with the beautiful and permanent forms of nature. The language, too, of these men is adopted (purified indeed from what appear to be its real defects, from all lasting and rational causes of dislike or disgust) because such men hourly communicate with the best objects from which the best part of language is originally derived; and because, from their rank in society and the sameness and narrow circle of their intercourse, being less under the influence of social vanity they convey their feelings and notions in simple and unelaborated expressions. Accordingly, such a language, arising out of repeated experience and regular feelings, is a more permanent, and a far more philosophical language, than that which is frequently substituted for it by Poets, who think that they are conferring honour upon themselves and their art, in proportion as they separate themselves from the sympathies of men, and indulge in arbitrary and capricious habits of expression, in order to furnish food for fickle tastes, and fickle appetites, of their own creation.[1]

I cannot, however, be insensible of the present outcry against the triviality and meanness both of thought and language, which some of my contemporaries have occasionally introduced into their metrical compositions; and I acknowledge that this defect, where it exists, is more dishonourable to the Writer's own character than false refinement or arbitrary innovation, though I should contend at the same time that it is far less pernicious in the sum of its consequences. From such verses the Poems in these volumes will be

1. [It is worth while here to observe that the affecting parts of Chaucer are almost always expressed in language pure and universally intelligible even to this day.—W.]

found distinguished at least by one mark of difference, that each of them has a worthy *purpose*. Not that I mean to say, that I always began to write with a distinct purpose formally conceived; but I believe that my habits of meditation have so formed my feelings, as that my descriptions of such objects as strongly excite those feelings, will be found to carry along with them a *purpose*. If in this opinion I am mistaken, I can have little right to the name of a Poet. For all good poetry is the spontaneous overflow of powerful feelings: but though this be true, Poems to which any value can be attached, were never produced on any variety of subjects but by a man, who being possessed of more than usual organic sensibility, had also thought long and deeply. For our continued influxes of feeling are modified and directed by our thoughts, which are indeed the representatives of all our past feelings; and, as by contemplating the relation of these general representatives to each other we discover what is really important to men, so, by the repetition and continuance of this act, our feelings will be connected with important subjects, till at length, if we be originally possessed of much sensibility, such habits of mind will be produced, that, by obeying blindly and mechanically the impulses of those habits, we shall describe objects, and utter sentiments, of such a nature and in such connection with each other, that the understanding of the being to whom we address ourselves, if he be in a healthful state of association, must necessarily be in some degree enlightened, and his affections ameliorated.

I have said that each of these poems has a purpose. I have also informed my Reader what this purpose will be found principally to be: namely, to illustrate the manner in which our feelings and ideas are associated in a state of excitement. But, speaking in language somewhat more appropriate, it is to follow the fluxes and refluxes of the mind when agitated by the great and simple affections of our nature. This object I have endeavoured in these short essays to attain by various means; by tracing the maternal passion through many of its more subtle windings, as in the poems of the IDIOT BOY and the MAD MOTHER; by accompanying the last struggles of a human being, at the approach of death, cleaving in solitude to life and society, as in the Poem of the FORSAKEN INDIAN; by showing, as in the Stanzas entitled WE ARE SEVEN, the perplexity and obscurity which in childhood attend our notion of death, or rather our utter inability to admit that notion; or by displaying the strength of fraternal, or to speak more philosophically, of moral attachment when early associated with the great and beautiful objects of nature, as in THE BROTHERS; or, as in the Incident of SIMON LEE, by placing my Reader in the way of receiving from ordinary moral sensations another and more salutary impression than we are accustomed to receive from them. It has also been part of my general purpose to attempt to sketch characters under the influence of less impassioned feelings, as in the TWO APRIL MORNINGS, THE FOUNTAIN, THE OLD MAN TRAVELLING, THE TWO THIEVES, &c. characters of which the elements are simple, belonging rather to nature than to manners, such as exist now, and will probably always exist, and which from their constitution may be distinctly and profitably contemplated. I will not abuse the indulgence of my Reader by dwelling longer upon this subject; but it is proper that I should mention one other circumstance which distinguishes these Poems from the popular Poetry of the day; it is this, that the feeling therein developed gives importance to the action and situation, and not the action and situation to the feeling. My meaning will be rendered perfectly intelligible by referring my Reader to the Poems entitled POOR SUSAN and the CHILDLESS FATHER, particularly to the last Stanza of the latter Poem.

I will not suffer a sense of false modesty to prevent me from asserting, that I point my Reader's attention to this mark of distinction, far less for the sake of these particular Poems than from the general importance of the subject. The subject is indeed important! For the human mind is capable of being excited without the application of gross and violent stimulants; and he must have a very faint perception of its beauty and dignity who does not know this, and who does not further know, that one being is elevated above another, in proportion as he possesses this capability. It has therefore appeared to me, that to endeavour to produce or enlarge this capability is one of the best services in which, at any period, a Writer can be engaged; but this service, excellent at all times, is especially so at the present day. For a multitude of causes, unknown to former times, are now acting with a combined force to blunt the discriminating powers of the mind, and unfitting it for all voluntary exertion to reduce it to a state of almost savage torpor. The most effective of these causes are the great national events which are daily taking place, and the increasing accumulation of men in cities, where the uniformity of their occupations produces a craving for extraordinary incident, which the rapid communication of intelligence hourly gratifies. To this tendency of life and manners the literature and theatrical exhibitions of the country have conformed themselves. The invaluable works of our elder writers, I had almost said the works of Shakespear and Milton, are driven into neglect by frantic novels, sickly and stupid German Tragedies, and deluges of idle and extravagant stories in verse.—When I think upon this degrading thirst after outrageous stimulation, I am almost ashamed to have spoken of the feeble effort with which I have endeavoured to counteract it; and, reflecting upon the magnitude of the general evil, I should be oppressed with no dishonorable melancholy, had I not a deep impression of certain inherent and indestructible qualities of the human mind, and likewise of certain powers in the great and permanent objects that act upon it, which are equally inherent and indestructible; and did I not further add to this impression a belief, that the time is approaching when the evil will be systematically opposed, by men of greater powers, and with far more distinguished success.

Having dwelt thus long on the subjects and aim of these Poems, I shall request the Reader's permission to apprize him of a few circumstances relating to their *style*, in order, among other reasons, that I may not be censured for not having performed what I never attempted. The Reader will find that personifications of abstract ideas rarely occur in these volumes; and, I hope, are utterly rejected as an ordinary device to elevate the style, and raise it above prose. I have proposed to myself to imitate, and, as far as is possible, to adopt the very language of men; and assuredly such personifications do not make any natural or regular part of that language. They are, indeed, a figure of speech occasionally prompted by passion, and I have made use of them as such; but I have endeavoured utterly to reject them as a mechanical device of style, or as a family language which Writers in metre seem to lay claim to by prescription. I have wished to keep my Reader in the company of flesh and blood, persuaded that by so doing I shall interest him. I am, however, well aware that others who pursue a different track may interest him likewise; I do not interfere with their claim, I only wish to prefer a different claim of my own. There will also be found in these volumes little of what is usually called poetic diction; I have taken as much pains to avoid it as others ordinarily take to produce it; this I have done for the reason already alleged, to bring my language near to the language of men, and further, because the pleasure which I have proposed to myself to impart is of a kind very different from that which is supposed by many persons to be the proper object of poetry. I do not know how, without being culpably particular, I can give my Reader a more exact notion of the style in which I wished these poems to be written, than by informing him that I have at all times endeavoured to look steadily at my subject, consequently, I hope that there is in these Poems little falsehood of description, and that my ideas are expressed in language fitted to their respective importance. Something I must have gained by this practice, as it is friendly to one property of all good poetry, namely good sense; but it has necessarily cut me off from a large portion of phrases and figures of speech which from father to son have long been regarded as the common inheritance of Poets. I have also thought it expedient to restrict myself still further, having abstained from the use of many expressions, in themselves proper and beautiful, but which have been foolishly repeated by bad Poets, till such feelings of disgust are connected with them as it is scarcely possible by any art of association to overpower.

If in a poem there should be found a series of lines, or even a single line, in which the language, though naturally arranged, and according to the strict laws of metre, does not differ from that of prose, there is a numerous class of critics, who, when they stumble upon these prosaisms, as they call them, imagine that they have made a notable discovery, and exult over the Poet as over a man ignorant of his own profession. Now these men would establish a canon of criticism which the Reader will conclude he must utterly reject, if he wishes to be pleased with these volumes. And it would

be a most easy task to prove to him, that not only the language of a
large portion of every good poem, even of the most elevated
character, must necessarily, except with reference to the metre, in
no respect differ from that of good prose, but likewise that some of
the most interesting parts of the best poems will be found to be
strictly the language of prose, when prose is well written. The truth
of this assertion might be demonstrated by innumerable passages
from almost all the poetical writings, even of Milton himself. I have
not space for much quotation; but, to illustrate the subject in a
general manner, I will here adduce a short composition of Gray,
who was at the head of those who, by their reasonings, have
attempted to widen the space of separation betwixt Prose and
Metrical composition, and was more than any other man curiously
elaborate in the structure of his own poetic diction.

> In vain to me the smiling mornings shine,
> And reddening Phoebus lifts his golden fire:
> The birds in vain their amorous descant join,
> Or cheerful fields resume their green attire.
> These ears, alas! for other notes repine;
> *A different object do these eyes require;*
> *My lonely anguish melts no heart but mine;*
> *And in my breast the imperfect joys expire;*
> Yet morning smiles the busy race to cheer,
> And new-born pleasure brings to happier men;
> The fields to all their wonted tribute bear;
> To warm their little loves the birds complain.
> *I fruitless mourn to him that cannot hear,*
> *And weep the more because I weep in vain.*

It will easily be perceived that the only part of this Sonnet which is
of any value is the lines printed in Italics: it is equally obvious, that,
except in the rhyme, and in the use of the single word "fruitless" for
fruitlessly, which is so far a defect, the language of these lines does
in no respect differ from that of prose.

By the foregoing quotation I have shown that the language of
Prose may yet be well adapted to Poetry; and I have previously
asserted that a large portion of the language of every good poem
can in no respect differ from that of good Prose. I will go further. I

do not doubt that it may be safely affirmed, that there neither is, nor can be, any essential difference between the language of prose and metrical composition. We are fond of tracing the resemblance between Poetry and Painting, and, accordingly, we call them Sisters: but where shall we find bonds of connection sufficiently strict to typify the affinity betwixt metrical and prose composition? They both speak by and to the same organs; the bodies in which both of them are clothed may be said to be of the same substance, their affections are kindred, and almost identical, not necessarily differing even in degree; Poetry[2] sheds no tears "such as Angels weep," but natural and human tears; she can boast of no celestial Ichor that distinguishes her vital juices from those of prose; the same human blood circulates through the veins of them both.

If it be affirmed that rhyme and metrical arrangement of them-selves constitute a distinction which overturns what I have been saying on the strict affinity of metrical language with that of prose, and paves the way for other artificial distinctions which the mind voluntarily admits, I answer that the language of such Poetry as I am recommending is, as far as is possible, a selection of the language really spoken by men; that this selection, wherever it is made with true taste and feeling, will of itself form a distinction far greater than would at first be imagined, and will entirely separate the composition from the vulgarity and meanness of ordinary life; and, if metre be superadded thereto, I believe that a dissimilitude will be produced altogether sufficient for the gratification of a rational mind. What other distinction would we have? Whence is it to come? And where is it to exist? Not, surely, where the Poet speaks through the mouths of his characters: it cannot be necessary here, either for elevation of style, or any of its supposed ornaments; for, if the Poet's subject be judiciously chosen, it will naturally, and

2. [I here use the word "Poetry" (though against my own judgment) as opposed to the word Prose, and synonymous with metrical composition. But much con-fusion has been introduced into criticism by this contradistinction of Poetry and Prose, instead of the more philosophical one of Poetry and Matter of Fact, or Science. The only strict antithesis to Prose is Metre; nor is this, in truth, a *strict* antithesis; because lines and passages of metre so naturally occur in writing prose, that it would be scarcely possible to avoid them, even were it desirable.—W.]

upon fit occasion, lead him to passions the language of which, if selected truly and judiciously, must necessarily be dignified and variegated, and alive with metaphors and figures. I forbear to speak of an incongruity which would shock the intelligent Reader, should the Poet interweave any foreign splendour of his own with that which the passion naturally suggests: it is sufficient to say that such addition is unnecessary. And, surely, it is more probable that those passages, which with propriety abound with metaphors and figures, will have their due effect, if, upon other occasions where the passions are of a milder character, the style also be subdued and temperate.

But, as the pleasure which I hope to give by the Poems I now present to the Reader must depend entirely on just notions upon this subject, and, as it is in itself of the highest importance to our taste and moral feelings, I cannot content myself with these detached remarks. And if, in what I am about to say, it shall appear to some that my labour is unnecessary, and that I am like a man fighting a battle without enemies, I would remind such persons that, whatever may be the language outwardly holden by men, a practical faith in the opinions which I am wishing to establish is almost unknown. If my conclusions are admitted, and carried as far as they must be carried if admitted at all, our judgments concerning the works of the greatest Poets both ancient and modern will be far different from what they are at present, both when we praise, and when we censure: and our moral feelings influencing, and influenced by these judgments will, I believe, be corrected and purified.

Taking up the subject, then, upon general grounds, I ask what is meant by the word Poet? What is a Poet? To whom does he address himself? And what language is to be expected from him? He is a man speaking to men: a man, it is true, endued with more lively sensibility, more enthusiasm and tenderness, who has a greater knowledge of human nature, and a more comprehensive soul, than are supposed to be common among mankind; a man pleased with his own passions and volitions, and who rejoices more than other men in the spirit of life that is in him; delighting to contemplate similar volitions and passions as manifested in the goings-on of the Universe, and habitually impelled to create them where he does not find them. To these qualities he has added a disposition to be affected more than other men by absent things as if they were present;[3] an ability of conjuring up in himself passions, which are indeed far from being the same as those produced by real events, yet (especially in those parts of the general sympathy which are pleasing and delightful) do more nearly resemble the passions produced by real events, than any thing which, from the motions of their own minds merely, other men are accustomed to feel in themselves; whence, and from practice, he has acquired a greater readiness and power in expressing what he thinks and feels, and especially those thoughts and feelings which, by his own choice, or from the structure of his own mind, arise in him without immediate external excitement.

But, whatever portion of this faculty we may suppose even the greatest Poet to possess, there cannot be a doubt but that the language which it will suggest to him, must, in liveliness and truth, fall far short of that which is uttered by men in real life, under the actual pressure of those passions, certain shadows of which the Poet thus produces, or feels to be produced, in himself.[4] However exalted a notion we would wish to cherish of the character of a Poet, it is obvious, that, while he describes and imitates passions, his situation is altogether slavish and mechanical, compared with the freedom and power of real and substantial action and suffering. So that it will be the wish of the Poet to bring his feelings near to those of the persons whose feelings he describes, nay, for short spaces of time perhaps, to let himself slip into an entire delusion, and even confound and identify his own feelings with theirs; modifying only the language which is thus suggested to him, by a consideration that he describes for a particular purpose, that of giving pleasure. Here, then, he will apply the principle on which I have so much insisted, namely, that of selection; on this he will depend for removing what would otherwise be painful or disgusting in the passion; he will feel that there is no necessity to trick out or to elevate nature: and, the more industriously he applies this principle, the deeper will be his

3. This echoes the passage from Quintilian quoted in the letter to Fox and used as epigraph to the edition of 1802.

4. Another echo of Quintilian, *Institutes*, X.vii.15.

faith that no words, which his fancy or imagination can suggest, will be to be compared with those which are the emanations of reality and truth.

But it may be said by those who do not object to the general spirit of these remarks, that, as it is impossible for the Poet to produce upon all occasions language as exquisitely fitted for the passion as that which the real passion itself suggests, it is proper that he should consider himself as in the situation of a translator, who deems himself justified when he substitutes excellences of another kind for those which are unattainable by him; and endeavours occasionally to surpass his original, in order to make some amends for the general inferiority to which he feels that he must submit. But this would be to encourage idleness and unmanly despair. Further, it is the language of men who speak of what they do not understand; who talk of Poetry as of a matter of amusement and idle pleasure; who will converse with us as gravely about a *taste* for Poetry, as they express it, as if it were a thing as indifferent as a taste for Rope-dancing, or Frontiniac[5] or Sherry. Aristotle, I have been told, hath said, that Poetry is the most philosophic of all writing:[6] it is so: its object is truth, not individual and local, but general, and operative; not standing upon external testimony, but carried alive into the heart by passion; truth which is its own testimony, which gives strength and divinity to the tribunal to which it appeals, and receives them from the same tribunal. Poetry is the image of man and nature. The obstacles which stand in the way of the fidelity of the Biographer and Historian, and of their consequent utility, are incalculably greater than those which are to be encountered by the Poet who has an adequate notion of the dignity of his art. The Poet writes under one restriction only, namely, that of the necessity of giving immediate pleasure to a human Being possessed of that information which may be expected from him, not as a lawyer, a physician, a mariner, an astronomer or a natural philosopher, but as a Man. Except this one restriction, there is no object standing

5. Frontignac is a muscat wine.
6. Aristotle (*Poetics*, 1451.b.5–7) says only that poetry is more philosophical than history. Coleridge echoes Wordsworth's misquotation in *Biographia Literaria* (ed. J. Shawcross [2 vols.; London: Oxford University Press, 1907], II, 101).

between the Poet and the image of things; between this, and the Biographer and Historian there are a thousand.

Nor let this necessity of producing immediate pleasure be considered as a degradation of the Poet's art. It is far otherwise. It is an acknowledgment of the beauty of the universe, an acknowledgment the more sincere, because it is not formal, but indirect; it is a task light and easy to him who looks at the world in the spirit of love: further, it is a homage paid to the native and naked dignity of man, to the grand elementary principle of pleasure, by which he knows, and feels, and lives, and moves. We have no sympathy but what is propagated by pleasure: I would not be misunderstood; but whereever we sympathize with pain it will be found that the sympathy is produced and carried on by subtle combinations with pleasure. We have no knowledge, that is, no general principles drawn from the contemplation of particular facts, but what has been built up by pleasure, and exists in us by pleasure alone. The Man of Science, the Chemist and Mathematician, whatever difficulties and disgusts they may have had to struggle with, know and feel this.[7] However painful may be the objects with which the Anatomist's knowledge is connected, he feels that his knowledge is pleasure; and where he has no pleasure he has no knowledge. What then does the Poet? He considers man and the objects that surround him as acting and re-acting upon each other, so as to produce an infinite complexity of pain and pleasure; he considers man in his own nature and in his ordinary life as contemplating this with a certain quantity of immediate knowledge, with certain convictions, intuitions, and deductions which by habit become of the nature of intuitions; he considers him as looking upon this complex scene of ideas and sensations, and finding every where objects that immediately excite in him sympathies which, from the necessities of his nature, are accompanied by an overbalance of enjoyment.

---

7. *Cf*. John Dennis, "Grounds of Criticism in Poetry" (1704): "The satisfaction that we receive from Geometry itself, comes from the Joy of having found out Truth, and the Desire of finding more. . . . Poetry attains its final end, which is the reforming the minds of men, by exciting of Passion. And here I dare be bold to affirm, that all Instruction whatever depends upon Passion" (*Works*, ed. E. N. Hooker [2 vols.; Baltimore: Johns Hopkins Press, 1939–1943], I, 337).

To this knowledge which all men carry about with them, and to these sympathies in which without any other discipline than that of our daily life we are fitted to take delight, the Poet principally directs his attention. He considers man and nature as essentially adapted to each other, and the mind of man as naturally the mirror of the fairest and most interesting qualities of nature. And thus the Poet, prompted by this feeling of pleasure which accompanies him through the whole course of his studies, converses with general nature with affections akin to those, which, through labour and length of time, the Man of Science has raised up in himself, by conversing with those particular parts of nature which are the objects of his studies. The knowledge both of the Poet and the Man of Science is pleasure; but the knowledge of the one cleaves to us as a necessary part of our existence, our natural and unalienable inheritance; the other is a personal and individual acquisition, slow to come to us, and by no habitual and direct sympathy connecting us with our fellow-beings. The Man of Science seeks truth as a remote and unknown benefactor; he cherishes and loves it in his solitude: the Poet, singing a song in which all human beings join with him, rejoices in the presence of truth as our visible friend and hourly companion. Poetry is the breath and finer spirit of all knowledge; it is the impassioned expression which is in the countenance of all Science. Emphatically may it be said of the Poet, as Shakespeare hath said of man, "that he looks before and after."[8] He is the rock of defence of human nature; an upholder and preserver, carrying every where with him relationship and love. In spite of difference of soil and climate, of language and manners, of laws and customs, in spite of things silently gone out of mind and things violently destroyed, the Poet binds together by passion and knowledge the vast empire of human society, as it is spread over the whole earth, and over all time. The objects of the Poet's thoughts are every where; though the eyes and senses of man are, it is true, his favourite guides, yet he will follow wheresoever he can find an atmosphere of sensation in which to move his wings. Poetry is the first and last of all knowledge—it is as immortal as the heart of man. If the labours of Men of Science should ever create any material

8. *Hamlet*, IV.iv.37.

revolution, direct or indirect, in our condition, and in the impressions which we habitually receive, the Poet will sleep then no more than at present, but he will be ready to follow the steps of the Man of Science, not only in those general indirect effects, but he will be at his side, carrying sensation into the midst of the objects of the Science itself. The remotest discoveries of the Chemist, the Botanist, or Mineralogist, will be as proper objects of the Poet's art as any upon which it can be employed, if the time should ever come when these things shall be familiar to us, and the relations under which they are contemplated by the followers of these respective Sciences shall be manifestly and palpably material to us as enjoying and suffering beings. If the time should ever come when what is now called Science, thus familiarized to men, shall be ready to put on, as it were, a form of flesh and blood, the Poet will lend his divine spirit to aid the transfiguration, and will welcome the Being thus produced, as a dear and genuine inmate of the household of man.—It is not, then, to be supposed that any one, who holds that sublime notion of Poetry which I have attempted to convey, will break in upon the sanctity and truth of his pictures by transitory and accidental ornaments, and endeavour to excite admiration of himself by arts, the necessity of which must manifestly depend upon the assumed meanness of his subject.

What I have thus far said applies to Poetry in general; but especially to those parts of composition where the Poet speaks through the mouths of his characters; and upon this point it appears to have such weight that I will conclude, there are few persons of good sense, who would not allow that the dramatic parts of composition are defective, in proportion as they deviate from the real language of nature, and are coloured by a diction of the Poet's own, either peculiar to him as an individual Poet, or belonging simply to Poets in general, to a body of men who, from the circumstance of their compositions being in metre, it is expected will employ a particular language.

It is not, then, in the dramatic parts of composition that we look for this distinction of language; but still it may be proper and necessary where the Poet speaks to us in his own person and character. To this I answer by referring my Reader to the description which I have before given of a Poet. Among the qualities which I have enumerated as principally conducing to form a Poet, is implied nothing differing in kind from other men, but only in degree. The sum of what I have there said is, that the Poet is chiefly distinguished from other men by a greater promptness to think and feel without immediate external excitement, and a greater power in expressing such thoughts and feelings as are produced in him in that manner. But these passions and thoughts and feelings are the general passions and thoughts and feelings of men. And with what are they connected? Undoubtedly with our moral sentiments and animal sensations, and with the causes which excite these; with the operations of the elements and the appearances of the visible universe; with storm and sun-shine, with the revolutions of the seasons, with cold and heat, with loss of friends and kindred, with injuries and resentments, gratitude and hope, with fear and sorrow. These, and the like, are the sensations and objects which the Poet describes, as they are the sensations of other men, and the objects which interest them. The Poet thinks and feels in the spirit of the passions of men. How, then, can his language differ in any material degree from that of all other men who feel vividly and see clearly? It might be *proved* that it is impossible. But supposing that this were not the case, the Poet might then be allowed to use a peculiar language when expressing his feelings for his own gratification, or that of men like himself. But Poets do not write for Poets alone, but for men. Unless therefore we are advocates for that admiration which depends upon ignorance, and that pleasure which arises from hearing what we do not understand, the Poet must descend from this supposed height, and, in order to excite rational sympathy, he must express himself as other men express themselves. To this it may be added, that while he is only selecting from the real language of men, or, which amounts to the same thing, composing accurately in the spirit of such selection, he is treading upon safe ground, and we know what we are to expect from him. Our feelings are the same with respect to metre; for, as it may be proper to remind the Reader, the distinction of metre is regular and uniform, and not like that which is produced by what is usually called poetic diction, arbitrary, and subject to infinite caprices upon which no calculation whatever can be made. In the one case, the Reader is utterly at the mercy of the Poet respecting what imagery or diction he may choose to connect with the passion, whereas, in the other, the metre obeys certain laws, to which the Poet and Reader both willingly submit because they are certain, and because no interference is made by them with the passion but such as the concurring testimony of ages has shown to heighten and improve the pleasure which co-exists with it.

It will now be proper to answer an obvious question, namely, Why, professing these opinions, have I written in verse? To this, in addition to such answer as is included in what I have already said, I reply in the first place, Because, however I may have restricted myself, there is still left open to me what confessedly constitutes the most valuable object of all writing, whether in prose or verse, the great and universal passions of men, the most general and interesting of their occupations, and the entire world of nature, from which I am at liberty to supply myself with endless combinations of forms and imagery. Now, supposing for a moment that whatever is interesting in these objects may be as vividly described in prose, why am I to be condemned, if to such description I have endeavoured to superadd the charm which, by the consent of all nations, is acknowledged to exist in metrical language? To this, by such as are unconvinced by what I have already said, it may be answered, that a very small part of the pleasure given by Poetry depends upon the metre, and that it is injudicious to write in metre, unless it be accompanied with the other artificial distinctions of style with which metre is usually accompanied, and that by such deviation more will be lost from the shock which will be thereby given to the Reader's associations, than will be counterbalanced by any pleasure which he can derive from the general power of numbers. In answer to those who still contend for the necessity of accompanying metre with certain appropriate colours of style in order to the accomplishment of its appropriate end, and who also, in my opinion, greatly under-rate the power of metre in itself, it might perhaps, as far as relates to these Poems, have been almost sufficient to observe, that poems are extant, written upon more humble subjects, and in a more naked and simple style than I have aimed at, which poems have continued to give pleasure from generation to generation. Now, if nakedness and simplicity be a defect, the fact here mentioned affords a strong presumption that poems somewhat less naked and simple are capable of affording pleasure at the present day; and, what I wished *chiefly* to attempt, at present, was to justify myself for having written under the impression of this belief.

But I might point out various causes why, when the style is manly, and the subject of some importance, words metrically arranged will long continue to impart such a pleasure to mankind as he who is sensible of the extent of that pleasure will be desirous to impart. The end of Poetry is to produce excitement in co-existence with an over-balance of pleasure. Now, by the supposition, excitement is an unusual and irregular state of the mind; ideas and feelings do not in that state succeed each other in accustomed order. But, if the words by which this excitement is produced are in themselves powerful, or the images and feelings have an undue proportion of pain connected with them, there is some danger that the excitement may be carried beyond its proper bounds. Now the co-presence of something regular, something to which the mind has been accustomed in various moods and in a less excited state, cannot but have great efficacy in tempering and restraining the passion by an intertexture of ordinary feeling, and of feeling not strictly and necessarily connected with the passion. This is un-questionably true, and hence, though the opinion will at first appear paradoxical, from the tendency of metre to divest language in a certain degree of its reality, and thus to throw a sort of half consciousness of unsubstantial existence over the whole composition, there can be little doubt but that more pathetic situations and sentiments, that is, those which have a greater proportion of pain connected with them, may be endured in metrical composition, especially in rhyme, than in prose. The metre of the old ballads is very artless; yet they contain many passages which would illustrate this opinion, and, I hope, if the following Poems be attentively perused, similar instances will be found in them. This opinion may be further illustrated by appealing to the Reader's own experience of the reluctance with which he comes to the re-perusal of the distressful parts of Clarissa Harlowe, or the Gamester. While

Shakespeare's writings, in the most pathetic scenes, never act upon us as pathetic beyond the bounds of pleasure—an effect which, in a much greater degree than might at first be imagined, is to be ascribed to small, but continual and regular impulses of pleasurable surprise from the metrical arrangement.—On the other hand (what it must be allowed will much more frequently happen) if the Poet's words should be incommensurate with the passion, and inadequate to raise the Reader to a height of desirable excitement, then, (unless the Poet's choice of his metre has been grossly injudicious) in the feelings of pleasure which the Reader has been accustomed to connect with metre in general, and in the feeling, whether cheerful or melancholy, which he has been accustomed to connect with that particular movement of metre, there will be found something which will greatly contribute to impart passion to the words, and to effect the complex end which the Poet proposes to himself.

If I had undertaken a systematic defence of the theory upon which these poems are written, it would have been my duty to develope the various causes upon which the pleasure received from metrical language depends. Among the chief of these causes is to be reckoned a principle which must be well known to those who have made any of the Arts the object of accurate reflection; I mean the pleasure which the mind derives from the perception of similitude in dissimilitude. This principle is the great spring of the activity of our minds, and their chief feeder. From this principle the direction of the sexual appetite, and all the passions connected with it, take their origin: it is the life of our ordinary conversation; and upon the accuracy with which similitude in dissimilitude, and dissimilitude in similitude are perceived, depend our taste and our moral feelings. It would not have been a useless employment to have applied this principle to the consideration of metre, and to have shown that metre is hence enabled to afford much pleasure, and to have pointed out in what manner that pleasure is produced. But my limits will not permit me to enter upon this subject, and I must content myself with a general summary.

I have said that Poetry is the spontaneous overflow of powerful feelings: it takes its origin from emotion recollected in tranquillity:

the emotion is contemplated till by a species of reaction the tranquillity gradually disappears, and an emotion, kindred to that which was before the subject of contemplation, is gradually produced, and does itself actually exist in the mind. In this mood successful composition generally begins, and in a mood similar to this it is carried on; but the emotion, of whatever kind and in whatever degree, from various causes is qualified by various pleasures, so that in describing any passions whatsoever, which are voluntarily described, the mind will upon the whole be in a state of enjoyment. Now, if Nature be thus cautious in preserving in a state of enjoyment a being thus employed, the Poet ought to profit by the lesson thus held forth to him, and ought especially to take care, that whatever passions he communicates to his Reader, those passions, if his Reader's mind be sound and vigorous, should always be accompanied with an overbalance of pleasure. Now the music of harmonious metrical language, the sense of difficulty overcome, and the blind association of pleasure which has been previously received from works of rhyme or metre of the same or similar construction, an indistinct perception perpetually renewed of language closely resembling that of real life, and yet, in the circumstance of metre, differing from it so widely, all these imperceptibly make up a complex feeling of delight, which is of the most important use in tempering the painful feeling which will always be found intermingled with powerful descriptions of the deeper passions. This effect is always produced in pathetic and impassioned poetry; while, in lighter compositions, the ease and gracefulness with which the Poet manages his numbers are themselves confessedly a principal source of the gratification of the Reader. I might perhaps include all which it is *necessary* to say upon this subject by affirming, what few persons will deny, that, of two descriptions, either of passions, manners, or characters, each of them equally well executed, the one in prose and the other in verse, the verse will be read a hundred times where the prose is read once. We see that Pope, by the power of verse alone, has contrived to render the plainest common sense interesting, and even frequently to invest it with the appearance of passion. In consequence of these convictions I related in metre the Tale of GOODY BLAKE AND HARRY GILL, which is one of the rudest of this collection. I wished to draw attention to the truth, that the power of the human imagination is sufficient to produce such changes even in our physical nature as might almost appear miraculous. The truth is an important one; the fact (for it is a *fact*) is a valuable illustration of it. And I have the satisfaction of knowing that it has been communicated to many hundreds of people who would never have heard of it, had it not been narrated as a Ballad, and in a more impressive metre than is usual in Ballads.

Having thus explained a few of the reasons why I have written in verse, and why I have chosen subjects from common life, and endeavoured to bring my language near to the real language of men, if I have been too minute in pleading my own cause, I have at the same time been treating a subject of general interest; and it is for this reason that I request the Reader's permission to add a few words with reference solely to these particular poems, and to some defects which will probably be found in them. I am sensible that my associations must have sometimes been particular instead of general, and that, consequently, giving to things a false importance, sometimes from diseased impulses I may have written upon unworthy subjects; but I am less apprehensive on this account, than that my language may frequently have suffered from those arbitrary connections of feelings and ideas with particular words and phrases, from which no man can altogether protect himself. Hence I have no doubt, that, in some instances, feelings even of the ludicrous may be given to my Readers by expressions which appeared to me tender and pathetic. Such faulty expressions, were I convinced they were faulty at present, and that they must necessarily continue to be so, I would willingly take all reasonable pains to correct. But it is dangerous to make these alterations on the simple authority of a few individuals, or even of certain classes of men; for where the understanding of an Author is not convinced, or his feelings altered, this cannot be done without great injury to himself: for his own feelings are his stay and support, and, if he sets them aside in one instance, he may be induced to repeat this act till his mind loses all confidence in itself, and becomes utterly debilitated. To this it may be added, that the Reader ought never to forget that he is himself exposed to the same errors as the Poet, and perhaps in a much greater degree: for there can be no presumption in saying, that it is not probable he will be so well acquainted with the various stages of meaning through which words have passed, or with the fickleness or stability of the relations of particular ideas to each other; and above all, since he is so much less interested in the subject, he may decide lightly and carelessly.

Long as I have detained my Reader, I hope he will permit me to caution him against a mode of false criticism which has been applied to Poetry in which the language closely resembles that of life and nature. Such verses have been triumphed over in parodies of which Dr. Johnson's stanza is a fair specimen.

> "I put my hat upon my head,
> And walk'd into the Strand,
> And there I met another man
> Whose hat was in his hand."

Immediately under these lines I will place one of the most justly admired stanzas of the "*Babes* in the Wood."

> "These pretty Babes with hand in hand
> Went wandering up and down;
> But never more they saw the Man
> Approaching from the Town."

In both these stanzas the words, and the order of the words, in no respect differ from the most unimpassioned conversation. There are words in both, for example, "the Strand," and "the Town," connected with none but the most familiar ideas; yet the one stanza we admit as admirable, and the other as a fair example of the superlatively contemptible. Whence arises this difference? Not from the metre, not from the language, not from the order of the words; but the *matter* expressed in Dr. Johnson's stanza is contemptible. The proper method of treating trivial and simple verses, to which Dr. Johnson's stanza would be a fair parallelism, is not to say, This is a bad kind of poetry, or This is not poetry; but This wants sense; it is neither interesting in itself, nor can *lead* to any thing interesting; the images neither originate in that sane state of feeling which arises out of thought, nor can excite thought or feeling in the Reader. This is the only sensible manner of dealing with such verses. Why trouble yourself about the species till you have previously decided upon the genus? Why take pains to prove that an ape is not a Newton, when it is self-evident that he is not a man?

I have one request to make of my Reader, which is, that in judging these Poems he would decide by his own feelings genuinely, and not by reflection upon what will probably be the judgment of others. How common is it to hear a person say, "I myself do not object to this style of composition, or this or that expression, but to such and such classes of people it will appear mean or ludicrous." This mode of criticism, so destructive of all sound unadulterated judgment, is almost universal: I have therefore to request, that the Reader would abide independently by his own feelings, and that if he finds himself affected he would not suffer such conjectures to interfere with his pleasure.

If an Author by any single composition has impressed us with respect for his talents, it is useful to consider this as affording a presumption, that, on other occasions where we have been displeased, he nevertheless may not have written ill or absurdly; and, further, to give him so much credit for this one composition as may induce us to review what has displeased us with more care than we should otherwise have bestowed upon it. This is not only an act of justice, but, in our decisions upon poetry especially, may conduce in a high degree to the improvement of our own taste: for an *accurate* taste in poetry, and in all the other arts, as Sir Joshua Reynolds has observed, is an *acquired* talent, which can only be produced by thought, and a long continued intercourse with the best models of composition. This is mentioned, not with so ridiculous a purpose as to prevent the most inexperienced Reader from judging for himself, (I have already said that I wish him to judge for himself;) but merely to temper the rashness of decision, and to suggest, that, if Poetry be a subject on which much time has not been bestowed, the judgment may be erroneous; and that in many cases it necessarily will be so.

I know that nothing would have so effectually contributed to further the end which I have in view, as to have shown of what kind the pleasure is, and how that pleasure is produced, which is confessedly produced by metrical composition essentially different from that which I have here endeavoured to recommend: for the Reader will say that he has been pleased by such composition; and what can I do more for him? The power of any art is limited; and he will suspect, that, if I propose to furnish him with new friends, it is only upon condition of his abandoning his old friends. Besides, as I have said, the Reader is himself conscious of the pleasure which he has received from such composition, composition to which he has peculiarly attached the endearing name of Poetry; and all men feel an habitual gratitude, and something of an honorable bigotry for the objects which have long continued to please them; we not only wish to be pleased, but to be pleased in that particular way in which we have been accustomed to be pleased. There is a host of arguments in these feelings; and I should be the less able to combat them successfully, as I am willing to allow, that, in order entirely to enjoy the Poetry which I am recommending, it would be necessary to give up much of what is ordinarily enjoyed. But, would my limits have permitted me to point out how this pleasure is produced, I might have removed many obstacles, and assisted my Reader in perceiving that the powers of language are not so limited as he may suppose; and that it is possible that poetry may give other enjoyments, of a purer, more lasting, and more exquisite nature. This part of my subject I have not altogether neglected; but it has been less my present aim to prove, that the interest excited by some other kinds of poetry is less vivid, and less worthy of the nobler powers of the mind, than to offer reasons for presuming, that, if the object which I have proposed to myself were adequately attained, a species of poetry would be produced, which is genuine poetry; in its nature well adapted to interest mankind permanently, and likewise important in the multiplicity and quality of its moral relations.

From what has been said, and from a perusal of the Poems, the Reader will be able clearly to perceive the object which I have proposed to myself: he will determine how far I have attained this object; and, what is a much more important question, whether it be worth attaining: and upon the decision of these two questions will rest my claim to the approbation of the public.

Lyrical Ballads, with Pastoral and other Poems (2 vols.; London, 1802), I, [i]–lxiv.

Appendix to the Preface (1802)

See Preface, page 54.—*"by what is usually called Poetic Diction."*

As perhaps I have no right to expect from a Reader of an Introduction to a volume of Poems that attentive perusal without which it is impossible, imperfectly as I have been compelled to express my meaning, that what I have said in the Preface should throughout be fully understood, I am the more anxious to give an exact notion of the sense in which I use the phrase *poetic diction*; and for this purpose I will here add a few words concerning the origin of the phraseology which I have condemned under that name.—The earliest Poets of all nations generally wrote from passion excited by real events; they wrote naturally, and as men: feeling powerfully as they did, their language was daring, and figurative. In succeeding times, Poets, and men ambitious of the fame of Poets, perceiving the influence of such language, and desirous of producing the same effect, without having the same animating passion, set themselves to a mechanical adoption of those figures of speech, and made use of them, sometimes with propriety, but much more frequently applied them to feelings and ideas with which they had no natural connection whatsoever. A language was thus insensibly produced, differing materially from the real language of men in *any situation*. The Reader or Hearer of this distorted language found himself in a perturbed and unusual state of mind: when affected by the genuine language of passion he had been in a perturbed and unusual state of mind also: in both cases he was willing that his common judgment and understanding should be laid asleep, and he had no instinctive and infallible perception of the true to make him reject the false; the one served as a passport for the other. The agitation and confusion of mind were in both cases delightful, and no wonder if he confounded the one with the other, and believed them both to be produced by the same, or similar causes. Besides, the Poet spake to him in the character of a man to be looked up to, a man of genius and authority. Thus, and from a variety of other causes, this distorted language was received with admiration; and Poets, it is probable, who had before contented themselves for the most part with misapplying only expressions which at first had been dictated by real passion, carried the abuse still further, and introduced phrases composed apparently in the spirit of the original figurative language of passion, yet altogether of their own invention, and distinguished by various degrees of wanton deviation from good sense and nature.

It is indeed true that the language of the earliest Poets was felt to differ materially from ordinary language, because it was the language of extraordinary occasions; but it was really spoken by men, language which the Poet himself had uttered when he had been affected by the events which he described, or which he had heard uttered by those around him. To this language it is probable that metre of some sort or other was early superadded. This separated the genuine language of Poetry still further from common life, so that whoever read or heard the poems of these earliest Poets felt himself moved in a way in which he had not been accustomed to be moved in real life, and by causes manifestly different from those which acted upon him in real life. This was the great temptation to all the corruptions which have followed: under the protection of this feeling succeeding Poets constructed a phraseology which had one thing, it is true, in common with the genuine language of poetry, namely, that it was not heard in ordinary conversation; that it was unusual. But the first Poets, as I have said, spake a language which, though unusual, was still the language of men. This circumstance, however, was disregarded by their successors; they found that they could please by easier means: they became proud of a language which they themselves had invented, and which was uttered only by themselves; and, with the spirit of a fraternity, they arrogated it to themselves as their own. In process of time metre became a symbol or promise of this unusual language, and whoever took upon him to write in metre, according as he possessed more or less of true poetic genius, introduced less or more of this adulterated phraseology into his compositions, and the true and the false became so inseparably interwoven that the taste of men was gradually perverted; and this language was received as a natural language; and at length, by the influence of books upon men, did to a certain degree really become so. Abuses of this kind were imported from one nation to another, and with the progress of refinement this diction became daily more and more corrupt, thrusting out of sight the plain humanities of nature by a motley masquerade of tricks, quaintnesses, hieroglyphics, and enigmas.

It would be highly interesting to point out the causes of the pleasure given by this extravagant and absurd language: but this is not the place; it depends upon a great variety of causes, but upon none perhaps more than its influence in impressing a notion of the peculiarity and exaltation of the Poet's character, and in flattering the Reader's self-love by bringing him nearer to a sympathy with that character; an effect which is accomplished by unsettling ordinary habits of thinking, and thus assisting the Reader to approach to that perturbed and dizzy state of mind in which if he does not find himself, he imagines that he is *balked* of a peculiar enjoyment which poetry can, and ought to bestow.

The sonnet which I have quoted from Gray, in the Preface, except the lines printed in Italics, consists of little else but this diction, though not of the worst kind; and indeed, if I may be permitted to say so, it is far too common in the best writers, both antient and modern. Perhaps I can in no way, by positive example, more easily give my Reader a notion of what I mean by the phrase *poetic diction* than by referring him to a comparison between the metrical paraphrases which we have of passages in the old and new Testament, and those passages as they exist in our common Translation. See Pope's "Messiah" throughout, Prior's "Did sweeter sounds adorn my flowing tongue,"[1] &c. &c. "Though I speak with the tongues of men and of angels," &c. &c. See 1st Corinthians,

1. *Works,* ed. H. B. Wright and M. K. Spears (2 vols.; Oxford: Clarendon Press, 1959), I, 207:

> Did sweeter Sounds adorn my flowing Tongue,
> Than ever Man pronounc'd or Angel sung:
> Had I all Knowledge, Human and Divine
> That Thought can reach, or Science can define....

chapter xiiith. By way of immediate example, take the following of Dr. Johnson:

> "Turn on the prudent Ant thy heedless eyes,
> Observe her labours, Sluggard, and be wise;
> No stern command, no monitory voice,
> Prescribes her duties, or directs her choice;
> Yet, timely provident, she hastes away
> To snatch the blessings of a plenteous day;
> When fruitful Summer loads the teeming plain,
> She crops the harvest and she stores the grain.
> How long shall sloth usurp thy useless hours,
> Unnerve thy vigour, and enchain thy powers?
> While artful shades thy downy couch enclose,
> And soft solicitation courts repose,
> Amidst the drowsy charms of dull delight,
> Year chases year with unremitted flight,
> Till want now following, fraudulent and slow,
> Shall spring to seize thee, like an ambushed foe."[2]

From this hubbub of words pass to the original. "Go to the Ant, thou Sluggard, consider her ways, and be wise: which having no guide, overseer, or ruler, provideth her meat in the summer, and gathereth her food in the harvest. How long wilt thou sleep, O Sluggard? when wilt thou arise out of thy sleep? Yet a little sleep, a little slumber, a little folding of the hands to sleep. So shall thy poverty come as one that travaileth, and thy want as an armed man." Proverbs, chap. vith.

One more quotation and I have done. It is from Cowper's verses supposed to be written by Alexander Selkirk:

> "Religion! what treasure untold
> Resides in that heavenly word!
> More precious than silver and gold,
> Or all that this earth can afford.
> But the sound of the church-going bell
> These valleys and rocks never heard,
> Ne'er sighed at the sound of a knell,
> Or smiled when a sabbath appeared.

---

2. *Poems*, ed. D. Nichol Smith and E. L. McAdam, pp. 151–152.

Ye winds, that have made me your sport,
Convey to this desolate shore
Some cordial endearing report
Of a land I must visit no more.
My Friends, do they now and then send
A wish or a thought after me?
O tell me I yet have a friend,
Though a friend I am never to see."[3]

I have quoted this passage as an instance of three different styles of composition. The first four lines are poorly expressed; some Critics would call the language prosaic; the fact is, it would be bad prose, so bad, that it is scarcely worse in metre. The epithet "church-going" applied to a bell, and that by so chaste a writer as Cowper, is an instance of the strange abuses which Poets have introduced into their language till they and their Readers take them as matters of course, if they do not single them out expressly as objects of admiration. The two lines "Ne'er sigh'd at the sound," &c. are, in my opinion, an instance of the language of passion wrested from its proper use, and, from the mere circumstance of the composition being in metre, applied upon an occasion that does not justify such violent expressions; and I should condemn the passage, though perhaps few Readers will agree with me, as vicious poetic diction. The last stanza is throughout admirably expressed: it would be equally good whether in prose or verse, except that the Reader has an exquisite pleasure in seeing such natural language so naturally connected with metre. The beauty of this stanza tempts me here to add a sentiment which ought to be the pervading spirit of a system, detached parts of which have been imperfectly explained in the Preface,—namely, that in proportion as ideas and feelings are valuable, whether the composition be in prose or in verse, they require and exact one and the same language.[4]

Lyrical Ballads, with Pastoral and other Poems (2 vols.; London, 1802), II, [237]–247.

3. *Poems*, ed. H. S. Milford (4th ed.; Oxford: Oxford University Press, 1934), p. 312, ll. 25–40.

4. Two passages were deleted from the Appendix before printing: another example of defective diction from a sonnet by Thomas Russell; and a diffident concluding paragraph. See W. Hale White, *A Description of the Wordsworth and Coleridge Manuscripts in the Possession of Mr. T. Norton Longman* (London, 1897), pp. 47–50.

Letter to John Wilson (June, 1802)

John Wilson, later to become "Christopher North" of Blackwood's Magazine, *was a seventeen-year-old student at Glasgow when he wrote to Wordsworth about the* Lyrical Ballads. *Wilson's letter, dated May 24, 1802, is some two thousand words long, almost half concerning the "Idiot Boy."* [1] *After apologizing for intruding, Wilson praises Wordsworth, questions him, and then instructs him. These excerpts are typical:* ". . . *disposition of the mind to assimilate the appearances of external nature to its own situation, is a fine subject for poetical allusion, and in several poems you have employed it with a most electrifying effect. But you have not stopped* here, *you have shown the effect which the qualities of external nature have in forming the human mind, and have presented us with several characters whose particular bias arose from that situation in which they were planted with respect to the scenery of nature." "May not the face of external nature through different quarters of the globe account for the dispositions of different nations?" Then Wilson leads into censure: The poems "represent the enjoyment resulting from cultivation of the social affections of our nature; they inculcate a conscientious regard to the rights of our fellow-men; they show that every creature on the face of the earth is entitled in some measure to our kindness. They prove that in every mind,* however *depraved, there exist some qualities deserving our esteem." But, says Wilson, "No feeling, no state of mind ought, in my opinion, to become the subject of poetry, that does not please." "We may lay this down as a general rule, that no description can please, where the sympathies of our soul are not excited, and no narration interest, where we do not enter into the feelings of some of the parties concerned." Neither he nor anyone he knows can enter into the feelings of Betty Foy in "The Idiot Boy": "Among all the people ever I knew to have read this poem, I never met one who did not rise rather displeased from the perusal of it . . . ." "You have delineated feelings which, though natural, do not please, but which create a certain degree of disgust and contempt."*

1. Wilson's letter is reprinted in Mary Gordon, *Christopher North* (New York, 1863), pp. 26–32.

Wordsworth received the letter on May 31 and replied to it within a week.[2]

Had it not been for a very amiable modesty you would not have imagined that your letter could give me any offence. It was on many accounts highly grateful to me. I was pleased to find that I had given so much pleasure to an ingenuous and able mind, and I further considered the enjoyment which you had had from my Poems as an earnest that others might be delighted with them in the same, or a like manner. It is plain from your letter that the pleasure which I have given you has not been blind or unthinking; you have studied the poems, and prove that you have entered into the spirit of them. They have not given you a cheap or vulgar pleasure; therefore I feel that you are entitled to my kindest thanks for having done some violence to your natural diffidence in the communication which you have made to me.

There is scarcely any part of your letter that does not deserve particular notice; but partly from some constitutional infirmities, and partly from certain habits of mind, I do not write any letters unless upon business, not even to my dearest friends. Except during absence from my own family I have not written five letters of friendship during the last five years. I have mentioned this in order that I may retain your good opinion, should my letter be less minute than you are entitled to expect. You seem to be desirous of my opinion on the influence of natural objects in forming the character of Nations. This cannot be understood without first considering their influence upon men in general, first, with reference to such subjects as are common to all countries; and, next, such as belong exclusively to any particular country, or in a greater degree to it than to another. Now it is manifest that no human being can be so besotted and debased by oppression, penury, or any other evil which unhumanizes man as to be utterly insensible to the colours, forms, or smell of flowers, the voices and motions of birds and beasts, the appearances of the sky and heavenly bodies, the general warmth

2. William Knight, *Life of Wordsworth* (3 vols.; Edinburgh, 1889), I, 397.

of a fine day, the terror and uncomfortableness of a storm, etc. etc. How dead soever many full-grown men may outwardly seem to these things, all are more or less affected by them; and in childhood, in the first practice and exercise of their senses, they must have been not the nourishers merely, but often the fathers of their passions. There cannot be a doubt that in tracts of country where images of danger, melancholy, and grandeur, or loveliness, softness, and ease prevail, they will make themselves felt powerfully in forming the characters of the people, so as to produce a uniformity of national character, where the nation is small and is not made up of men who, inhabiting different soils, climates, etc., by their civil usages and relations, materially interfere with each other. It was so formerly, no doubt, in the Highlands of Scotland; but we cannot perhaps observe it in our own island at the present day, because, even in the most sequestered places, by manufactures, traffic, religion, law, interchange of inhabitants, etc., distinctions are done away with which would otherwise have been strong and obvious. This complex state of society does not, however, prevent the characters of individuals from frequently receiving a strong bias, not merely from the impressions of general nature, but also from local objects and images. But it seems that to produce these effects, in the degree in which we frequently find them to be produced, there must be a peculiar sensibility of original organization combining with moral accidents, as is exhibited in *The Brothers* and in *Ruth*; I mean, to produce this in a marked degree; not that I believe that any man was ever brought up in the country without loving it, especially in his better moments, or in a district of particular grandeur or beauty, without feeling some stronger attachment to it on that account than he would otherwise have felt. I include, you will observe, in these considerations, the influence of climate, changes in the atmosphere and elements, and the labours and occupations which particular districts require.

You begin what you say upon *The Idiot Boy* with this observation, that nothing is a fit subject for poetry which does not please. But here follows a question, Does not please whom? Some have little knowledge of natural imagery of any kind, and, of course, little relish for it; some are disgusted with the very mention of the words "pastoral poetry," "sheep," or "shepherds"; some cannot tolerate a poem with a ghost or any supernatural agency in it; others would shrink from an animated description of the pleasures of love, as from a thing carnal and libidinous; some cannot bear to see delicate and refined feelings ascribed to men in low conditions of society, because their vanity and self-love tell them that these belong only to themselves and men like themselves in dress, station, and way of life; others are disgusted with the naked language of some of the most interesting passions of men, because either it is indelicate, or gross, or vulgar; as many fine ladies could not bear certain expressions in *The Mother*[3] and *The Thorn*, and as in the instance of Adam Smith, who, we are told, could not endure the ballad of *Clym of the Clough*, because the author had not written like a gentleman.[4] Then there are professional and national prejudices forevermore. Some take no interest in the description of a particular passion or quality, as love of solitariness, we will say, genial activity of fancy, love of nature, religion, and so forth, because they have little or nothing of it in themselves; and so on without end. I return then to the question, please whom? or what? I answer, human nature, as it has been and ever will be. But where are we to find the best measure of this? I answer, from within; by stripping our own hearts naked, and by looking out of ourselves towards men who lead the simplest lives, and those most according to nature; men who have never known false refinements, wayward and artificial desires, false criticisms, effeminate habits of thinking and feeling, or who, having known these things, have outgrown them. This latter class is the most to be depended upon, but it is very small in number. People in our rank in life are perpetually falling into one sad mistake, namely, that of supposing that human nature and the persons they associate with

3. The title "The Mad Mother" was later changed to "Her Eyes are Wild."

4. Clym of the Clough is a Robin Hood-like character in ballads about Adam Bell, popular in northern counties. Adam Smith's comments are in a series of anecdotes about the great economist published in the Edinburgh *Bee* (May, 1791), 1–8; and reprinted in the *European Magazine*, XX (August, 1791), 133–136. Wordsworth alludes to this statement: "It is the duty of a poet to write like a gentleman. I dislike that homely style which some think fit to call the language of nature and simplicity, and so forth" (*European Magazine*, XX, 135). Clym is given as an example. Adam Smith's anecdotes will be recalled in 1815; see below, p. 171.

are one and the same thing. Whom do we generally associate with? Gentlemen, persons of fortune, professional men, ladies, persons who can afford to buy, or can easily procure, books of half-a-guinea price, hot-pressed, and printed upon superfine paper. These persons are, it is true, a part of human nature, but we err lamentably if we suppose them to be fair representatives of the vast mass of human existence. And yet few ever consider books but with reference to their power of pleasing these persons and men of a higher rank; few descend lower, among cottages and fields, and among children. A man must have done this habitually before his judgment upon *The Idiot Boy* would be in any way decisive with me. I *know* I have done this myself habitually; I wrote the poem with exceeding delight and pleasure, and whenever I read it I read it with pleasure. You have given me praise for having reflected faithfully in my Poems the feelings of human nature. I would fain hope that I have done so. But a great Poet ought to do more than this: he ought, to a certain degree, to rectify men's feelings, to give them new compositions of feeling, to render their feelings more sane, pure, and permanent, in short, more consonant to nature, that is, to eternal nature, and the great moving spirit of things. He ought to travel before men occasionally as well as at their sides. I may illustrate this by a reference to natural objects. What false notions have prevailed from generation to generation as to the true character of the Nightingale. As far as my Friend's Poem in the *Lyrical Ballads* is read, it will contribute greatly to rectify these. You will recollect a passage in Cowper, where, speaking of rural sounds, he says:

> And *even* the boding owl
> That hails the rising moon has charms for me.[5]

Cowper was passionately fond of natural objects, yet you see he mentions it as a marvellous thing that he could connect pleasure with the cry of the owl. In the same poem he speaks in the same manner of that beautiful plant, the gorse; making in some degree an amiable boast of his loving it, *unsightly* and unsmooth as it is. There are many aversions of this kind, which, though they have

5. "The Task," ll. 205–206 (*Poems*, ed. H. Milford [4th ed.; Oxford: Oxford University Press, 1934], p. 133).

some foundation in nature, have yet so slight a one that, though they may have prevailed hundreds of years, a philosopher will look upon them as accidents. So with respect to many moral feelings, either of love or dislike. What excessive admiration was paid in former times to personal prowess and military success; it is so with the latter even at the present day, but surely not nearly so much as heretofore. So with regard to birth, and innumerable other modes of sentiment, civil and religious. But you will be inclined to ask by this time how all this applies to *The Idiot Boy*. To this I can only say that the loathing and disgust which many people have at the sight of an idiot, is a feeling which, though having some foundation in human nature, is not necessarily attached to it in any virtuous degree, but is owing in a great measure to a false delicacy, and, if I may say it without rudeness, a certain want of comprehensiveness of thinking and feeling. Persons in the lower classes of society have little or nothing of this: if an idiot is born in a poor man's house, it must be taken care of, and cannot be boarded out, as it would be by gentlefolks, or sent to a public or private asylum for such unfortunate beings. Poor people, seeing frequently among their neighbours such objects, easily forget whatever there is of natural disgust about them, and have therefore a sane state, so that without pain or suffering they perform their duties towards them. I could with pleasure pursue this subject, but I must now strictly adopt the plan which I proposed to myself when I began to write this letter, namely, that of setting down a few hints or memorandums, which you will think of for my sake.

I have often applied to idiots, in my own mind, that sublime expression of Scripture, that *their life is hidden with God*. They are worshipped, probably from a feeling of this sort, in several parts of the East. Among the Alps, where they are numerous, they are considered, I believe, as a blessing to the family to which they belong. I have, indeed, often looked upon the conduct of fathers and mothers of the lower classes of society towards idiots as the great triumph of the human heart. It is there that we see the strength, disinterestedness, and grandeur of love; nor have I ever been able to contemplate an object that calls out so many excellent and virtuous sentiments without finding it hallowed thereby, and having something in me which bears down before it, like a deluge, every feeble sensation of disgust and aversion.

There are, in my opinion, several important mistakes in the latter part of your letter which I could have wished to notice; but I find myself much fatigued. These refer both to the Boy and the Mother. I must content myself simply with observing that it is probable that the principle cause of your dislike to this particular poem lies in the *word* Idiot. If there had been any such word in our language *to which we had attached passion*, as lack-wit, half-wit, witless, etc., I should have certainly employed it in preference; but there is no such word. Observe (this is entirely in reference to this particular poem), my "Idiot" is not one of those who cannot articulate, or of those that are usually disgusting in their persons:

> Whether in cunning or in joy,
> And then his words were not a few, etc.[6]

and the last speech at the end of the poem. The boy whom I had in my mind was by no means disgusting in his appearance, quite the contrary; and I have known several with imperfect faculties who are handsome in their persons and features. There is one, at present, within a mile of my own house, remarkably so, though he has something of a stare and vacancy in his countenance. A friend of mine knowing that some persons had a dislike to the poem, such as you have expressed, advised me to add a stanza, describing the person of the boy so as entirely to separate him in the imaginations of my readers from that class of idiots who are disgusting in their persons; but the narration in the poem is so rapid and impassioned, that I could not find a place in which to insert the stanza without checking the progress of the poem and so leaving a deadness upon the feeling. This poem has, I know, frequently produced the same effect as it did upon you and your friends; but there are many also to whom it affords exquisite delight, and who, indeed, prefer it to any other of my poems. This proves that the feelings there delineated are such as men *may* sympathise with. This is enough for my purpose. It is not enough for me as a Poet, to delineate merely such feelings as all men

6. These lines are not in sequence, but apparently random selections: the first is line 378; the second, line 65 (*Poetical Works*, II, 78, 69).

do sympathise with; but it is also highly desirable to add to these others, such as all men *may* sympathise with, and such as there is reason to believe they would be better and more moral beings if they did sympathise with.

I conclude with regret, because I have not said one half of what I intended to say; but I am sure you will deem my excuse sufficient, when I inform you that my head aches violently, and I am in other respects unwell. I must, however, again give you my warmest thanks for your kind letter. I shall be happy to hear from you again, and do not think it unreasonable that I should request a letter from you when I feel that the answer which I may make to it will not perhaps be above three or four lines. This I mention to you with frankness, and you will not take it ill after what I have before said of my remissness in writing letters.

Early Letters, pp. 292–298.

Letter to Lady Beaumont (May 21, 1807)

Sir George and Lady Beaumont had been close friends and patrons of the Wordsworths since 1803. At the time of this letter, the Wordsworths were living on the Beaumonts' estate, Coleorton, while the Beaumonts summered in the Lake District. Poems in Two Volumes, *which included "Ode to Duty," "Stanzas on Peele Castle," and the "Intimations Ode," appeared in May, 1807. Within a month, Lady Beaumont reported the reactions of her friends, including the comments of her sister Mrs. Fermor, alluded to in the letter.*

Though I am to see you so soon I cannot but write a word or two, to thank you for the interest you take in my Poems as evinced by your solicitude about their immediate reception. I write partly to thank you for this and to express the pleasure it has given me, and partly to remove any uneasiness from your mind which the disappointments you sometimes meet with in this labour of love may occasion. I see that you have many battles to fight for me; more than in the ardour and confidence of your pure and elevated mind you had ever thought of being summoned to; but be assured that this opposition is nothing more than what I distinctly foresaw that you and my other Friends would have to encounter. I say this, not to give myself credit for an eye of prophecy, but to allay any vexatious thoughts on my account which this opposition may have produced in you. It is impossible that any expectations can be lower than mine concerning the immediate effect of this little work upon what is called the Public. I do not here take into consideration the envy and malevolence, and all the bad passions which always stand in the way of a work of any merit from a living Poet; but merely think of the pure absolute honest ignorance, in which all worldlings of every rank and situation must be enveloped, with respect to the thoughts, feelings, and images, on which the life of my Poems depends. The things which I have taken, whether from within or without,—what have they to do with routs, dinners, morning calls, hurry from door to door, from street to street, on foot or in Carriage; with Mr. Pitt or Mr. Fox, Mr. Paul or Sir Francis Burdett, the Westminster Election or the Borough of Honiton;[1] in a word, for I cannot stop to make my way through the hurry of images that present themselves to me, what have they to do with endless talking about things nobody cares anything for except as far as their own vanity is concerned and this with persons they care nothing for but as their vanity or *selfishness* is concerned; what have they to do (to say all at once) with a life without love? in such a life there can be no thought; for we have no thought (save thoughts of pain) but as far as we have love and admiration.[2] It is an awful truth, that there neither is, nor can be, any genuine enjoyment of Poetry among nineteen out of twenty of those persons who live, or wish to live, in the broad light of the world—among those who either are, or are striving to make themselves, people of consideration in society. This is a truth, and an awful one, because to be incapable of a feeling of Poetry in my sense of the word is to be without love of human nature and reverence for God.[3]

1. James Paull and Sir Francis Burdett, earlier bosom friends but now competitors in the Westminster election, fought a duel May 2 in which each shot the other in a leg. Thomas, Lord Cochrane, was a third candidate in the election, preferring to give up his seat for the Borough of Honiton because he was constantly besieged by office seekers there.

2. The manuscript version of *Excursion*, IV.763–765 reads:

> "We live by Admiration and by Love;
> And, even as these are well and wisely fixed,
> In dignity of being we ascend."

> (*Poetical Works*, V, 133.)

3. This key concept, whether called "primal sympathy" or "imaginative love," pervasive in Wordsworth's poems of this period, is heralded in a letter from Coleridge to his brother in March 1798:

> I devote myself to such works as encroach not on the antisocial passions—in poetry, to elevate the imagination & set the affections in right tune by the beauty of the inanimate impregnated, as with a living soul, by the presence of Life. . . . I love fields & woods & mountains with almost a visionary fondness—and because I have found benevolence & quietness growing within

Upon this I shall insist elsewhere; at present let me confine myself to my object, which is to make you, my dear Friend, as easy-hearted as myself with respect to these Poems. Trouble not yourself upon their present reception; of what moment is that compared with what I trust is their destiny, to console the afflicted, to add sunshine to daylight by making the happy happier, to teach the young and the gracious of every age, to see, to think and feel, and therefore to become more actively and securely virtuous; this is their office, which I trust they will faithfully perform long after we (that is, all that is mortal of us) are mouldered in our graves. I am well aware how far it would seem to many I overrate my own exertions when I speak in this way, in direct connection with the Volumes I have just made public.

I am not, however, afraid of such censure, insignificant as probably the majority of those poems would appear to very

---

me as that fondness has increased, therefore I should wish to be the means of implanting it in others—& to destroy the bad passions not by combating them, but by keeping them in inaction.

Coleridge then quotes the lines that originally concluded "The Ruined Cottage":

> Not useless do I deem
> These shadowy Sympathies with things that hold
> An inarticulate Language: for the Man
> Once taught to love such objects, as excite
> No morbid passions, no disquietude,
> No vengeance & no hatred, needs must feel
> The Joy of that pure principle of Love
> So deeply, that, unsatisfied with aught
> Less pure & exquisite, he cannot chuse
> But seek for objects of a kindred Love
> In fellow-natures, & a kindred Joy.
> Accordingly, he by degrees perceives
> His feelings of aversion softened down,
> A holy tenderness pervade his frame!
> His sanity of reason not impair'd,
> Say rather that his thoughts now flowing clear
> From a clear fountain flowing, he looks round—
> He seeks for Good & finds the Good he seeks.

Wordsworth—(*Collected Letters*, ed. E. L. Griggs
[6 vols.; Oxford: Clarendon Press,
1956–1964], I, 397–398).

respectable persons; I do not mean London wits and witlings, for these have too many bad passions about them to be respectable even if they had more intellect than the benign laws of providence will allow to such a heartless existence as theirs is;[4] but grave, kindly-natured, worthy persons, who would be pleased if they could. I hope that these Volumes are not without some recommendations, even for Readers of this class, but their imagination has slept; and the voice which is the voice of my Poetry without Imagination cannot be heard.

Leaving these, I was going to say a word to such Readers as Mr. Rogers.[5] Such!—how would he be offended if he knew I considered him only as a representative of a class, and not an unique! "Pity," says Mr. R., "that so many trifling things should be admitted to obstruct the view of those that have merit"; now, let this candid judge take, by way of example, the sonnets, which, probably, with the exception of two or three other Poems for which I will not contend appear to him the most trifling, as they are the shortest, I would say to him, omitting things of higher consideration, there is one thing which must strike you at once if you will only read these poems,—that those to Liberty, at least, have a connection with, or a bearing upon, each other, and therefore, if individually they want weight, perhaps, as a Body, they may not be so deficient, at least this ought to induce you to suspend your judgement, and qualify it so far as to allow that the writer aims at least at comprehensiveness. But dropping this, I would boldly say at once, that these Sonnets, while they each fix the attention upon some important sentiment separately considered, do at the same time collectively

4. See Coleridge's "Ode: Dejection":
>   And would we aught behold, of higher worth,
>   Than that inanimate cold world allowed
>   To the poor loveless ever-anxious crowd,
>   Ah! from the soul itself must issue forth
>   A light, a glory, a fair luminous cloud
>   Enveloping the Earth—
>   (*Poems*, ed. E. H. Coleridge [2 vols.; Oxford: Clarendon Press, 1912], I, 365.)

5. Samuel Rogers, poet ("Pleasures of Memory") and banker, popular in literary and social circles alike.

make a Poem on the subject of civil Liberty and national independence, which, either for simplicity of style or grandeur of moral
sentiment, is, alas! likely to have few parallels in the Poetry of the
present day. Again, turn to the "Moods of my own Mind." There is
scarcely a Poem here of above thirty Lines, and very trifling these
poems will appear to many; but, omitting to speak of them
individually, do they not, taken collectively, fix the attention upon a
subject eminently poetical, viz., the interest which objects in nature
derive from the predominance of certain affections more or less
permanent, more or less capable of salutary renewal in the mind of
the being contemplating these objects? This is poetic, and essentially
poetic, and why? because it is creative.

But I am wasting words, for it is nothing more than you know,
and if said to those for whom it is intended, it would not be understood.

I see by your last Letter that Mrs. Fermor has entered into the
spirit of these "Moods of my own Mind." Your transcript from her
Letter gave me the greatest pleasure; but I must say that even she
has something yet to receive from me. I say this with confidence,
from her thinking that I have fallen below myself in the Sonnet
beginning—"With ships the sea was sprinkled far and nigh."[6] As
to the other which she objects to, I will only observe that there is a
misprint in the last line but two, "And *though* this wilderness" for
"And *through* this wilderness"—that makes it unintelligible. This
latter Sonnet for many reasons, though I do not abandon it, I will

6.   With Ships the sea was sprinkled far and nigh,
            Like stars in heaven, and joyously it showed;
            Some lying fast at anchor in the road,
            Some veering up and down, one knew not why.
            A goodly Vessel did I then espy
            Come like a giant from a haven broad;
            And lustily along the bay she strode,
            Her tackling rich, and of apparel high.
            This Ship was nought to me, nor I to her,
            Yet I pursued her with a Lover's look;
            This Ship to all the rest did I prefer:
            When will she turn, and whither? She will brook
            No tarrying; where She comes the winds must stir:
            On went She, and due north her journey took.
                                        (*Poetical Works*, III, 18.)

not now speak of; but upon the other, I could say something important in conversation, and will attempt now to illustrate it by a comment which I feel will be very inadequate to convey my meaning. There is scarcely one of my Poems which does not aim to direct the attention to some moral sentiment, or to some general principle, or law of thought, or of our intellectual constitution. For instance in the present case, who is there that has not felt that the mind can have no rest among a multitide of objects, of which it either cannot make one whole, or from which it cannot single out one individual, whereupon may be concentrated the attention divided among or distracted by a multitude? After a certain time we must either select one image or object, which must put out of view the rest wholly, or must subordinate them to itself while it stands forth as a Head:

> Now glowed the firmament
> With living sapphires! Hesperus, that *led*
> The starry host, rode brightest; till the Moon,
> Rising in clouded majesty, at length,
> Apparent *Queen*, unveiled *her peerless* light,
> And o'er the dark her silver mantle threw.[7]

Having laid this down as a general principle, take the case before us. I am represented in the Sonnet as casting my eyes over the sea, sprinkled with a multitude of Ships, like the heavens with stars, my mind may be supposed to float up and down among them in a kind of dreamy indifference with respect either to this or that one, only in a pleasurable state of feeling with respect to the whole prospect. "Joyously it showed," this continued till that feeling may be supposed to have passed away, and a kind of comparative listlessness or apathy to have succeeded, as at this line, "Some veering up and down, one knew not why." All at once, while I am in this state, comes forth an object, an individual, and my mind, sleepy and unfixed, is awakened and fastened in a moment. "Hesperus, that *led* The starry host," is a poetical object, because the glory of his own Nature gives him the pre-eminence the moment he appears; he calls forth the poetic faculty, receiving its exertions as a tribute; but this Ship in the Sonnet may, in a manner

7. *Paradise Lost*, IV, 604–609.

still more appropriate, be said to come upon a mission of the poetic Spirit, because in its own appearance and attributes it is barely sufficiently distinguished to rouse the creative faculty of the human mind; to exertions at all times welcome, but doubly so when they come upon us when in a state of remissness. The mind being once fixed and rouzed, all the rest comes from itself; it is merely a lordly Ship, nothing more:

> This ship was nought to me, nor I to her,
> Yet I pursued her with a lover's look.

My mind wantons with grateful joy in the exercise of its own powers, and, loving its own creation,

> This ship to all the rest I did prefer,

making her a sovereign or a regent, and thus giving body and life to all the rest; mingling up this idea with fondness and praise—

> where she comes the winds must stir;

and concluding the whole with

> On went She, and due north her journey took.

Thus taking up again the Reader with whom I began, letting him know how long I must have watched this favorite Vessel, and inviting him to rest his mind as mine is resting.

Having said so much upon a mere 14 lines, which Mrs. Fermor did not approve, I cannot but add a word or two upon my satisfaction in finding that my mind has so much in common with hers, and that we participate so many of each other's pleasures. I collect this from her having singled out the two little Poems, the Daffodils, and the Rock crowned with snowdrops.[8] I am·sure that whoever is much pleased with either of these quiet and tender delineations must be fitted to walk through the recesses of my poetry with delight, and will there recognise, at every turn, something or other in which, and over which, it has that property and right which knowledge and love confer. The line, "Come, blessed barrier, etc.," in the sonnet upon Sleep,[9] which Mrs. F. points out, had before

8. "I wandered lonely as a cloud" and "Who fancied what a pretty sight" (*Poetical Works*, II, 216–217, 148–149).

9. "Come, blessed barrier between day and day" (*Poetical Works*, III, 9).

been mentioned to me by Coleridge, and indeed by almost everybody who had heard it, as eminently beautiful. My letter (as this 2nd sheet, which I am obliged to take, admonishes me) is growing to an enormous length; and yet, saving that I have expressed my calm confidence that these Poems will live, I have said nothing which has a particular application to the object of it, which was to remove all disquiet from your mind on account of the condemnation they may at present incur from that portion of my contemporaries who are called the Public. I am sure, my dear Lady Beaumont, if you attach any importance to it it can only be from an apprehension that it may affect me, upon which I have already set you at ease, or from a fear that this present blame is ominous of their future or final destiny. If this be the case, your tenderness for me betrays you; be assured that the decision of these persons has nothing to do with the Question; they are altogether incompetent judges. These people in the senseless hurry of their idle lives do not *read* books, they merely snatch a glance at them that they may talk about them. And even if this were not so, never forget what I believe was observed to you by Coleridge, that every great and original writer, in proportion as he is great or original, must himself create the taste by which he is to be relished; he must teach the art by which he is to be seen; this, in a certain degree, even to all persons, however wise and pure may be their lives, and however unvitiated their taste; but for those who dip into books in order to give an opinion of them, or talk about them to take up an opinion—for this multitude of unhappy, and misguided, and misguiding beings, an entire regeneration must be produced; and if this be possible, it must be a work of *time*. To conclude, my ears are stone-dead to this idle buzz, and my flesh as insensible as iron to these petty stings; and after what I have said I am sure yours will be the same. I doubt not that you will share with me an invincible confidence that my writings (and among them these little Poems) will co-operate with the benign tendencies in human nature and society, wherever found; and that they will, in their degree, be efficacious in making men wiser, better, and happier. Farewell; I will not apologise for this Letter, though its length demands an apology. * * *

Middle Years, I, 125 131.

Reply to "Mathetes" (1809–1810)

Coleridge's weekly journal The Friend *appeared in twenty-seven numbers between June 1, 1809, and March 15, 1810. Its discursive essays covered a variety of topics, from freedom of the press to travel and biography. Most of the material was by Coleridge himself, dictated to Wordsworth's sister-in-law Sara Hutchinson, but Wordsworth contributed poems and two untitled essays. The first essay, called here "Reply to 'Mathetes,'" was published in two parts, December 14, 1809, and January 4, 1810. The second, now called "Essay upon Epitaphs," appeared in the issue for February 22, 1810, and will be discussed later. The occasion of the "Reply to 'Mathetes'" was a letter written for* The Friend *by the same John Wilson who had written to Wordsworth in 1802 and had since become a close neighbor. Signing himself "Mathetes" ("learner"), Wilson asked* The Friend *to enlist the aid of a contemporary teacher who would advise youth on how to discriminate between false and desirable goals in a dissolute age. Wordsworth, replying as that teacher, advised him to trust himself: "a good and greatly gifted nature" must believe in the perfectibility of man; progress to this "unattainable perfection" follows a course like that of a river, meandering slowly yet inexorably, with "an accompanying impulse that will insure its advancement hereafter." Youth, says Wordsworth, does not need any teacher other than nature, for the youthful mind is "rich in health of body and animal spirits, in its sensibility to the impressions of the natural universe, in the conscious growth of knowledge, in lively sympathy and familiar communion with the generous actions recorded in history, and with the high passions of poetry." The selection given here represents about one-fourth of the total essay and shows Wordsworth's concern for the imaginative process.*

* * * I spoke of a few simple questions—the question involved in this deliberation[1] *is* simple; but at the same time it is high and awful: and I would gladly know whether an answer can be returned

1. The problem is the active vs. the contemplative life.

satisfactory to the mind.—We will for a moment suppose that it can not; that there is a startling and a hesitation.—Are we then to despond? to retire from all contest? and to reconcile ourselves at once to cares without generous hope, and to efforts in which there is no more Moral life than that which is found in the business and labours of the unfavoured and unaspiring many? No—but, if the enquiry have not been on just grounds satisfactorily answered, we may refer confidently our Youth to that Nature of which he deems himself an enthusiastic follower, and one who wishes to continue no less faithful and enthusiastic.—We would tell him that there are paths which he has not trodden; recesses which he has not penetrated, that there is a beauty which he has not seen, a pathos which he has not felt—a sublimity to which he hath not been raised. If he have trembled, because there has occasionally taken place in him a lapse, of which he is conscious; if he foresee open or secret attacks, which he has had intimations that he will neither be strong enough to resist, nor watchful enough to elude, let him not hastily ascribe this weakness, this deficiency, and the painful apprehensions accompanying them, in any degree to the virtues or noble qualities with which Youth by Nature is furnished; but let him first be assured, before he looks about for the means of attaining the insight, the discriminating powers, and the confirmed wisdom of Manhood, that his soul has more to demand of the appropriate excellences of Youth, than Youth has yet supplied to it;—that the evil under which he labours is not a superabundance of the instincts and the animating spirit of that age, but a falling short, or a failure.—But what can he gain from this admonition? he cannot recal past time; he cannot begin his journey afresh; he cannot untwist the links by which, in no undelightful harmony, images and sentiments are wedded in his mind. Granted that the sacred light of Childhood is and must be for him no more than a remembrance. He may, notwithstanding, be remanded to Nature; and with trust-worthy hopes; founded less upon his sentient than upon his intellectual Being—to Nature, not as leading on insensibly to the society of Reason; but to Reason and Will, as leading back to the wisdom of Nature. A re-union, in this order accomplished, will bring reformation and timely support; and the two powers of Reason and Nature, thus reciprocally teacher and taught, may advance together in a track to which there is no limit.

We have been discoursing (by implication at least) of Infancy, Childhood, Boyhood, and Youth, of pleasures lying upon the unfolding Intellect plenteously as morning dew-drops—of knowledge inhaled insensibly like a fragrance—of dispositions stealing into the Spirit like music from unknown quarters—of images uncalled for and rising up like exhalations—of hopes plucked like beautiful wild flowers from the ruined tombs that border the high-ways of antiquity, to make a garland for a living forehead;—in a word, we have been treating of Nature as a Teacher of Truth through joy and through gladness, and as a Creatress of the faculties by a process of smoothness and delight. We have made no mention of fear, shame, sorrow, nor of ungovernable and vexing thoughts; because, although these have been and have done mighty service, they are overlooked in that stage of life when youth is passing into manhood—overlooked, or forgotten. We now apply for succour which we need, to a faculty that works after a different course: that faculty is Reason: she gives much spontaneously, but she seeks for more; she works by thought, through feeling; yet in thoughts she begins and ends.

A familiar incident may elucidate this contrast in the operations of Nature, may render plain the manner in which a process of intellectual improvements, the reverse of that which Nature pursues is by Reason introduced: There never perhaps existed a School-boy who, having when he retired to rest, carelessly blown out his candle, and having chanced to notice as he lay upon his bed in the ensuing darkness, the sullen light which had survived the extinguished flame, did not, at some time or other, watch that light as if his mind were bound to it by a spell. It fades and revives— gathers to a point—seems as if it would go out in a moment—again recovers it's strength, nay becomes brighter than before: it continues to shine with an endurance, which in its apparent weakness is a mystery—it protracts its existence so long, clinging to the power which supports it, that the Observer, who had laid down in his bed so easy-minded, becomes sad and melancholy: his sympathies are touched—it is to him an intimation and an image of departing

human life,—the thought comes nearer to him—it is the life of a
venerated Parent, of a beloved Brother or Sister, or of an aged
Domestic; who are gone to the grave, or whose destiny it soon may
be thus to linger, thus to hang upon the last point of mortal existence,
thus finally to depart and be seen no more—This is Nature teaching
seriously and sweetly through the affections—melting the heart,
and, through that instinct of tenderness, developing the understanding.—In this instance the object of solicitude is the bodily
life of another. Let us accompany this same Boy to that period
between Youth and Manhood, when a solicitude may be awakened
for the moral life of himself.—Are there any powers by which,
beginning with a sense of inward decay that affects not however the
natural life, he could call up to mind the same image and hang
over it with an equal interest as a visible type of his own perishing
Spirit? Oh! surely, if the being of the individual be under his own
care—if it be his first care—if duty begin from the point of
accountableness to our Conscience, and, through that, to God and
human Nature;—if without such primary sense of duty, all
secondary care of Teacher, of Friend, or Parent, must be baseless
and fruitless; if, lastly, the motions of the Soul transcend in worth
those of the animal functions, nay give to them their sole value;
then truly are there such powers: and the image of the dying taper
may be recalled and contemplated, though with no sadness in the
nerves, no disposition to tears, no unconquerable sighs, yet with a
melancholy in the soul, a sinking inward into ourselves from thought
to thought, a steady remonstrance, and a high resolve.—Let then
the Youth go back, as occasion will permit, to Nature and to
Solitude, thus admonished by Reason, and relying upon this
newly-acquired support. A world of fresh sensations will gradually
open upon him as his mind puts off its infirmities, and as instead of
being propelled restlessly towards others in admiration, or too hasty
love, he makes it his prime business to understand himself. New
sensations, I affirm, will be opened out—pure, and sanctioned by
that reason which is their original Author; and precious feelings of
disinterested, that is self-disregarding joy and love may be regenerated and restored:—and, in this sense, he may be said to
measure back the track of life he has trod.

In such disposition of mind let the Youth return to the visible Universe; and to conversation with ancient Books; and to those, if such there be, which in the present day breathe the ancient spirit: and let him feed upon that beauty which unfolds itself, *not* to his eye as it sees carelessly the things which cannot possibly go unseen, and are remembered or not as accident shall decide, but to the thinking mind; which searches, discovers, and treasures up,—infusing by meditation into the objects with which it converses an intellectual life; whereby they remain planted in the memory, now, and for ever. Hitherto the Youth, I suppose, has been content for the most part, to look at his own mind, after the manner in which he ranges along the Stars in the firmament with naked unaided sight: let him now apply the telescope of Art—to call the invisible Stars out of their hiding places; and let him endeavour to look through the system of his being, with the organ of Reason; summoned to penetrate, as far as it has power, in discovery of the impelling forces and the governing laws.

These expectations are not immoderate: they demand nothing more than the perception of a few plain truths; namely, that knowledge efficacious for the production of virtue, is the ultimate end of all effort, the sole dispenser of complacency and repose. A perception also is implied of the inherent superiority of Contemplation to Action. The FRIEND does not in this contradict his own words, where he has said heretofore, that "doubtless it is nobler to Act than to Think."[2] In those words, it was his purpose to censure that barren contemplation, which rests satisfied with itself in cases where the thoughts are of such quality that they may be, and ought to be, embodied in Action. But he speaks now of the general superiority of thought to action;—as preceeding and governing all action that moves to salutary purposes: and, secondly, as leading to elevation, the absolute possession of the individual mind, and to a consistency or harmony of the Being within itself, which no outward agency can reach to disturb or to impair:—and lastly as producing works

---

2. *The Friend*, September 21, 1809: "Doubtless, to act is nobler than to think; but as the old man doth not become a Child by means of his second Childishness, as little can a Nation exempt itself from the necessity of thinking, which has once learnt to think" (p. 86).

of pure science; or of the combined faculties of imagination, feeling, and reason;—works which, both from their independence in their origin upon accident, their nature, their duration, and the wide spread of their influence, are entitled rightly to take place of the noblest and most beneficent deeds of Heroes, Statesmen, Legislators, or Warriors. * * *

The Friend (1809–1810), pp. 309–313.

Essay upon Epitaphs—I (1810)

The second of Wordsworth's essays for The Friend *appeared in the issue for February 22, 1810, following two of his translations of epitaphs by the early seventeenth-century Italian poet Gabriello Chiabrera. Dorothy Wordsworth said he had not intended to publish it at that time, "but Coleridge was in such bad spirits that when the time came he was utterly unprovided . . . so my brother's essay, being ready, was sent off. . . . My brother has written two more essays on the same subject, which will appear when there is need."[1] The two other essays were not published in Wordsworth's lifetime. When he was annotating a friend's memoir of him, he said: "I should have written many things like 'Essay upon Epitaphs' out of kindness to [Coleridge] in* The Friend, *but he always put me off by saying, 'You must wait till my principles are laid down and then I shall be happy to have your contributions.' But the principles never were laid down and the work fell to the ground. As I never was fond of writing prose and required some incitement to do so, I rather regret having been prevented in this way by my dear Friend."[2] The published essay is given here in its entirety, but omitted from the unpublished essays are many random epitaphs and analyses of them that Wordsworth amassed to illustrate his points—representing perhaps half of the unpublished essays' total length. The first essay was reprinted with* The Excursion *in 1814. The others were printed posthumously in* Prose Works of Wordsworth (*ed. A. B. Grosart [3 vols.; London, 1876], II, 40–75).*

In this, and some preceding Numbers, has been given a selection of Epitaphs from the Italian Poet CHIABRERA; in one instance imitated, and in the others carefully translated. The perusal of the original collection afforded me so much pleasure that I was induced to think upon the nature of that species of composition with more

1. *Middle Years,* I, 358–359.
2. *Times Literary Supplement,* April 28, 1950, p. 261.

care than I had previously bestowed upon the Subject: the result of my reflections may perhaps be interesting to the Readers of THE FRIEND. An attempt will be made to unfold the Laws of Taste and Criticism systematically, as soon as certain topics, which have already been entered upon, shall be concluded: in the mean while, I wish to avail myself of the present occasion to tempt the more practised Reader into a short prelusive exercise of powers which he will hereafter be called upon to put forth in good earnest; and, in respect to those Persons who are unfamiliar with such speculations, my labour, in the present Essay, may be likened to that of a Teacher of Geology, who, to awaken the curiosity of his Pupils, and to induce them to prepare for the study of the inner constitution of the Planet, lectures with a few specimens of fossils and minerals in his hand, arranged in their several classes, and the beauty of which he points out to their attention.

"To define an Epitaph," says Dr. Johnson, "is useless; every one knows that it is an inscription on a Tomb. An Epitaph, therefore, implies no particular character of writing, but may be composed in verse or prose. It is indeed commonly panegyrical; because we are seldom distinguished with a Stone but by our Friends; but it has no rule to restrain or mollify it, except this, that it ought not to be longer than common beholders may have leisure or patience to peruse."[3] From this introduction the Critic immediately proceeds to a review of the metrical Epitaphs of Pope. This summary opinion is delivered with such laxity that, even on that account, the passage would not have deserved to be quoted, if it had not been forced upon the notice of our Countrymen, by the place which it occupies in the book entitled, "The Lives of the most eminent English Poets," by the same Writer. I now solicit the Reader's attention to a more comprehensive view of the subject; and shall endeavour to treat it with more precision.

It needs scarcely be said, that an Epitaph presupposes a Monument upon which it is to be engraven. Almost all Nations have wished that certain external signs should point out the places where their Dead are interred. Among savage Tribes unacquainted with

3. "Life of Pope," *Lives*, ed. G. B. Hill (3 vols.; Oxford: Clarendon Press, 1905), III, 254.

Letters, this has mostly been done either by rude stones placed near the Graves, or by Mounds of earth raised over them. This custom proceeded obviously from a twofold desire; first, to guard the remains of the deceased from irreverant approach or from savage violation; and, secondly, to preserve their memory. Never any, says Cambden, neglected burial but some savage Nations;[4] as the Bactrians which cast their dead to the dogs; some varlet Philosophers, as Diogenes, who desired to be devoured of fishes; some dissolute Courtiers, as Mecaenas, who was wont to say, Non tumulum curo; sepelit natura relictos.

I'm careless of a Grave:—Nature her dead will save.

As soon as Nations had learned the use of letters, Epitaphs were inscribed upon these Monuments; in order that their intention might be more surely and adequately fulfilled. I have derived Monuments and Epitaphs from two sources of feeling: but these do in fact resolve themselves into one. The invention of Epitaphs, Weever, in his discourse of funeral Monuments, says rightly, "proceeded from the presage or fore-feeling of Immortality, implanted in all men naturally, and is referred to the Scholars of Linus the Theban Poet, who flourished about the year of the World two thousand seven hundred; who first bewailed this Linus their Master, when he was slain, in doleful verses then called of him Oelina, afterwards Epitaphia, for that they were first sung at burials, after engraved upon the Sepulchres."[5]

And, verily, without the consciousness of a principle of Immortality in the human soul,[6] Man could never have had awakened in him the desire to live in the remembrance of his fellows; mere love, or the yearning of Kind towards Kind, could not have produced it. The Dog or Horse perishes in the field, or in the stall, by the side of his Companions, and is incapable of anticipating the sorrow

4. Wordsworth refers to only those parts of Cambden quoted by John Weever, *Ancient Funerall Monuments* (London, 1631), and adopts Weever's translation of the quotation here (which is in Latin in Cambden).

5. Weever, *Ancient Funerall Monuments*, p. 9.

6. Cf. the following passages and the "Intimations Ode" with its Fenwick notes, and also "There Was a Boy" (*Poetical Works*, II, 206).

with which his surrounding Associates shall bemoan his death, or pine for his loss; he cannot pre-conceive this regret, he can form no thought of it; and therefore cannot possibly have a desire to leave such regret or remembrance behind him. Add to the principle of love, which exists in the inferior animals, the faculty of reason which exists in Man alone; will the conjunction of these account for the desire? Doubtless it is a necessary consequence of this conjunction, yet not I think as a direct result, but only to be come at through an intermediate thought, viz. that of an intimation or assurance within us, that some part of our nature is imperishable. At least the precedence in order of birth, of one feeling to the other is unquestionable. If we look back upon the days of childhood, we shall find that the time is not in remembrance when, with respect to our own individual Being, the mind was without this assurance; whereas, the wish to be remembered by our Friends or Kindred after Death, or even in Absence, is, as we shall discover, a sensation that does not form itself till the *social* feelings have been developed, and the Reason has connected itself with a wide range of objects. Forlorn, and cut off from communication with the best part of his nature, must that Man be, who should derive the sense of immortality, as it exists in the mind of a child, from the same unthinking gaiety or liveliness of animal Spirits with which the Lamb in the meadow, or any other irrational Creature, is endowed; who should ascribe it, in short, to blank ignorance in the Child; to an inability arising from the imperfect state of his faculties to come, in any point of his being, into contact with a notion of Death; or to an unreflecting acquiescence in what has been instilled in to him! Has such an unfolder of the mysteries of Nature, though he may have forgotten his former self, ever noticed the early, obstinate, and unappeasable inquisitiveness of Children upon the subject of origination? This single fact proves outwardly the monstrousness of those suppositions: for, if we had no direct external testimony that the minds of very young Children meditate feelingly upon Death and Immortality, these enquiries, which we all know they are perpetually making concerning the *whence*, do necessarily include correspondent habits of interrogation concerning the *whither*. Origin and tendency are notions inseparably co-relative.

Never did a Child stand by the side of a running Stream, pondering within himself what power was the feeder of the perpetual current, from what never-wearied sources the body of water was supplied, but he must have been inevitably propelled to follow this question by another: "towards what abyss is it in progress? what receptacle can contain the mighty influx?" and the spirit of the answer must have been, though the word might be Sea or Ocean, accompanied perhaps with an image gathered from a Map, or from the real object in Nature—these might have been the *letter*, but the *spirit* of the answer must have been *as* inevitably, a receptacle without bounds or dimensions, nothing less than infinity. We may, then, be justified in asserting that the sense of Immortality, if not co-existent and twin birth with Reason, is among the earliest of its Offspring: and we may further assert, that from these conjoined, and under their countenance, the human affections are gradually formed and opened out. This is not the place to enter into the recesses of these investigations; but the subject requires me here to make a plain avowal that, for my own part, it is to me inconceivable, that the sympathies of love towards each other, which grow with our growth, could ever attain any new strength, or even preserve the old, after we had received from the outward senses the impression of Death, and were in the habit of having that impression daily renewed and its accompanying feeling brought home to ourselves, and to those we love; if the same were not counteracted by those communications with our internal Being, which are anterior to all these experiences, and with which revelation coincides, and has through that coincidence alone (for otherwise it could not possess it) a power to affect us. I confess, with me the conviction is absolute, that, if the impression and sense of Death were not thus counterbalanced, such a hollowness would pervade the whole system of things, such a want of correspondence and consistency, a disproportion so astounding betwixt means and ends, that there could be no repose, no joy. Were we to grow up unfostered by this genial warmth, a frost would chill the spirit, so penetrating and powerful, that there could be no notions of the life of love; and infinitely less could we have any wish to be remembered after we had passed away from a world in which each man had moved about like a shadow.

Simonides, it is related, upon landing in a strange Country, found the Corse of an unknown person, lying by the Sea side; he buried it, and was honoured throughout Greece for the piety of that Act.[7] Another ancient Philosopher, chancing to fix his eyes upon a dead Body, regarded the same with slight, if not with contempt; saying, "see the Shell of the flown Bird." But it is not to be supposed that the moral and tender hearted Simonides was incapable of the lofty movements of thought, to which that other Sage gave way at the moment while his soul was intent only upon the indestructible being; or, on the other hand, that he, in whose sight a lifeless human Body was of no more value than the worthless Shell from which the living fowl had departed, would not, in a different mood of mind, have been affected by those earthly considerations which had incited the philosophic Poet to the performance of that pious duty; and with regard to this latter, we may be assured that, if he had been destitute of the capability of communing with the more exalted thoughts that appertain to human Nature, he would have cared no more for the Corse of the Stranger than for the dead body of a Seal or Porpoise which might have been cast up by the Waves. We respect the corporeal frame of Man, not merely because it is the habitation of a rational, but of an immortal Soul. Each of these Sages was in sympathy with the best feelings of our Nature; feelings which, though they seem opposite to each other, have another and a finer connection than that of contrast.—It is a connection formed through the subtle progress by which, both in the natural and the moral world, qualities pass insensibly into their contraries, and things revolve upon each other. As, in sailing upon the orb of this Planet, a voyage, towards the regions where the sun sets, conducts gradually to the quarter where we have been accustomed to behold it come forth at its rising; and, in like manner, a voyage towards the east, the birth-place in our imagination of the morning, leads finally to the quarter where the Sun is last seen when he departs from our eyes; so, the contemplative soul, travelling in the direction of mortality, advances to the Country of everlasting Life; and, in

7. The sonnet "I find it written of Simonides" tells the same story (*Poetical Works*, III, 408). The source could have been Valerius Maximus, I, vii; or Cicero, *De Divinatione*, I, xxvii.

like manner, may she continue to explore those chearful tracts, till she is brought back, for her advantage and benefit, to the land of transitory things—of sorrow and of tears.

On a midway point, therefore, which commands the thoughts and feelings of the two Sages whom we have represented in contrast, does the Author of that species of composition, the Laws of which it is our present purpose to explain, take his stand. Accordingly, recurring to the twofold desire, namely, to guard the remains of the deceased, and to preserve their memory, which has been deduced from the higher feeling, namely, the consciousness of immortality, it may be said, that a sepulchral Monument is a tribute to a Man as a human Being; and that an Epitaph (in the ordinary meaning attached to the word) includes this general feeling and something more; and is a record to preserve the memory of the dead, as a tribute due to his individual worth, for a satisfaction to the sorrowing hearts of the Survivors, and for the common benefit of the living: which record is to be accomplished, not in a general manner, but in *close connection with the bodily remains of the deceased:* and these, it may be added, among the modern Nations of Europe are deposited within, or contiguous to their places of worship. In ancient times, as is well known, it was the custom to bury the dead beyond the Walls of Towns and Cities; and among the Greeks and Romans they were frequently interred by the way-sides.

I could here pause with pleasure, and invite the Reader to indulge with me in contemplation of the advantages which must have attended such a practice. I could ruminate upon the beauty which the Monuments, thus placed, must have borrowed from the surrounding images of Nature—from the trees, the wild flowers, from a stream running perhaps within sight or hearing, from the beaten road stretching its weary length hard by. Many tender similitudes must these objects have presented to the mind of the Traveller, leaning upon one of the Tombs, or reposing in the coolness of its shade, whether he had halted from weariness or in compliance to the invitation, "Pause Traveller!" so often found upon the Monuments. And to its Epitaph also must have been supplied strong appeals to visible appearances or immediate impressions, lively and affecting analogies of Life as a Journey—Death as a Sleep

overcoming the tired Wayfarer—of Misfortune as a Storm that
falls suddenly upon him—of Beauty as a Flower that passeth away,
or of innocent pleasure as one that may be gathered—of Virtue
that standeth firm as a Rock against the beating Waves;—of Hope
"undermined insensibly like the Poplar by the side of the River
that has fed it," or blasted in a moment like a Pine-tree by the stroke
of lightening upon the Mountain top—of admonitions and heart-
stirring remembrances, like a refreshing Breeze that comes without
warning, or the taste of the waters of an unexpected Fountain.
These, and similar suggestions must have given, formerly, to the
language of the senseless stone a voice enforced and endeared by the
benignity of that Nature with which it was in unison.—We in
modern times have lost much of these advantages: and they are but
in a small degree counterbalanced to the Inhabitants of large Towns
and Cities, by the custom of depositing the Dead within, or contiguous to, their places of worship; however splendid or imposing
may be the appearances of those Edifices, or however interesting or
salutary the recollections associated with them. Even were it not
true that Tombs lose their monitory virtue when thus obtruded upon
the notice of Men occupied with the cares of the World, and too
often sullied and defiled by those cares, yet still, when Death is in
our thoughts, nothing can make amends for the want of the soothing
influences of Nature, and for the absence of those types of renovation
and decay, which the fields and woods offer to the notice of the
serious and contemplative mind. To feel the force of this sentiment,
let a man only compare in imagination the unsightly manner in
which our Monuments are crowded together in the busy, noisy,
unclean, and almost grassless Church-yard of a large Town, with the
still seclusion of a Turkish Cemetry, in some remote place, and yet
further sanctified by the Grove of Cypress in which it is embosomed.
Thoughts in the same temper as these, have already been expressed
with true sensibility by an ingenuous Poet of the present day. The
subject of his Poem is "All Saint's Church, Derby:"[8] he has been
deploring the forbidden and unseemly appearance of its burial-
ground, and uttering a wish, that in past times the practices had

8. John Edwards, a liquor merchant in Derby, published *All Saints' Church,
Derby* in 1805.

been adopted of interring the Inhabitants of large Towns in the
Country.—

> "Then in some rural, calm, sequestered spot,
> Where healing Nature her benignant look
> Ne'er changes, save at that lorn season, when,
> With tresses drooping o'er her sable stole,
> She yearly mourns the mortal doom of man,
> Her noblest work, (so Israel's virgins erst,
> With annual moan upon the mountains wept
> Their fairest gone) there in that rural scene,
> So placid, so congenial to the wish
> The Christian feels, of peaceful rest within
> The silent grave, I would have stray'd:
>
> .   .   .   .
>
> —wandered forth, where the cold dew of heaven
> Lay on the humbler graves around, what time
> The pale moon gazed upon the turfy mounds,
> Pensive, as though like me, in lonely muse,
> 'Twere brooding on the Dead inhum'd beneath.
> There, while with him, the holy Man of Uz,
> O'er human destiny I sympathiz'd,
> Counting the long, long periods prophecy
> Decrees to roll, ere the great day arrives
> Of resurrection, oft the blue-eyed Spring
> Had met me with her blossoms, as the Dove
> Of old, return'd with olive leaf, to cheer
> The Patriarch mourning o'er a world destroy'd:
> And I would bless her visit; for to me
> 'Tis sweet to trace the consonance that links
> As one, the works of Nature and the word
> Of God."—   JOHN EDWARDS.

A Village Church-yard, lying as it does in the lap of Nature, may
indeed be most favourably contrasted with that of a Town of
crowded Population; and Sepulture therein combines many of the
best tendencies which belong to the mode practised by the Ancients,
with others peculiar to itself. The sensations of pious chearfulness,
which attend the celebration of the Sabbath-day in rural places, are
profitably chastised by the sight of the Graves of Kindred and

Friends, gathered together in that general Home towards which the thoughtful yet happy Spectators themselves are journeying. Hence a Parish Church, in the stillness of the Country, is a visible centre of a community of the living and the dead; a point to which are habitually referred the nearest concerns of both.

As, then, both in Cities and in Villages, the Dead are deposited in close connection with our places of worship, with us the composition of an Epitaph naturally turns still more than among the Nations of Antiquity, upon the most serious and solemn affections of the human mind; upon departed Worth—upon personal or social Sorrow and Admiration—upon Religion individual and social—upon Time, and upon Eternity. Accordingly it suffices, in ordinary cases, to secure a composition of this kind from censure, that it contains nothing that shall shock or be inconsistent with this spirit. But to entitle an Epitaph to praise more than this is necessary. It ought to contain some Thought or Feeling belonging to the mortal or immortal part of our Nature touchingly expressed; and if that be done, however general or even trite the sentiment may be, every man of pure mind will read the words with pleasure and gratitude. A Husband bewails a wife; a Parent breathes a sigh of disappointed Hope over a lost Child; a Son utters a sentiment of filial reverence for a departed Father or Mother; a Friend perhaps inscribes an encomium recording the companionable qualities, or the solid virtues, of the Tenant of the Grave, whose departure has left a sadness upon his memory. This, and a pious admonition to the Living, and a humble expression of Christian confidence in Immortality, is the language of a thousand Church yards; and it does not often happen that any thing, in a greater degree discriminate or appropriate to the Dead or to the Living, is to be found in them. This want of discrimination has been ascribed by the Critic above quoted, to two causes; first, the scantiness of the Objects of human praise; and, secondly, to the want of variety in the Characters of Men; or to use his own words, "to the fact, that the greater part of Mankind have no Character at all."9 This is language which may

9. In concluding the "Life of Pope," Dr. Johnson quotes from Pope's line 2 of Moral Essay II ("Most women have no characters at all . . ."): "The difficulty in writing epitaphs is to give a particular and appropriate praise. This, however, is

be holden without blame among the generalities of common conversation; but does not become a Critic and a Moralist speaking seriously upon a serious Subject. The objects of admiration in Human Nature are not scanty but abundant; and every Man has a Character of his own, to the eye that has skill to perceive it. The real cause of the acknowledged want of discrimination in sepulchral memorials is this: That to analyse the Characters of others, especially of those whom we love, is not a common or natural employment of Men, at any time. We are not anxious unerringly to understand the constitution of the Minds of those who have soothed, who have cheered, who have supported us; with whom we have been long and daily pleased or delighted. The affections are their own justification. The Light of Love in our Hearts is a satisfactory evidence that there is a flame of worth in the minds of our friends or kindred, whence that Light has proceeded. We shrink from the thought of placing their merits and defects to be weighed against each other in the nice balance of pure intellect; nor do we find much temptation to detect the shades by which a good quality or virtue is discriminated in them from an excellence known by the same general name as it exists in the mind of another; and least of all do we incline to these refinements when under the pressure of Sorrow, Admiration, or Regret, or when actuated by any of those feelings which incite men to prolong the memory of their Friends and Kindred, by records placed in the bosom of the all-uniting and equalizing Receptacle of the Dead.

The first requisite, then, in an Epitaph is, that it should speak, in a tone which shall sink into the heart, the general language of humanity as connected with the subject of Death—the source from which an Epitaph proceeds, of death and of life. To be born and to die are the two points in which all men feel themselves to be in

----

not always to be performed . . . for the greater part of mankind 'have no character at all,' have little that distinguishes them from others equally good or bad, and therefore nothing can be said of them which may not be applied with equal propriety to a thousand more . . . . The scantiness of human praises can scarcely be made more apparent than by remarking how often Pope has, in the few epitaphs which he composed, found it necessary to borrow from himself" (*Lives*, ed. G. B. Hill, III, 263–264).

absolute coincidence. This general language may be uttered so strikingly as to entitle an Epitaph to high praise; yet it cannot lay claim to the highest unless other excellencies be superadded. Passing through all intermediate steps, we will attempt to determine at once what these excellencies are, and wherein consists the perfection of this species of composition. It will be found to lie in a due proportion of the common or universal feeling of humanity to sensations excited by a distinct and clear conception, conveyed to the Reader's mind, of the Individual, whose death is deplored and whose memory is to be preserved; at least of his character as, after death, it appeared to those who loved him and lament his loss. The general sympathy ought to be quickened, provoked, and diversified, by particular thoughts, actions, images,—circumstances of age, occupation, manner of life, prosperity which the Deceased had known, or adversity to which he had been subject; and these ought to be bound together and solemnized into one harmony by the general sympathy. The two powers should temper, restrain, and exalt each other. The Reader ought to know who and what the Man was whom he is called upon to think of with interest. A distinct conception should be given (implicitly where it can, rather than explicitly) of the Individual lamented. But the Writer of an Epitaph is not an Anatomist who dissects the internal frame of the mind; he is not even a Painter who executes a portrait at leisure and in entire tranquillity: his delineation, we must remember, is performed by the side of the Grave; and, what is more, the grave of one whom he loves and admires. What purity and brightness is that virtue cloathed in, the image of which must no longer bless our living eyes! The character of a deceased Friend or beloved Kinsman is not seen, no—nor ought to be seen, other than as a Tree through a tender haze or a luminous mist, that spiritualizes and beautifies it; that takes away indeed, but only to the end that the parts which are not abstracted may appear more dignified and lovely, may impress and affect the more. Shall we say then that this is not truth, not a faithful image; and that accordingly the purposes of commemoration cannot be answered?—It *is* truth, and of the highest order! for, though doubtless things are not apparent which did exist, yet, the object being looked at through this medium, parts and proportions are brought into distinct view which before had been only imperfectly or unconsciously seen: it is truth hallowed by love—the joint offspring of the worth of the Dead and the affections of the Living! This may easily be brought to the test. Let one, whose eyes have been sharpened by personal hostility to discover what was amiss in the character of a good man, hear the tidings of his death, and what a change is wrought in a moment!—Enmity melts away; and, as it disappears, unsightliness, disproportion, and deformity, vanish; and, through the influence of commiseration, a harmony of love and beauty succeeds. Bring such a Man to the Tomb-stone on which shall be inscribed an Epitaph on his Adversary, composed in the spirit which we have recommended. Would he turn from it as from an idle tale? Ah! no—the thoughtful look, the sigh, and perhaps the involuntary tear, would testify that it had a sane, a generous, and good meaning; and that on the Writer's mind had remained an impression which was a true abstract of the character of the deceased; that his gifts and graces were remembered in the simplicity in which they ought to be remembered. The composition and quality of the mind of a virtuous man, contemplated by the side of the Grave where his body is mouldering, ought to appear and be felt as something midway between what he was on Earth walking about with his living frailties, and what he may be presumed to be as a Spirit in Heaven.

It suffices, therefore, that the Trunk and the main Branches of the Worth of the Deceased be boldly and unaffectedly represented. Any further detail, minutely and scrupulously pursued, especially if this be done with laborious and antithetic discriminations, must inevitably frustrate it's own purpose; forcing the passing Spectator to this conclusion,—either that the Dead did not possess the merits ascribed to him, or that they who have raised a monument to his memory and must therefore be supposed to have been closely connected with him, were incapable of perceiving those merits; or at least during the act of composition had lost sight of them; for, the Understanding having been so busy in it's petty occupation, how could the heart of the Mourner be other than cold? and in either of these cases, whether the fault be on the part of the buried Person or the Survivors, the Memorial is unaffecting and profitless.

Much better is it to fall short in discrimination than to pursue it too far, or to labour it unfeelingly. For in no place are we so much disposed to dwell upon those points, of nature and condition, wherein all Men resemble each other, as in the Temple where the universal Father is worshipped, or by the side of the Grave which gathers all Human Beings to itself, and "equalizes the lofty and the low."[10] We suffer and we weep with the same heart; we love and are anxious for one another in one spirit; our hopes look to the same quarter; and the virtues by which we are all to be furthered and supported, as patience, meekness, good-will, temperance, and temperate desires, are in an equal degree the concern of us all. Let an Epitaph then, contain at least these acknowledgments to our common nature; nor let the sense of their importance be sacrificed to a balance of opposite qualities or minute distinctions in individual character; which if they do not, (as will for the most part be the case) when examined, resolve themselves into a trick of words, will, even when they are true and just, for the most part be grievously out of place; for, as it is probable that few only have explored these intricacies of human nature, so can the tracing of them be interesting only to a few. But an Epitaph is not a proud Writing shut up for the studious; it is exposed to all, to the wise and the most ignorant; it is condescending, perspicuous, and lovingly solicits regard; it's story and admonitions are brief, that the thoughtless, the busy and indolent, may not be deterred, nor the impatient tired; the stooping Old Man cons the engraven record like a second horn-book;—the Child is proud that he can read it—and the Stranger is introduced by it's mediation to the company of a Friend: it is concerning all, and for all:—in the Church-yard it is open to the day; the sun looks down upon the stone, and the rains of Heaven beat against it.

Yet, though the Writer who would excite sympathy is bound in this case more than in any other, to give proof that he himself has been moved, it is to be remembered, that to raise a Monument is a sober and a reflective act; that the inscription which it bears is intended to be permanent and for universal perusal; and that, for this reason, the thoughts and feelings expressed should be permanent also—liberated from that weakness and anguish of sorrow which

10. "Epitaphs from Chiabrera, IV," l. 24 (*Poetical Works*, IV, 250).

is in nature transitory, and which with instinctive decency retires from notice. The passions should be subdued, the emotions controlled; strong indeed, but nothing ungovernable or wholly involuntary. Seemliness requires this, and truth requires it also: for how can the Narrator otherwise be trusted? Moreover, a Grave is a tranquillizing object; resignation, in course of time, springs up from it as naturally as the wild flowers, besprinkling the turf with which it may be covered, or gathering round the monument by which it is defended. The very form and substance of the monument which has received the inscription, and the appearance of the letters, testifying with what a slow and laborious hand they must have been engraven, might seem to reproach the Author who had given way upon this occasion to transports of mind, or to quick turns of conflicting passion; though the same might constitute the life and beauty of a funeral Oration or elegiac Poem.

These sensations and judgements, acted upon perhaps unconsciously, have been one of the main causes why Epitaphs so often personate the Deceased, and represent him as speaking from his own Tomb-stone. The departed Mortal is introduced telling you himself that his pains are gone; that a state of rest is come; and he conjures you to weep for him no longer. He admonishes with the voice of one experienced in the vanity of those affections which are confined to earthly objects, and gives a verdict like a superior Being, performing the office of a Judge, who has no temptations to mislead him, and whose decision cannot but be dispassionate. Thus is Death disarmed of its sting, and affliction unsubstantialized. By this tender fiction the Survivors bind themselves to a sedater sorrow, and employ the intervention of the imagination in order that the reason may speak her own language earlier than she would otherwise have been enabled to do. This shadowy interposition also harmoniously unites the two worlds of the Living and the Dead by their appropriate affections. And I may observe, that here we have an additional proof of the propriety with which sepulchral inscriptions were referred to the consciousness of Immortality as their primal source.

I do not speak with a wish to recommend that an Epitaph should be cast in this mould preferably to the still more common one, in which what is said comes from the Survivors directly; but rather to point out how natural those feelings are which have induced men, in all states and ranks of Society, so frequently to adopt this mode. And this I have done chiefly in order that the laws, which ought to govern the composition of the other, may be better understood. This latter mode, namely, that in which the Survivors speak in their own Persons, seems to me upon the whole greatly preferable: as it admits a wider range of notices; and, above all, because, excluding the fiction which is the ground-work of the other, it rests upon a more solid basis.

Enough has been said to convey our notion of a perfect Epitaph; but it must be observed that one is meant which will best answer the *general* ends of that species of composition. According to the course pointed out, the worth of private life, through all varieties of situation and character, will be most honourably and profitably preserved in memory. Nor would the model recommended less suit public Men, in all instances save those persons who by the greatness of their services in the employments of Peace or War, or by the surpassing excellence of their works in Art, Literature, or Science, have made themselves not only universally known, but have filled the heart of their Country with everlasting gratitude. Yet I must here pause to correct myself. In describing the general tenor of thought which Epitaphs ought to hold, I have omitted to say, that, if it be the *actions* of a Man, or even some *one* conspicuous or beneficial act of local or general utility which has distinguished him and excited a desire that he should be remembered, then, of course ought the attention to be directed chiefly to those actions or that act; and such sentiments dwelt upon as naturally arise out of them or it. Having made this necessary distinction I proceed.—The mighty Benefactors of mankind, as they are not only known by the immediate Survivors, but will continue to be known familiarly to latest Posterity, do not stand in need of biographic sketches, in such a place; nor of delineations of character to individualize them. This is already done by their actions, in the Memories of Men. Their naked names, and a grand comprehensive sentiment of civic Gratitude, patriotic Love, or human Admiration; or the utterance of some elementary Principle most essential in the constitution of true Virtue; or an intuition, communicated in adequate words, of

the sublimity of intellectual power;—these are the only tribute
which can here be paid—the only offering that upon such an Altar
would not be unworthy!

> What needs my Shakespeare for his honoured bones
> The labour of an age in piled stones,
> Or that his hallowed reliques should be hid
> Under a star-y-pointing pyramid?
> Dear Son of Memory, great Heir of Fame,
> What need'st thou such weak witness of thy name?
> Thou in our wonder and astonishment
> Hast built thyself a live-long Monument.
> And so sepulchred, in such pomp dost lie,
> That Kings for such a Tomb would wish to die.[11]

The Friend (1809–1810), pp. 402–416.

11. Milton, "On Shakespear. 1630," ll. 1–8, 15–16.

Essay upon Epitaphs—II

* * * I gladly avail myself of this opportunity to place in a clear view the power and majesty of impassioned faith, whatever be its object: to shew how it subjugates the lighter motions of the mind, and sweeps away superficial difference in things. And this I have done, not to lower the witling and the worldling in their own esteem, but with a wish to bring the ingenuous into still closer communion with those primary sensations of the human heart, which are the vital springs of sublime and pathetic composition, in this and in every other kind. And as from these primary sensations such composition speaks, so, unless correspondent ones listen promptly and submissively in the inner cell of the mind to whom it is addressed, the voice cannot be heard; its highest powers are wasted.

These suggestions may be further useful to establish a criterion of sincerity, by which a writer may be judged; and this is of high import. For, when a man is treating an interesting subject, or one which he ought not to treat at all unless he be interested, no faults have such a killing power as those which prove that he is not in earnest, that he is acting a part, has leisure for affectation, and feels that without it he could do nothing. This is one of the most odious of faults; because it shocks the moral sense, and is worse in a sepulchral inscription, precisely in the same degree as that mode of composition calls for sincerity more urgently than any other. And indeed where the internal evidence proves that the writer was moved, in other words where this charm of sincerity lurks in the language of a tombstone and secretly pervades it, there are no errors in style or manner for which it will not be, in some degree, a recompence; but without habits of reflection a test of this inward simplicity cannot be come at; and as I have said, I am now writing with a hope to assist the well-disposed to attain it.

Let us take an instance where no one can be at a loss. The following lines are said to have been written by the illustrious

107

Marquis of Montrose with the point of his sword, upon being informed of the death of his master, Charles I:

> Great, good, and just, could I but rate
> My griefs, and thy so rigid fate;
> I'd weep the world to such a strain,
> As it should deluge once again.
> But since thy loud-tongued blood demands supplies,
> More from Briareus' hands than Argus' eyes,
> I'll sing thy obsequies with trumpets' sounds
> And write thy epitaph with blood and wounds.[1]

These funereal verses would certainly be wholly out of their place upon a tombstone; but who can doubt that the writer was transported to the height of the occasion? that he was moved as it became an heroic soldier, holding those principles and opinions, to be moved? His soul labours;—the most tremendous event in the history of the planet—namely, the deluge, is brought before his imagination by the physical image of tears,—a connection awful from its very remoteness and from the slender band that unites the ideas:—it passes into the region of fable likewise; for all modes of existence that forward his purpose are to be pressed into the service. The whole is instinct with spirit, and every word has its separate life; like the chariot of the Messiah, and the wheels of that chariot, as they appeared to the imagination of Milton aided by that of the prophet Ezekiel. It had power to move of itself, but was conveyed by cherubs.

> —with stars their bodies all
> And wings were set with eyes, with eyes the wheels
> Of beryl, and careering fires between.[2]

Compare with the above verses of Montrose the following epitaph upon Sir Philip Sidney, which was formerly placed over his grave in St. Paul's Church.

> England, Netherland, the Heavens, and the Arts,
> The Soldiers, and the World, have made six parts

1. See *Poems of James Graham, Marquis of Montrose*, ed. J. L. Weir (London: John Murray, 1938), pp. 33, 60–61.
2. *Paradise Lost*, VI, 754–756.

Of noble Sidney; for who will suppose
That a small heap of stones can Sidney enclose?
England hath his Body, for she it fed,
Netherland his Blood, in her defence shed:
The Heavens have his Soul, the Arts have his Fame,
The Soldiers the grief, the World his good Name.[3]

There were many points in which the case of Sidney resembled that of Charles I. He was a sovereign, but of a nobler kind—a sovereign in the hearts of men; and after his premature death he was truly, as he hath been styled, "the world-mourned Sidney." So fondly did the admiration of his contemporaries settle upon him, that the sudden removal of a man so good, great, and thoroughly accomplished, wrought upon many even to repining, and to the questioning the dispensations of Providence. Yet he, whom Spenser and all the men of genius of his age had tenderly bemoaned, is thus commemorated upon his tombstone; and to add to the indignity, the memorial is nothing more than the second-hand coat of a French commander! It is a servile translation from a French epitaph, which says Weever, "was by some English Wit happily imitated and ingeniously applied to the honour of our worthy chieftain."[4] Yet Weever in a foregoing paragraph thus expresses himself upon the same subject; giving without his own knowledge, in my opinion, an example of the manner in which an epitaph ought to have been composed: "But I cannot pass over in silence Sir Philip Sidney, the elder brother, being (to use Camden's words) the glorious star of this family, a lively pattern of virtue, and the lovely joy of all the learned sort; who fighting valiantly with the enemy before Zutphen in Geldesland, dyed manfully. This is that Sidney, whom, as God's will was, he should therefore be born into the world even to shew unto our age a sample of ancient virtues: so His good pleasure was, before any man looked for it, to call for him again and take him out of the world, as being more worthy of heaven than earth. Thus we may see perfect virtue suddenly vanisheth out of sight, and the best men continue not long."[5]

There can be no need to analyze this simple effusion of the

3. John Weever, *Ancient Funerall Monuments* (London, 1631), p. 321.
4. *Ibid.*, p. 320.   5. *Ibid.*

moment in order to contrast it with the laboured composition before given; the difference will flash upon the Reader at once. But I may say it is not likely that such a frigid composition as the former would have ever been applied to a man whose death had so stirred up the hearts of his contemporaries, if it had not been felt that something different from that nature which each man carried in his own breast was in his case requisite; and that a certain straining of mind was inseparable from the subject. Accordingly, an epitaph is adopted in which the Writer had turned from the genuine affections and their self-forgetting inspirations, to the end that his understanding, or the faculty designated by the word *head* as opposed to *heart*, might curiously construct a fabric to be wondered at. Hyperbole in the language of Montrose is a mean instrument made mighty because wielded by an afflicted soul, and strangeness is here the order of Nature. Montrose stretched after remote things, but was at the same time propelled towards them; the French Writer goes deliberately in search of them: no wonder then if what he brings home does not prove worth the carriage.

Let us return to an instance of common life. I quote it with reluctance, not so much for its absurdity as that the expression in one place will strike at first sight as little less than impious; and it is indeed, though unintentionally so, most irreverent. But I know no other example that will so forcibly illustrate the important truth I wish to establish. The following epitaph is to be found in a church-yard in Westmoreland; which the present Writer has reason to think of with interest as it contains the remains of some of his ancestors and kindred. The date is 1673.

> Under this Stone, Reader, inter'd doth lye,
>   Beauty and Virtue's true epitomy.
> At her appearance the noone-son
>   Blush'd and shrunk in 'cause quite undon.
> In her concentered did all graces dwell:
>   God pluck'd my rose that He might take a smel.
> I'll say no more: but weeping wish I may
> Soone with thy dear chaste ashes com to lay.
>   Sic efflevit Maritus.

Can anything go beyond this in extravagance? yet, if the funda-mental thoughts be translated into a natural style, they will be found reasonable and affecting—"The woman who lies here interred, was in my eyes a perfect image of beauty and virtue; she was to me a brighter object than the sun in heaven: God took her, who was my delight, from this earth to bring her nearer to Himself. Nothing further is worthy to be said than that weeping I wish soon to lie by thy dear chaste ashes. Thus did the husband pour out his tears."

These verses are preceded by a brief account of the lady, in Latin prose, in which the little that is said is the uncorrupted language of affection. But, without this introductory communication I should myself have had no doubt, after recovering from the first shock of surprize and disapprobation, that this man, notwithstanding his extravagant expressions, was a sincere mourner; and that his heart, during the very act of composition, was moved. These fantastic images, though they stain the writing, stained not her soul,—they did not even touch it; but hung like globules of rain suspended above a green leaf, along which they may roll and leave no trace that they have passed over it. This simple-hearted man must have been betrayed by a common notion that what was natural in prose would be out of place in verse;—that it is not the Muse which puts on the garb but the garb which makes the Muse. And having adopted this notion at a time when vicious writings of this kind accorded with the public taste, it is probable that, in the excess of his modesty, the blankness of his inexperience, and the intensity of his affection, he thought that the further he wandered from Nature in his language the more would he honour his departed consort, who now appeared to him to have surpassed humanity in the excellence of her endowments. The quality of his fault and its very excess are both in favour of this conclusion.

Let us contrast this epitaph with one taken from a celebrated Writer of the last century.

> *To the memory of LUCY LYTTLETON, Daughter &c. who departed this life &c. aged 20. Having employed the short time assigned to her here in the uniform practice of religion and virtue.*

> Made to engage all hearts, and charm all eyes,
> Though meek, magnanimous; though witty, wise;
> Polite, as all her life in Courts had been;
> Yet good, as she the world had never seen;

> The noble fire of an exalted mind,
> With gentle female tenderness combined.
> Her speech was the melodious voice of love,
> Her song the warbling of the vernal grove;
> Her eloquence was sweeter than her song,
> Soft as her heart, and as her reason strong;
> Her form each beauty of the mind express'd,
> Her mind was Virtue by the Graces drest.[6]

The prose part of this inscription has the appearance of being intended for a tomb-stone; but there is nothing in the verse that would suggest such a thought. The composition is in the style of those laboured portraits in words which we sometimes see placed at the bottom of a print to fill up lines of expression which the bungling Artist had left imperfect. We know from other evidence that Lord Lyttleton dearly loved his wife; he has indeed composed a monody to her memory,[7] which proves this, and she was an amiable woman; neither of which facts could have been gathered from these inscriptive verses. This epitaph would derive little advantage from being translated into another style as the former was; for there is no under current; no skeleton or staminae of thought and feeling. The Reader will perceive at once that nothing in the heart of the Writer had determined either the choice, the order or the expression, of the ideas; that there is no interchange of action from within and from without; that the connections are mechanical and arbitrary, and the lowest kind of these—heart and eyes: petty alliterations, as meek and magnanimous, witty and wise, combined with oppositions in thoughts where there is no necessary or natural opposition. Then follow voice, song, eloquence, form, mind—each enumerated by a separate act as if the Author had been making a *Catalogue Raisonné.*

These defects run through the whole; the only tolerable verse is,

> Her speech was the melodious voice of love.

Observe, the question is not which of these epitaphs is better or

---

6. *Works of the English Poets* (London, 1790), LXIV, 331–332; Lucy was Lyttleton's wife. The fuller title of the epitaph included: "Daughter of Hugh Fortescue . . . ."

7. *Ibid.*, pp. 311–322. See J. R. Sutherland, *Preface to Eighteenth Century Poetry* (Oxford: Clarendon Press, 1948), pp. 72–73.

worse; but which faults are of a worse kind. In the former case we
have a mourner whose soul is occupied by grief and urged forward
by his admiration. He deems in his simplicity that no hyberole can
transcend the perfections of her whom he has lost; for the version
which I have given fairly demonstrates that, in spite of his outrageous expressions, the under current of his thoughts was natural
and pure. We have therefore in him the example of a mind during
the act of composition misled by false taste to the highest possible
degree; and, in that of Lord Lyttleton, we have one of a feeling
heart, not merely misled, but wholly laid asleep by the same power.
Lord Lyttleton could not have written in this way upon such a
subject, if he had not been seduced by the example of Pope, whose
sparkling and tuneful manner had bewitched the men of letters his
contemporaries, and corrupted the judgment of the nation through
all ranks of society. So that a great portion of original genius was
necessary to embolden a man to write faithfully to Nature upon
any affecting subject if it belonged to a class of composition in
which Pope had furnished examples.

I am anxious not to be misunderstood. It has already been stated
that in this species of composition above every other, our sensations
and judgments depend upon our opinion or feeling of the Author's
state of mind.[8] Literature is here so far identified with morals, the
quality of the act so far determined by our notion of the aim and
purpose of the agent, that nothing can please us, however well
executed in its kind, if we are persuaded that the primary virtues
of sincerity, earnestness and a moral interest in the main object are
wanting. Insensibility here shocks us, and still more so if manifested
by a Writer going wholly out of his way in search of supposed
beauties, which if he were truly moved he could set no value upon,
could not even think of. We are struck in this case not merely with
a sense of disproportion and unfitness, but we cannot refrain from
attributing no small part of his intellectual to a moral demerit.
And here the difficulties of the question begin, namely in ascertaining
what errors in the choice of or the mode of expressing the thoughts,
most surely indicate the want of that which is most indispensible.
Bad taste, whatever shape it may put on, is injurious to the heart

8. See above, pp. 103–104.

and the understanding. If a man attaches much interest to the faculty of taste as it exists in himself and employs much time in those studies of which this faculty (I use the word taste in its comprehensive though most unjustifiable sense) is reckoned the arbiter, certain it is his moral notions and dispositions must either be purified and strengthened or corrupted and impaired. How can it be otherwise, when his ability to enter into the spirit of works in literature must depend upon his feelings, his imagination and his understanding, that is upon his recipient, upon his creative or active and upon his judging powers, and upon the accuracy and compass of his knowledge, in fine upon all that makes up the moral and intellectual man. What is true of individuals is equally true of nations. Nevertheless a man called to a task in which he is not practised, may have his expression thoroughly defiled and clogged by the style prevalent in his age, yet still, through the force of circumstances that have roused him, his under feeling may remain strong and pure; yet this may be wholly concealed from common view. Indeed the favourite style of different ages is so different and wanders so far from propriety that if it were not that first rate Writers in all nations and tongues are governed by common principles, we might suppose that truth and nature were things not to be looked for in books; hence to an unpractised Reader the productions of every age will present obstacles in various degrees hard to surmount; a deformity of style not the worst in itself but of that kind with which he is least familiar will on the one hand be most likely to render him insensible to a pith and power which may be within, and on the other hand he will be the least able to see through that sort of falsehood which is most prevalent in the works of his own time. Many of my Readers, to apply these general observations to the present case, must have derived pleasure from the epitaph of Lord Lyttleton and no doubt will be startled at the comparison I have made; but bring it to the test recommended it will then be found that its faults, though not in degree so intolerable, are in kind more radical and deadly than those of the strange composition with which it has been compared.

The course which we have taken having brought us to the name of this distinguished Writer—Pope—I will in this place give a few observations upon his Epitaphs,—the largest collection we have in our language, from the pen of any Writer of eminence. As the epitaphs of Pope and also those of Chiabrera, which occasioned this dissertation, are in metre, it may be proper here to enquire how far the notion of a perfect epitaph, as given in a former Paper, may be modified by the choice of metre for the vehicle, in preference to prose. If our opinions be just, it is manifest that the basis must remain the same in either case; and that the difference can only lie in the superstructure; and it is equally plain, that a judicious man will be less disposed in this case than in any other to avail himself of the liberty given by metre to adopt phrases of fancy, or to enter into the more remote regions of illustrative imagery. For the occasion of writing an epitaph is matter-of-fact in its intensity, and forbids more authoritatively than any other species of composition all modes of fiction, except those which the very strength of passion has created; which have been acknowledged by the human heart, and have become so familiar that they are converted into substantial realities. When I come to the epitaphs of Chiabrera, I shall perhaps give instances in which I think he has not written under the impression of this truth; where the poetic imagery does not elevate, deepen, or refine the human passion, which it ought always to do or not to act at all, but excludes it. In a far greater degree are Pope's epitaphs debased by faults into which he could not I think have fallen if he had written in prose as a plain man and not as a metrical Wit. I will transcribe from Pope's Epitaphs the one upon Mrs. Corbet (who died of a cancer), Dr. Johnson having extolled it highly and pronounced it the best of the collection.[9]

> Here rests a woman, good without pretence,
> Blest with plain reason and with sober sense;
> No conquest she but o'er herself desir'd;
> No arts essayed, but not to be admir'd.
> Passion and pride were to her soul unknown,
> Convinc'd that virtue only is our own.
> So unaffected, so compos'd a mind,
> So firm yet soft, so strong yet so refin'd,
> Heaven as its purest gold by tortures tried,
> The saint sustain'd it, but the woman died.[10]

9. *Lives*, ed. G. B. Hill (3 vols.; Oxford: Clarendon Press, 1905), III, 262.
10. *Ibid.*

This *may* be the best of Pope's Epitaphs; but if the standard which we have fixed be a just one, it cannot be approved of. First, it must be observed, that in the epitaphs of this Writer, the true impulse is wanting, and that his motions must of necessity be feeble. For he has no other aim than to give a favourable portrait of the character of the deceased. Now mark the process by which this is performed. Nothing is represented implicitly, that is, with its accompaniment of circumstances, or conveyed by its effects. The Author forgets that it is a living creature that must interest us and not an intellectual existence, which a mere character is. Insensible to this distinction the brain of the Writer is set at work to report as flatteringly as he may of the mind of his subject; the good qualities are separately abstracted (can it be otherwise than coldly and unfeelingly?) and put together again as coldly and unfeelingly. The epitaph now before us owes what exemption it may have from these defects in its general plan to the excruciating disease of which the lady died; but it is liable to the same censure, and is, like the rest, further objectionable in this; namely, that the thoughts have their nature changed and moulded by the vicious expression in which they are entangled, to an excess rendering them wholly unfit for the place they occupy.

> Here rests a woman, good without pretence,
> Blest with plain reason—

from which *sober sense* is not sufficiently distinguishable. This verse and a half, and the one "so unaffected, so composed a mind," are characteristic, and the expression is true to nature; but they are, if I may take the liberty of saying it, the only parts of the epitaph which have this merit. Minute criticism is in its nature irksome, and as commonly practiced in books and conversation, is both irksome and injurious. Yet every mind must occasionally be exercised in this discipline, else it cannot learn the art of bringing words rigorously to the test of thoughts; and these again to a comparison with things, their archetypes, contemplated first in themselves, and secondly in relation to each other; in all which processes the mind must be skilful, otherwise it will be perpetually imposed upon. In the next couplet the word *conquest*, is applied in a manner that would have been displeasing even from its triteness in a copy of complimentary verses to a fashionable Beauty; but to talk of making conquests in an epitaph is not to be endured. "No arts essayed, but not to be admired,"—are words expressing that she had recourse to artifices to conceal her amiable and admirable qualities; and the context implies that there was a merit in this; which surely no sane mind would allow. But the meaning of the Author, simply and honestly given, was nothing more than that she shunned admiration, probably with a more apprehensive modesty than was common; and more than this would have been inconsistent with the praise bestowed upon her—that she had an unaffected mind. This couplet is further objectionable, because the sense of love and peaceful admiration which such a character naturally inspires, is disturbed by an oblique and ill-timed stroke of satire. She is not praised so much as others are blamed, and is degraded by the Author in thus being made a covert or stalking-horse for gratifying a propensity the most abhorrent from her own nature—"Passion and pride were to her soul unknown." It cannot be meant that she had no passions, but that they were moderate and kept in subordination to her reason; but the thought is not here expressed; nor is it clear that a conviction in the understanding that "virtue only is our own," though it might suppress her pride, would be itself competent to govern or abate many other affections and passions to which our frail nature is, and ought in various degrees, to be subject. In fact, the Author appears to have had no precise notion of his own meaning. If she was "good without pretence," it seems unnecessary to say that she was not proud. Dr. Johnson, making an exception of the verse, "Convinced that virtue only is our own," praises this epitaph for "containing nothing taken from common places."[11] Now in fact, as may be deduced from the principles of this discourse, it is not only no fault but a primary requisite in an epitaph that it shall contain thoughts and feelings which are in their substance common-place, and even trite. It is grounded upon the universal intellectual property of man,—sensations which all men have felt and feel in some degree daily and hourly;—truths whose very interest and importance have caused them to be unattended

11. *Ibid.*

to, as things which could take care of themselves. But it is required that these truths should be instinctively ejaculated or should rise irresistibly from circumstances; in a word that they should be uttered in such connection as shall make it felt that they are not adopted, not spoken by rote, but perceived in their whole compass with the freshness and clearness of an original intuition.[12] The Writer must introduce the truth with such accompaniment as shall imply that he has mounted to the sources of things, penetrated the dark cavern from which the river that murmurs in every one's ear has flowed from generation to generation. The line "Virtue only is our own,"—is objectionable, not from the common-placeness of the truth, but from the vapid manner in which it is conveyed. A similar sentiment is expressed with appropriate dignity in an epitaph by Chiabrera, where he makes the Archbishop of Albino say of himself, that he was

> . . . smitten by the great ones of the world,
> But did not fall; for virtue braves all shocks,
> Upon herself resting immoveably.[13]

"So firm yet soft, so strong yet so refined": These intellectual operations (while they can be conceived of as operations of intellect at all, for in fact one half of the process is mechanical, words doing their own work and one half of the line manufacturing the rest) remind me of the motions of a Posture-master, or of a man balancing a sword upon his finger, which must be kept from falling at all hazards. "The saint sustained it, but the woman died." Let us look steadily at this antithesis: the *saint*, that is her soul strengthened by religion, supported the anguish of her disease with patience and resignation; but the *woman*, that is her body (for if anything else is

---

12. Cf. *The Friend*, September 14, 1809: "So to represent familiar objects as to awaken the minds of others to a like freshness of sensation concerning them . . . this is the prime merit of Genius, and its most unequivocal mode of manifestation" (p. 76). With slight revision, this statement refers to Wordsworth in *Biographia Literaria*, ed. J. Shawcross (2 vols.; London: Oxford University Press, 1907), I, 59–60.

13. "Epitaphs from Chiabrera, III," ll. 10–12 (*Poetical Works*, IV, 249). This poem had preceded the published "Essay upon Epitaphs" in *The Friend*, February 22, 1810, p. 402.

meant by the word woman, it contradicts the former part of the proposition and the passage is nonsense), was overcome. Why was not this simply expressed; without playing with the Reader's fancy, to the delusion and dishonour of his understanding, by a trifling epigramatic point? But alas! ages must pass away before men will have their eyes open to the beauty and majesty of Truth, and will be taught to venerate Poetry no further than as she is a handmaid pure as her mistress—the noblest handmaid in her train!

Prose Works of Wordsworth, ed. A. B. Grosart (3 vols.; London, 1876), II, 48–59.

Essay upon Epitaphs—III

I vindicate the rights and dignity of Nature; and as long as I condemn nothing without assigning reasons not lightly given, I cannot suffer any individual, however highly and deservedly honoured by my countrymen, to stand in my way. If my notions are right, the epitaphs of Pope cannot well be too severely condemned; for not only are they almost wholly destitute of those universal feelings and simple movements of mind which we have called for as indispensible, but they are little better than a tissue of false thoughts, languid and vague expressions, unmeaning antithesis, and laborious attempts at discrimination. Pope's mind had been employed chiefly in observation upon the vices and follies of men. Now, vice and folly are in contradiction with the moral principle which can never be extinguished in the mind; and therefore, wanting the contrast, are irregular, capricious, and inconsistent with themselves. If a man has once said (see FRIEND, No. ...), "Evil, be thou my good!"[1] and has acted accordingly, however strenuous may have been his adherence to this principle, it will be well known by those who have had an opportunity of observing him narrowly that there have been perpetual obliquities in his course; evil passions thwarting each other in various ways; and now and then, revivals of his better nature, which check him for a short time or lead him to remeasure his steps:—not to speak of the various necessities of counterfeiting virtue, which the furtherance of his schemes will impose upon him, and the division which will be consequently introduced into his nature.

It is reasonable then that Cicero, when holding up Catiline to detestation; and (without going to such an extreme case) that

1. *The Friend*, September 21, 1809: "He, who has once said with his whole heart, Evil be thou my Good! has removed a world of Obstacles by the very decision, that he will have no Obstacles but those of force and brute matter" (p. 84). The original source, of course, is *Paradise Lost*, IV, 110.

120

Dryden and Pope, when they are describing characters like Buckingham, Shaftsbury, and the Duchess of Marlborough,[2] should represent qualities and actions at war with each other and with themselves; and that the page should be suitably crowded with antithetical expressions. But all this argues an obtuse moral sensibility and a consequent want of knowledge, if applied where virtue ought to be described in the language of affectionate admiration. In the mind of the truly great and good everything that is of importance is at peace with itself; all is stillness, sweetness and stable grandeur. Accordingly the contemplation of virtue is attended with repose. A lovely quality, if its loveliness be clearly perceived, fastens the mind with absolute sovereignity upon itself; permitting or inciting it to pass, by smooth gradation or gentle transition, to some other kindred quality. Thus a perfect image of meekness (I refer to an instance before given) when looked at by a tender mind in its happiest mood, might easily lead on to thoughts of magnanimity; for assuredly there is nothing incongruous in those virtues. But the mind would not then be separated from the person who is the object of its thoughts; it would still be confined to that person or to others of the same general character; that is, would be kept within the circle of qualities which range themselves quietly by each other's sides. Whereas, when meekness and magnanimity are represented antithetically, the mind is not only carried from the main object, but is compelled to turn to a subject in which the quality exists divided from some other as noble, its natural ally: a painful feeling! that checks the course of love, and repels the sweet thoughts that might be settling round the person whom it was the Author's wish to endear to us; but for whom, after this interruption, we no longer care. If then a man, whose duty it is to praise departed excellence not without some sense of regret or sadness, to do this or to be silent, should upon all occasions exhibit that mode of connecting thoughts, which is only natural while we are delineating vice under certain relations, we may be assured that the nobler

2. Buckingham and Shaftesbury are Zimri and Achitophel in Dryden's "Absalom and Achitophel"; the Duchess of Marlborough was supposedly the original of Atossa in Pope's "Moral Essay II (To a Lady on the Characters of Women)," ll. 115–150.

sympathies are not alive in him; that he has no clear insight into the internal constitution of virtue; nor has himself been soothed, cheared, harmonized, by those outward effects which follow everywhere her goings,—declaring the presence of the invisible Deity. And though it be true that the most admirable of them must fall far short of perfection, and that the majority of those whose work is commemorated upon their tombstones must have been persons in whom good and evil were intermixed in various proportions and stood in various degrees of opposition to each other, yet the Reader will remember what has been said before upon that medium of love, sorrow and admiration, through which a departed friend is viewed; how it softens down or removes these harshnesses and contradictions, which moreover must be supposed never to have been grievous: for there can be no true love but between the good; and no epitaph ought to be written upon a bad man, except for a warning.

The purpose of the remarks given in the last Essay was chiefly to assist the Reader in separating truth and sincerity from falsehood and affectation; presuming that if the unction of a devout heart be wanting everything else is of no avail. It was shewn that a current of just thought and feeling may flow under a surface of illustrative imagery so impure as to produce an effect the opposite of that which was intended. Yet, though this fault may be carried to an intolerable *degree*, the Reader will have gathered that in our estimation it is not *in kind* the most offensive and injurious. We have contrasted it in its excess with instances where the genuine current or vein was wholly wanting; where the thoughts and feelings had no vital union, but were artificially connected, or formally accumulated, in a manner that would imply discontinuity and feebleness of mind upon any occasion, but still more reprehensible here!

I will proceed to give milder examples not in this last kind but in the former; namely of failure from various causes where the groundwork is good.

> Take holy earth! all that my soul holds dear:
> Take that best gift which Heaven so lately gave:
> To Bristol's fount I bore with trembling care,
> Her faded form. She bow'd to taste the wave—
> And died. Does youth, does beauty read the line?

Does sympathetic fear their breasts alarm?
Speak, dead Maria! breathe a strain divine;
Even from the grave thou shalt have power to charm.
Bid them in duty's sphere as meekly move:
And if so fair, from vanity as free,
As firm in friendship, and as fond in love;
Tell them, tho' 'tis an awful thing to die,
('Twas e'en to thee) yet, the dread path once trod;
Heaven lifts its everlasting portals high,
And bids "the pure in heart behold their God."[3]

This epitaph has much of what we have demanded; but it is debased in some instances by weakness of expression, in others by false prettiness. "She bow'd to taste the wave, and died." The plain truth was, she drank the Bristol waters which failed to restore her, and her death soon followed; but the expression involves a multitude of petty occupations for the fancy. "She bow'd": was there any truth in this? "to taste the wave": the water of a mineral spring which must have been drunk out of a goblet. Strange application of the word "wave" and "died": This would have been a just expression if the water had killed her; but, as it is, the tender thought involved in the disappointment of a hope however faint is left unexpressed; and a shock of surprise is given, entertaining perhaps to a light fancy but to a steady mind unsatisfactory, because false. "Speak! dead Maria, breathe a strain divine"! This sense flows nobly from the heart and the imagination; but perhaps it is not one of those impassioned thoughts which should be fixed in language upon a sepulchral stone. It is in its nature too poignant and transitory. A husband meditating by his wife's grave would throw off such a feeling and would give voice to it; and it would be in its place in a Monody to her memory; but if I am not mistaken, ought to have been suppressed here, or uttered after a different manner. The implied impersonation of the deceased (according to the tenor of what has before been said) ought to have been more general and shadowy.

3. William Mason's epitaph on his wife's monument in Bristol Cathedral was widely known. See J. W. Draper, *William Mason* (New York: New York University Press, 1924), p. 70.

And if so fair, from vanity as free,
As firm in friendship and as fond in love;
Tell them—

These are two sweet verses, but the word "fair" is improper; for unquestionably it was not intended that their title to receive this assurance should depend at all upon their personal beauty. Moreover in this couplet and in what follows, the long suspension of the sense excites the expectation of a thought less common than the concluding one; and is an instance of a failure in doing what is most needful and most difficult in an epitaph to do; namely to give to universally received truths a pathos and spirit which shall re-admit them into the soul like revelations of the moment.

I have said that this excellence is difficult to attain; and why? Is it because nature is weak? No! Where the soul has been thoroughly stricken (and Heaven knows the course of life must have placed all men, at some time or other, in that condition) there is never a want of *positive* strength; but because the adversary of Nature (call that adversary Art or by what name you will) is *comparatively* strong. The far-searching influence of the power, which, for want of a better name, we will denominate Taste, is in nothing more evinced than in the changeful character and complexion of that species of composition which we have been reviewing. Upon a call so urgent, it might be expected that the affections, the memory, and the imagination would be *constrained* to speak their genuine language. Yet, if the few specimens which have been given in the course of this enquiry, do not demonstrate the fact, the Reader need only look into any collection of Epitaphs to be convinced, that the faults predominant in the literature of every age will be as strongly reflected in the sepulchral inscriptions as any where; nay perhaps more so, from the anxiety of the Author to do justice to the occasion: and especially if the composition be in verse; for then it comes more avowedly in the shape of a work of art; and of course, is more likely to be coloured by the work of art holden in most esteem at the time. In a bulky volume of Poetry entitled ELEGANT EXTRACTS IN VERSE,[4]

4. *Elegant Extracts: or, Useful and Entertaining Pieces of Poetry, Selected for the Improvement of Young Persons.* Compiled first by Vicissimus Knox about 1770, the book had passed through some twenty ever enlarging editions by 1809, when it

which must be known to most of my Readers, as it is circulated everywhere and in fact constitutes at this day the poetical library of our Schools, I find a number of epitaphs in verse, of the last century; and there is scarcely one which is not thoroughly tainted by the artifices which have over-run our writings in metre since the days of Dryden and Pope. Energy, stillness, grandeur, tenderness, those feelings which are the pure emanations of Nature, those thoughts which have the infinitude of truth, and those expressions which are not what the garb is to the body but what the body is to the soul,[5] themselves a constituent part and power or function in the thought—all these are abandoned for their opposites,—as if our countrymen, through successive generations, had lost the sense of solemnity and pensiveness (not to speak of deeper emotions) and resorted to the tombs of their forefathers and contemporaries, only to be tickled and surprised. Would we not recoil from such gratification, in such a place, if the general literature of the country had not co-operated with other causes insidiously to weaken our sensibilities and deprave our judgments? Doubtless, there are shocks of event and circumstance, public and private, by which for all minds the truths of Nature will be elicited; but sorrow for that individual or people to whom these special interferences are necessary, to bring them into communion with the inner spirit of things! for such intercourse must be profitless in proportion as it is unfrequently irregular and transient. Words are too awful an instrument for good and evil, to be trifled with; they hold above all other external powers a dominion over thoughts. If words be not (recurring to a metaphor before used) an incarnation of the thought, but only a clothing for it, then surely will they prove an ill gift; such a one as those possessed vestments, read of in the stories of superstitious times, which had power to consume and to alienate from

---

consisted of four parts: I. Sacred and Moral; II. Didactive, Descriptive, Narrative, and Pathetic; III. Dramatic, chiefly from Shakespeare; and IV. Sentimental, Lyrical and Ludicrous (including odes, sonnets, and epitaphs). See Edmund Blunden, "Elegant Extracts," *Essays on the 18th Century* (Oxford: Clarendon Press, 1945), pp. 225–237.

5. Wordsworth here opposes Pope's theory of poetic language, particularly the notion that "expression is the dress of thought" ("Essay on Criticism," II, 118).

his right mind the victim who put them on. Language, if it do not uphold, and feed, and leave in quiet, like the power of gravitation or the air we breathe, is a counter-spirit, unremittingly and noiselessly at work, to subvert, to lay waste, to vitiate, and to dissolve. From a deep conviction then that the excellence of writing, whether in prose or verse, consists in a conjunction of Reason and Passion, a conjunction which must be of necessity benign; and that it might be deduced from what has been said that the taste, intellectual power and morals of a country are inseparably linked in mutual dependence, I have dwelt thus long upon this argument. And the occasion justifies me; for how could the tyranny of bad taste be brought home to the mind more aptly than by showing in what degree the feelings of nature yield to it when we are rendering to our friends the solemn testimony of our love? more forcibly than by giving proof that thoughts cannot, even upon this impulse, assume an outward life without a transmutation and a fall. * * *

Prose Works of Wordsworth, ed. A. B. Grosart (3 vols.; London, 1876), II, 60–65.

Preface to *The Excursion* (1814)

The Excursion appeared in an expensive quarto edition July, 1814. As the Preface says, the poem was intended as the middle segment of a three-part work. The first part was to be "The Recluse," quoted extensively in the Preface but not published until 1884, still unfinished. The third part was apparently never begun. "The Recluse," conceived as early as 1797, had grown to thirteen hundred lines in the spring of 1798. Wordsworth worked on it until his return from Germany in 1799, then put it aside to compose the poem that became The Prelude, called "the preparatory poem" in the Preface.

The Title-page announces that this is only a Portion of a Poem; and the Reader must be here apprized that it belongs to the second part of a long and laborious Work, which is to consist of three parts.—The Author will candidly acknowledge that, if the first of these had been completed, and in such a manner as to satisfy his own mind, he should have preferred the natural order of publication, and have given that to the World first; but, as the second division of the Work was designed to refer more to passing events, and to an existing state of things, than the others were meant to do, more continuous exertion was naturally bestowed upon it, and greater progress made here than in the rest of the Poem; and as this part does not depend upon the preceding, to a degree which will materially injure its own peculiar interest, the Author, complying with the earnest entreaties of some valued Friends, presents the following Pages to the Public.

It may be proper to state whence the Poem, of which The Excursion is a part, derives its Title of THE RECLUSE.—Several years ago, when the Author retired to his native Mountains, with the hope of being enabled to construct a literary Work that might live, it was a reasonable thing that he should take a review of his own Mind, and examine how far Nature and Education had qualified him for such employment. As subsidiary to this preparation, he undertook to record, in Verse, the origin and progress of his own powers, as far as he was acquainted with them. That Work, addressed to a dear Friend, most distinguished for his knowledge and genius, and to whom the Author's Intellect is deeply indebted, has been long finished; and the result of the investigation which gave rise to it was a determination to compose a philosophical Poem, containing views of Man, Nature, and Society; and to be entitled, The Recluse; as having for its principal subject the sensations and opinions of a Poet living in retirement.—The preparatory Poem is biographical, and conducts the history of the Author's mind to the point when he was emboldened to hope that his faculties were sufficiently matured for entering upon the arduous labour which he had proposed to himself; and the two Works have the same kind of relation to each other, if he may so express himself, as the Anti-chapel has to the body of a gothic Church. Continuing this allusion, he may be permitted to add, that his minor Pieces, which have been long before the Public, when they shall be properly arranged, will be found by the attentive Reader to have such connection with the main Work as may give them claim to be likened to the little Cells, Oratories, and sepulchral Recesses, ordinarily included in those Edifices.

The Author would not have deemed himself justified in saying, upon this occasion, so much of performances either unfinished, or unpublished, if he had not thought that the labour bestowed by him upon what he has heretofore and now laid before the Public, entitled him to candid attention for such a statement as he thinks necessary to throw light upon his endeavours to please, and he would hope, to benefit his countrymen.—Nothing further need be added, than that the first and third parts of the Recluse will consist chiefly of meditations in the Author's own Person; and that in the intermediate part (The Excursion) the intervention of Characters speaking is employed, and something of a dramatic form adopted.

It is not the Author's intention formally to announce a system: it was more animating to him to proceed in a different course; and if he shall succeed in conveying to the mind clear thoughts, lively images, and strong feelings, the Reader will have no difficulty in extracting the system for himself. And in the mean time the following passage, taken from the conclusion of the first Book of the Recluse, may be acceptable as a kind of *Prospectus* of the design and scope of the whole Poem.

"On Man, on Nature, and on Human Life
Musing in Solitude, I oft perceive
Fair trains of imagery before me rise,
Accompanied by feelings of delight
Pure, or with no unpleasing sadness mixed;
And I am conscious of affecting thoughts
And dear remembrances, whose presence soothes
Or elevates the Mind, intent to weigh
The good and evil of our mortal state.
—To these emotions, whencesoe'er they come,
Whether from breath of outward circumstance,
Or from the Soul—an impulse to herself,
I would give utterance in numerous Verse.
—Of Truth, of Grandeur, Beauty, Love, and Hope—
And melancholy Fear subdued by Faith;
Of blessed consolations in distress;
Of moral strength, and intellectual power;
Of joy in widest commonalty spread;
Of the individual Mind that keeps her own
Inviolate retirement, subject there
To Conscience only, and the law supreme
Of that Intelligence which governs all;
I sing:—"fit audience let me find though few!"[1]

So prayed, more gaining than he asked, the Bard,
Holiest of Men.—Urania, I shall need
Thy guidance, or a greater Muse, if such
Descend to earth or dwell in highest heaven!
For I must tread on shadowy ground, must sink
Deep—and, aloft ascending, breathe in worlds
To which the heaven of heavens is but a veil.
All strength—all terror, single or in bands,

1. *Paradise Lost*, VII, 31: "fit audience, though few."

That ever was put forth in personal form;
Jehovah—with his thunder, and the choir
Of shouting Angels, and the empyreal thrones,
I pass them, unalarmed. Not Chaos, not
The darkest pit of lowest Erebus,
Nor aught of blinder vacancy—scooped out
By help of dreams, can breed such fear and awe
As fall upon us often when we look
Into our Minds, into the Mind of Man,
My haunt, and the main region of my Song.
—Beauty—a living Presence of the earth,
Surpassing the most fair ideal Forms
Which craft of delicate Spirits hath composed
From earth's materials—waits upon my steps;
Pitches her tents before me as I move,
An hourly neighbour. Paradise, and groves
Elysian, Fortunate Fields—like those of old
Sought in the Atlantic Main, why should they be
A history only of departed things,
Or a mere fiction of what never was?
For the discerning intellect of Man,
When wedded to this goodly universe
In love and holy passion, shall find these
A simple produce of the common day.
—I, long before the blissful hour arrives,
Would chaunt, in lonely peace, the spousal verse
Of this great consummation:—and, by words
Which speak of nothing more than what we are,
Would I arouse the sensual from their sleep
Of Death, and win the vacant and the vain
To noble raptures; while my voice proclaims
How exquisitely the individual Mind
(And the progressive powers perhaps no less
Of the whole species) to the external World
Is fitted:—and how exquisitely, too,
Theme this but little heard of among Men,
The external World is fitted to the Mind;
And the creation (by no lower name
Can it be called) which they with blended might
Accomplish:—this is our high argument.

—Such grateful haunts foregoing, if I oft
Must turn elsewhere—to travel near the tribes
And fellowships of men, and see ill sights
Of madding passions mutually inflamed;
Must hear Humanity in fields and groves
Pipe solitary anguish; or must hang
Brooding above the fierce confederate storm
Of sorrow, barricadoed evermore
Within the walls of Cities; may these sounds
Have their authentic comment,—that, even these
Hearing, I be not downcast or forlorn!
—Come thou prophetic Spirit, that inspir'st
The human Soul of universal earth,
Dreaming on things to come; and dost possess
A metropolitan Temple in the hearts
Of mighty Poets; upon me bestow
A gift of genuine insight; that my Song
With star-like virtue in its place may shine;
Shedding benignant influence,—and secure,
Itself, from all malevolent effect
Of those mutations that extend their sway
Throughout the nether sphere!—And if with this
I mix more lowly matter; with the thing
Contemplated, describe the Mind and Man
Contemplating; and who, and what he was,
The transitory Being that beheld
This Vision,—when and where, and how he lived;—
Be not this labour useless. If such theme
May sort with highest objects, then, dread Power,
Whose gracious favour is the primal source
Of all illumination, may my Life
Express the image of a better time,
More wise desires, and simpler manners;—nurse
My Heart in genuine freedom:—all pure thoughts
Be with me;—so shall thy unfailing love
Guide, and support, and cheer me to the end!"

The Excursion (London, 1814), pp. [vii]–xiv.

Letter to Catherine Clarkson
(January, 1815)

Catherine Buck Clarkson, a close friend of Dorothy Wordsworth's since 1800, was the wife of Thomas Clarkson, a leading English abolitionist who, with William Smith, played a large part in obtaining the abolition of slavery in Great Britain. William Smith, the spokesman for Dissenting churches in Parliament and a Unitarian leader, fathered five daughters, one of whom, Frances, became the mother of Florence Nightingale. His daughter Parthenope ("Patty") offered the criticism Wordsworth answers here. Henry Crabb Robinson, a mutual friend of the Clarksons and the Wordsworths, says in his diary for January 3, 1815, that Mrs. Clarkson was upset by "an exceedingly sensible letter from Miss Smith in which the radical objection made by the Eclectic Review" *against* The Excursion "*was also urged by her though a Unitarian, and with great force.*"[1] *The* Eclectic Review *was at this time an organ of liberal Dissenters generally. Its review objected to the poem because it (1) treated nature as God; (2) represented a love of nature as a sanctifying process; and (3) ignored scriptural revelation.*[2]

I don't know that it is quite *fair* to sit down to answer a letter of friendship the moment it is received; but allow me to do so in this case.—Unitarian hymns must by their dispassionate monotony have deprived your Friend's ear of all compass, which implies of all discrimination. To you I will whisper, that the Excursion has one merit if it has no other, a versification to which for *variety* of musical effect no Poem in the language furnishes a parallel. Tell Patty

1. *Henry Crabb Robinson on Books and their Writers,* ed. E. J. Morley (3 vols.; London: J. M. Dent, 1938), I, 159.
2. The review is reprinted in Elsie Smith, *Estimate of William Wordsworth* (Oxford: Blackwell, 1932), pp. 175–181.

Smith this (the name is a secret with me) and make her stare; and exhort her to study with her fingers till she has learned to confess it to herself. Miss S's notion of poetical imagery is probably taken from the Pleasures of Hope or Gertrude of Wyoming; see for instance stanza first of said poem.[3] There is very little imagery of that kind; but, I am far from subscribing to your concession that there is little imagery in the Poem; either collateral in the way of metaphor coloring the style; illustrative in the way of simile; or directly under the shape of description or incident: there is a great deal; though not quite so much as will be found in the other parts of the Poem where the subjects are more lyrically treated and where there is less narration; or description turning upon manners, and those repeated actions which constitute habits, or a course of life.— Poetic Passion (Dennis has well observed)[4] is of two kinds imaginative and enthusiastic; and merely human & ordinary; of the former it is only to be feared that there is too great a proportion. But all this must inevitably be lost upon Miss P. S—

The Soul, dear Mrs C. may be re-given when it has been taken away, my own Solitary is an instance of this; but a Soul that has been dwarfed by a course of bad culture cannot after a certain age, be expanded into one of even ordinary proportion.—Mere error of

3. These poems by Thomas Campbell achieved instant popularity when published in 1799 and 1809 respectively. The first stanza of "Pleasures of Hope":

> At summer eve, when Heaven's ethereal bow
> Spans with bright arch the glittering hills below,
> Why to yon mountain turns the musing eye,
> Whose sunbright summit mingles with the sky?
> Why do those cliffs of shadowy tint appear
> More sweet than all the landscape smiling near?
> 'Tis distance lends enchantment to the view,
> And robes the mountain in its azure hue.
> (*Poetical Works of Thomas Campbell*, ed. J. L. Robertson [London: Oxford University Press, 1907], p. 2.)

4. "I call that ordinary Passion, whose Cause is clearly comprehended by him who feels it, whether it be Admiration, Terror or Joy; and I call the very same Passions Enthusiasms, when their Cause is not clearly comprehended by him who feels them" ("Advancement and Reformation of Modern Poetry" [1701], *Critical Works*, ed. E. N. Hooker [2 vols.; Baltimore: Johns Hopkins Press, 1939–1943], I, 216).

opinion, mere apprehension of ill consequences from supposed mistaken views on my part, could never have rendered your correspondent blind to the innumerable analogies and types of infinity, insensible to the countless awakenings to noble aspiration, which I have transfused into that Poem from the Bible of the Universe as it speaks to the ear of the intelligent, as it lies open to the eyes of the humble-minded. I have alluded to the Ladys errors of opinion—she talks of my being a worshipper of Nature—a passionate expression uttered incautiously in the Poem upon the Wye[5] has led her into this mistake, she, reading in cold-heartedness and substituting the letter for the spirit. Unless I am greatly mistaken, there is nothing of this kind in the Excursion. There is indeed a passage towards the end of the 4th. Book where the Wanderer introduces the simile of the Boy and the Shell, and what follows,[6] that has something, ordinarily but absurdly called *Spinosistic*. But the intelligent reader will easily see the *dramatic* propriety of the Passage. The Wanderer in the beginning of the book had given vent to his own devotional feelings and announced in some degree his own creed; he is here preparing the way for more distinct conceptions of the Deity by reminding the Solitary of such religious feelings as cannot but exist in the minds of those who affect atheism. She condemns me for not distinguishing between nature as the work of God and God himself. But where does she find this doctrine inculcated? Where does she gather that the Author of the Excursion looks upon nature and God as the same? He does not indeed consider the Supreme Being as bearing the same relation to the universe as a watch-maker bears to a watch. In fact, there is nothing in the course of religious education adopted in this country and in the use made by us of the holy scriptures that appears to me so injurious as the perpetually talking about *making* by God—Oh! that your Correspondent had heard a conversation which I had in bed with my sweet little Boy, four and a half years old, upon this subject the

5. "I, so long/A worshipper of Nature" in "Lines . . . Tintern Abbey," ll. 151–152 (*Poetical Works*, II, 263).

6. "Even such a shell the universe itself / Is to the ear of Faith," IV, 1141–1142 (*Poetical Works*, V, 145).

other morning. "How did God make me? Where is God? How does he speak? He never spoke to *me*." I told him that God was a spirit, that he was not like his flesh which he could touch; but more like his thoughts in his mind which he could not touch.—The wind was tossing the fir trees, and the sky and light were dancing about in their dark branches, as seen through the window—Noting these fluctuations he exclaimed eagerly—"There's a bit of him I see it there!" This is not meant entirely for Father's prattle; but, for Heaven's sake, in your religious talk with children say as little as possible about *making*. One of the main objects of the Recluse is, to reduce the calculating understanding to its proper level among the human faculties—Therefore my Book must be disliked by the Unitarians, as their religion rests entirely on that basis; and therefore is, in fact, no religion at all—but—I won't say what. I have done little or nothing towards your request of furnishing you with arguments to cope with my antagonist. Read the Book if it pleases you; the construction of the language is uniformly perspicuous; at least I have taken every possible pains to make it so, therefore you will have no difficulty here. The impediments you may meet with will be of two kinds, such as exist in the ode which concludes my 2d volume of poems.[7] This poem rests entirely upon two recollections of childhood, one that of a splendour in the objects of sense which is passed away, and the other an indisposition to bend to the law of death as applying to our own particular case. A Reader who has not a vivid recollection of these feelings having existed in his mind in childhood cannot understand that poem. So also with regard to some of those elements of the human soul whose importance is insisted upon in the Excursion. And some of those images of sense which are dwelt upon as holding that relation to immortality and infinity which I have before alluded to; if a person has not been in the way of receiving these images, it is not likely that he can form such an adequate conception of them as will bring him into lively sympathy with the Poet. For instance one who has never heard the echoes of the flying Raven's voice in a mountainous Country, as

7. The Intimations Ode was the concluding poem of *Poems in Two Volumes* (1807).

described at the close of the 4th Book will not perhaps be able to relish that illustration;[8] yet every one must have been in the way of perceiving similar effects from different causes;—but I have tired myself, and must have tired you.—

One word upon ordinary or popular passion. Could your correspondent read the description of Robert,[9] and the fluctuations of hope and fear in Margaret's mind, and the gradual decay of herself and her dwelling without a bedimmed eye, then I pity her. Could she read the distress of the Solitary after the loss of his Family and the picture of his quarrel with his own conscience (though this tends more to meditative passion) without some agitation then I envy not her tranquillity. Could the anger of Ellen before she sate down to weep over her Babe, though she were but a poor serving-maid, be found in a book, and that book be said to be without passion, then, thank Heaven! that the person so speaking is neither my Wife nor my Sister, nor one whom (unless I could work in her a great alteration) I am forced daily to converse with. What thinks she of those Relatives about the little Infant, who was unexpectedly given, and suddenly taken away? But too much of this—Farewell. I wish I could have written you a more satisfactory letter. Lamb is justifiably enraged at the spurious Review which his Friends expect to be his.[10] No Newmarket jockey, no horse-stealer was ever able to play a hundredth part of the tricks upon the person of an unhappy beast than the Bavius of the Quarterly Review has done for that sweet composition. So I will not scruple to style it, though I never saw it. And worst of all, Lamb kept no copy and the original manuscript we fear destroyed.—As to the Edinburgh Review I hold the Author of it in entire contempt, and therefore shall not pollute my fingers with the touch of it. There is one sentence in the Excursion ending in "sublime attractions of the grave"[11] which, if

8. IV, 1175–1187 (Poetical Works, V, 146).

9. The allusions in sequence are to Book I generally; II, 873–880; VI, 976–977; and VII, 677–794.

10. Lamb's review of The Excursion was rewritten by William Gifford, editor of the Quarterly Review. Wordsworth is echoing a letter from Lamb (Works, ed. E. V. Lucas [7 vols.; London: Methuen, 1903–1905], VI, 452–453).

11. IV, 238 (Poetical Works, V, 116).

the poem had contained nothing else that I valued, would have made it almost a matter of religion with me to keep out of the way of the best stuff which so mean a mind as Mr Jeffrey's could produce in connection with it. His impertinences, to use the mildest term, if once they had a place in my memory, would, for a time at least stick there. You cannot scower a spot of this kind out of your mind as you may a stain out of your clothes. If the mind were under the power of the will I should read Mr Jeffrey merely to expose his stupidity to his still more stupid admirers. This not being the case, as I said before, I shall not pollute my fingers with touching his book. Give my affectionate regards to Henry Robinson, and the same to Mr Clarkson. Remember me also kindly to your Father.—I am sure you are competent to write the Review as well as I could wish to have it done. I am very sorry for the indisposition under which your last was written. Headaches are plaguey things. I hope you are better—

Sunday Morning—I have just read over this Letter; it is a sad jumble of stuff and as ill expressed.—I should not send it but in compliance with the wish of Mary and Dorothy. The reason of the thing being so bad is that your Friends remarks were so monstrous. To talk of the offense of writing the Excursion and the difficulty of forgiving the Author is carrying audacity and presumption to a heighth of which I did not think any *Woman* was capable. Had my Poem been much coloured by Books, as many parts of what I have to write must be, I should have been accused as Milton has been of Pedantry, and of having a mind which could not support itself but by other mens labours.—Do not you perceive that my conversations almost all take place out of Doors, and all with grand objects of nature surrounding the speakers for the express purpose of their being alluded to in illustration of the subjects treated of. *Much* imagery from books would have been an impertinence and an incumbrance: where it was required it is found. As to passion; it is never to be lost sight of, that the Excursion is *part* of a work; that in its plan it is conversational; and that if I had introduced stories exciting curiosity, and filled with violent conflicts of passion and a rapid interchange of striking incidents, these things could have never harmonized with the rest of the work and all further discourse, comment, or reflections must have been put a stop to.—This I write for you and not for your friend; with whom if you would take my advice, you will neither converse by Letter nor *viva voce* upon a subject which she is in every respect disqualified to treat. farewell. * * *

Some Letters of the Wordsworth Family, ed. L. N. Broughton (Ithaca: Cornell University Press, 1942), pp. 56–60.

Preface to *Poems* (1815)

Wordsworth's Poems . . . in Two Volumes *appeared in an edition of five hundred copies in late March, 1815, announcing on its title page "A New Preface and a Supplementary Essay." The 1802 Preface was included, but now at the end of Volume II. The poems were rearranged into a dozen categories: "Poems Referring to the Period of Childhood," "Juvenile Pieces," "Poems Founded on the Affections," "Poems of the Fancy," "Poems of the Imagination," "Poems Proceeding from Sentiment and Reflection," "Miscellaneous Sonnets," "Sonnets Dedicated to Liberty," "Poems on the Naming of Places," "Inscriptions," "Poems Referring to the Period of Old Age," "Epitaphs and Elegiac Poems." This arrangement, as the Preface says, has reference to (1) the powers of the mind predominant in the poems; (2) their form; or (3) the subjects to which they relate. A fourth, historical, principle is reflected in the author dating the poems (unreliably) in the table of contents, thus referring to the growth of his poetic powers. The Supplementary Essay attacks critics and reviews English poetry since the Renaissance in order to vindicate the superiority of original over popular poetry. The 1800 Preface had said that a systematic defense of the theory behind the* Lyrical Ballads *would require a full account of the state of taste, which in turn would require examining the relation between language and mind and also tracing revolutions in literature and society. The 1815 Preface examines the relation between language and mind, while the Supplementary Essay examines revolutions in literature and—to a lesser extent—society. The Preface and Essay may thus be considered Wordsworth's summation of his case for posterity.*

The observations prefixed to that portion of these Volumes, which was published many years ago, under the title of "Lyrical Ballads," have so little of a special application to the greater part, perhaps, of this collection, as subsequently enlarged and diversified, that they could not with any propriety stand as an Introduction to it. Not deeming it, however, expedient to suppress that exposition, slight and imperfect as it is, of the feelings which had determined the choice of the subjects, and the principles which had regulated the composition of those Pieces, I have transferred it to the end of the second Volume, to be attended to, or not, at the pleasure of the Reader.

In the Preface to that part of "The Recluse," lately published under the title of "The Excursion," I have alluded to a meditated arrangement of my minor Poems, which should assist the attentive Reader in perceiving their connection with each other, and also their subordination to that Work.[1] I shall here say a few words explanatory of this arrangement, as carried into effect in the present Volumes.

The powers requisite for the production of poetry are,[2] first, those of observation and description, i.e. the ability to observe with accuracy things as they are in themselves, and with fidelity to describe them, unmodified by any passion or feeling existing in the mind of the Describer: whether the things depicted be actually present to the senses, or have a place only in the memory. This power, though indispensable to a Poet, is one which he employs only in submission to necessity, and never for a continuance of time; as its exercise supposes all the higher qualities of the mind to be passive, and in a state of subjection to external objects, much in the same way as the Translator or Engraver ought to be to his Original. 2dly, Sensibility,—which, the more exquisite it is, the wider will be the range of a Poet's perceptions; and the more will he be incited to observe objects, both as they exist in themselves and as re-acted upon by his own mind. (The distinction between poetic and human sensibility has been marked in the character of the Poet delineated

1. See above, p. 128.

2. Earlier classifications were concerned with qualities evident in a writer's poems; e.g., Joseph Warton classified English poets as: sublime and pathetic; moral, ethical, panegyrical; witty, elegant in taste, lively fanciful in describing familiar life; and mere versifiers ("Genius and Writings of Pope," *Eighteenth Century Critical Essays*, ed. Scott Elledge [2 vols.; Ithaca: Cornell University Press, 1961], II, 720). Or, they were lists of abstractions; e.g., Rapin specified wit, imagination, elevation of soul, and great judgment with vivacity (*Reflections on Aristotle's Treatise of Poesie*, tr. Thomas Rymer [London, 1694], Chap. II).

in the original preface, before-mentioned).³ 3rdly, Reflection,—
which makes the Poet acquainted with the value of actions, images,
thoughts, and feelings; and assists the sensibility in perceiving their
connection with each other. 4thly, Imagination and Fancy,—to
modify, to create, and to associate. 5thly, Invention,—by which
characters are composed out of materials supplied by observation;
whether of the Poet's own heart and mind, or of external life and
nature; and such incidents and situations produced as are most
impressive to the imagination, and most fitted to do justice to the
characters, sentiments, and passions, which the Poet undertakes to
illustrate. And, lastly, Judgment,—to decide how and where, and
in what degree, each of these faculties ought to be exerted; so that
the less shall not be sacrificed to the greater; nor the greater,
slighting the less, arrogate, to its own injury, more than its due. By
judgment, also, is determined what are the laws and appropriate
graces of every species of composition.

The materials of Poetry, by these powers collected and produced,
are cast, by means of various moulds, into divers forms. The moulds
may be enumerated, and the forms specified, in the following order.⁴
1st, the Narrative,—including the Epopoeia, the Historic Poem,
the Tale, the Romance, the Mock-heroic, and, if the spirit of Homer
will tolerate such neighbourhood, that dear production of our days,
the metrical Novel. Of this Class, the distinguishing mark, is, that
the Narrator, however liberally his speaking agents be introduced, is
himself the source from which every thing primarily flows. Epic
Poets, in order that their mode of composition may accord with the
elevation of their subject, represent themselves as *singing* from the
inspiration of the Muse, Arma virum que *cano*;⁵ but this is a fiction,
in modern times, of slight value: The Iliad or the Paradise Lost
would gain little in our estimation by being chaunted. The other
poets who belong to this class are commonly content to *tell* their

3. See above, p. 48.
4. Cf. Rapin, who distinguishes between epic and tragic poetry, lumping lesser
kinds under one head or the other: elegy, ode, eclogue (Wordsworth's "idyllium"),
satire, and epigram. He considers the madrigal, the roundelay, the sonnet, and
the ballad "a sort of *imperfect* Poems" (*Reflections on Aristotle's Treatise of Poesie*, p. 77).
5. "I sing of arms and the man" (opening line of the *Aeneid*).

tale;—so that of the whole it may be affirmed that they neither require nor reject the accompaniment of music.

2ndly, The Dramatic,—consisting of Tragedy, Historic Drama, Comedy, and Masque; in which the poet does not appear at all in his own person, and where the whole action is carried on by speech and dialogue of the agents; music being admitted only incidentally and rarely. The Opera may be placed here, in as much as it proceeds by dialogue; though depending, to the degree that it does, upon music, it has a strong claim to be ranked with the Lyrical. The characteristic and impassioned Epistle, of which Ovid and Pope have given examples, considered as a species of monodrama, may, without impropriety, be placed in this class.

3rdly, The Lyrical,—containing the Hymn, the Ode, the Elegy, the Song, and the Ballad; in all which, for the production of their *full* effect, an accompaniment of music is indispensable.

4thly, The Idyllium,—descriptive chiefly either of the processes and appearances of external nature, as the "Seasons" of Thomson; or of characters, manners, and sentiments, as are Shenstone's School-mistress, The Cotter's Saturday Night of Burns, The Twa Dogs of the same Author; or of these in conjunction with the appearances of Nature, as most of the pieces of Theocritus, the Allegro and Penseroso of Milton, Beattie's Minstrel, Goldsmith's "Deserted Village." The Epitaph, the Inscription, the Sonnet, most of the epistles of poets writing in their own persons, and all loco-descriptive poetry, belong to this class.

5thly, Didactic,—the principal object of which is direct instruction; as the Poem of Lucretius, the Georgics of Virgil, "the Fleece" of Dyer, Mason's "English Garden," &c.

And, lastly, philosophical satire, like that of Horace and Juvenal; personal and occasional Satire rarely comprehending sufficient of the general in the individual to be dignified with the name of Poetry.

Out of the three last classes has been constructed a composite species, of which Young's Night Thoughts and Cowper's Task are excellent examples.[6]

It is deducible from the above, that poems, apparently miscel-

6. We would now call this type descriptive-meditative.

laneous, may with propriety be arranged either with reference to the powers of mind *predominant* in the production of them; or to the mould in which they are cast; or, lastly, to the subjects to which they relate. From each of these considerations, the following Poems have been divided into classes; which, that the work may more obviously correspond with the course of human life, for the sake of exhibiting in it the three requisites of a legitimate whole, a beginning, a middle, and an end, have been also arranged, as far as it was possible, according to an order of time, commencing with Childhood, and terminating with Old Age, Death, and Immortality. My guiding wish was, that the small pieces of which these volumes consist, thus discriminated, might be regarded under a two-fold view; as composing an entire work within themselves, and as adjuncts to the philosophical Poem, "The Recluse." This arrangement has long presented itself habitually to my own mind. Nevertheless, I should have preferred to scatter the contents of these volumes at random, if I had been persuaded that, by the plan adopted, any thing material would be taken from the natural effect of the pieces, individually, on the mind of the unreflecting Reader. I trust there is a sufficient variety in each class to prevent this; while, for him who reads with reflection, the arrangement will serve as a commentary unostentatiously directing his attention to my purposes, both particular and general. But, as I wish to guard against the possibility of misleading by this classification, it is proper first to remind the Reader, that certain poems are placed according to the powers of mind, in the Author's conception, predominant in the production of them; *predominant*, which implies the exertion of other faculties in less degree. Where there is more imagination than fancy in a poem it is placed under the head of imagination, and vice versa. Both the above Classes might without impropriety have been enlarged from that consisting of "Poems founded on the Affections"; as might this latter from those, and from the class "Proceeding from Sentiment and Reflection." The most striking characteristics of each piece, mutual illustration, variety, and proportion, have governed me throughout.

It may be proper in this place to state, that the Extracts[7] in the

7. From "Evening Walk" and "Descriptive Sketches" (1793).

2nd Class entitled "Juvenile Pieces," are in many places altered from the printed copy, chiefly by omission and compression. The slight alterations of another kind were for the most part made not long after the publication of the Poems from which the Extracts are taken. These Extracts seem to have a title to be placed here as they were the productions of youth, and represent implicitly some of the features of a youthful mind, at a time when images of nature supplied to it the place of thought, sentiment, and almost of action; or, as it will be found expressed, of a state of mind when

> "the sounding cataract
> Haunted me like a passion: the tall rock,
> The mountain, and the deep and gloomy wood,
> Their colours and their forms were then to me
> An appetite, a feeling and a love,
> That had no need of a remoter charm,
> By thought supplied, or any interest
> Unborrowed from the eye"—[8]

I will own that I was much at a loss what to select of these descriptions; and perhaps it would have been better either to have reprinted the whole, or suppressed what I have given.

None of the other Classes, except those of Fancy and Imagination, require any particular notice. But a remark of general application may be made. All Poets, except the dramatic, have been in the practice of feigning that their works were composed to the music of the harp or lyre: with what degree of affectation this has been done in modern times, I leave to the judicious to determine.[9] For my own part, I have not been disposed to violate probability so far, or to make such a large demand upon the Reader's charity. Some of these pieces are essentially lyrical; and, therefore, cannot have their due force without a supposed musical accompaniment; but, in much the greatest part, as a substitute for the classic lyre or romantic harp, I require nothing more than an animated or impassioned recitation, adapted to the subject. Poems, however humble in their kind, if they be good in that kind, cannot read

8. "Lines . . . Tintern Abbey," ll. 76–83 (*Poetical Works*, II, 261).

9. See G. N. Shuster, *The English Ode from Milton to Keats* (New York: Columbia University Press, 1940), p. 237.

themselves: the law of long syllable and short must not be so inflexible—the letter of metre must not be so impassive to the spirit of versification—as to deprive the Reader of a voluntary power to modulate, in subordination to the sense, the music of the poem;— in the same manner as his mind is left at liberty, and even summoned, to act upon its thoughts and images. But, though the accompaniment of a musical instrument be frequently dispensed with, the true Poet does not therefore abandon his privilege distinct from that of the mere Proseman;

> "He murmurs near the running brooks
> A music sweeter than their own."[10]

I come now to the consideration of the words Fancy and Imagination, as employed in the classification of the following Poems. "A man," says an intelligent Author, has "imagination," in proportion as he can distinctly copy in idea the impressions of sense: it is the faculty which *images* within the mind the phenomena of sensation. A man has fancy in proportion as he can call up, connect, or associate, at pleasure, those internal images ($\phi \alpha \nu \tau \alpha \zeta \epsilon \iota \nu$ is to cause to appear) so as to complete ideal representations of absent objects. Imagination is the power of depicting, and fancy of evoking and combining. The imagination is formed by patient observation; the fancy by a voluntary activity in shifting the scenery of the mind. The more accurate the imagination, the more safely may a painter, or a poet, undertake a delineation, or a description, without the presence of the objects to be characterized. The more versatile the fancy, the more original and striking will be the decorations produced.—*British Synonyms discriminated, by W. Taylor.*[11]

Is not this as if a man should undertake to supply an account of a building, and be so intent upon what he had discovered of the foundation as to conclude his task without once looking up at the superstructure? Here, as in other instances throughout the volume, the judicious Author's mind is enthralled by Etymology; he takes up the original word as his guide, his conductor, his escort, and too

10. "A Poet's Epitaph," ll. 39–40 (*Poetical Works*, IV, 66).
11. William Taylor of Norwich, *English Synonymes Discriminated* (London, 1813), pp. 242–243.

often does not perceive how soon he becomes its prisoner, without liberty to tread in any path but that to which it confines him. It is not easy to find out how imagination, thus explained, differs from distinct remembrance of images; or fancy from quick and vivid recollection of them: each is nothing more than a mode of memory. If the two words bear the above meaning, and no other, what term is left to designate that Faculty of which the Poet is "all compact";[12] he whose eye glances from earth to heaven, whose spiritual attributes body-forth what his pen is prompt in turning to shape; or what is left to characterise fancy, as insinuating herself into the heart of objects with creative activity?—Imagination, in the sense of the word as giving title to a Class of the following Poems, has no reference to images that are merely a faithful copy, existing in the mind, of absent external objects; but is a word of higher import, denoting operations of the mind upon those objects, and processes of creation or of composition, governed by certain fixed laws. I proceed to illustrate my meaning by instances. A parrot *hangs* from the wires of his cage by his beak or by his claws; or a monkey from the bough of a tree by his paws or his tail. Each creature does so literally and actually. In the first Eclogue of Virgil, the Shepherd, thinking of the time when he is to take leave of his Farm, thus addresses his Goats;

> "Non ego vos posthac viridi projectus in antro
> Dumosa *pendere* procul de rupe videbo,"[13]

> —"half way up
> *Hangs* one who gathers samphire,"[14]

is the well-known expression of Shakespear, delineating an ordinary image upon the Cliffs of Dover. In these two instances is a slight exertion of the faculty which I denominate imagination, in the use of one word: neither the goats nor the samphire-gatherer do literally hang, as does the parrot or the monkey; but, presenting to the senses something of such an appearance, the mind in its activity, for its own gratification, contemplates them as hanging.

12. *Midsummer Night's Dream*, V.i.7–17.

13. "Never again, stretched out in my green hollow, will I see you way out there *hanging* from the bush-covered crag" (ll. 75–76).

14. *King Lear*, IV.vi.14: "half way down / Hangs one that gathers samphire . . ."

"As when far off at Sea a Fleet descried
Hangs in the clouds, by equinoxial winds
Close sailing from Bengala or the Isles
Of Ternate or Tydore, whence Merchants bring
Their spicy drugs; they on the trading flood
Through the wide Ethiopian to the Cape
Ply, stemming nightly toward the Pole: so seem'd
Far off the flying Fiend."[15]

Here is the full strength of the imagination involved in the word, *hangs*, and exerted upon the whole image: First, the Fleet, an aggregate of many Ships, is represented as one mighty Person, whose track, we know and feel, is upon the waters; but, taking advantage of its appearance to the senses, the Poet dares to represent it as *hanging in the clouds*, both for the gratification of the mind in contemplating the image itself, and in reference to the motion and appearance of the sublime object to which it is compared.

From images of sight we will pass to those of sound:

"Over his own sweet voice the Stock-dove *broods*";[16]

of the same bird,

"His voice was *buried* among trees,
Yet to be come at by the breeze";[17]

"O, Cuckoo! shall I call thee *Bird*,
Or but a wandering *Voice*?"[18]

The Stock-dove is said to *coo*, a sound well imitating the note of the bird; but, by the intervention of the metaphor *broods*, the affections are called in by the imagination to assist in marking the manner in which the Bird reiterates and prolongs her soft note, as if herself delighting to listen to it, and participating of a still and quiet satisfaction, like that which may be supposed inseparable from the continuous process of incubation. "His voice was buried among trees," a metaphor expressing the love of *seclusion* by which this Bird is marked; and characterising its note as not partaking

15. *Paradise Lost*, II, 636–643.
16. "Resolution and Independence," l. 5 (*Poetical Works*, II, 235).
17. "O Nightingale! thou surely art," ll. 13–14 (*Poetical Works*, II, 214).
18. "To the Cuckoo," ll. 3–4 (*Poetical Works*, II, 207).

of the shrill and the piercing, and therefore more easily deadened by the intervening shade; yet a note so peculiar, and withal so pleasing, that the breeze, gifted with that love of the sound which the Poet feels, penetrates the shade in which it is entombed, and conveys it to the ear of the listener.

> Shall I call thee Bird
> Or but a wandering Voice?

This concise interrogation characterises the seeming ubiquity of the voice of the Cuckoo, and dispossesses the creature almost of a corporeal existence; the imagination being tempted to this exertion of her power by a consciousness in the memory that the Cuckoo is almost perpetually heard throughout the season of Spring, but seldom becomes an object of sight.

Thus far of images independent of each other, and immediately endowed by the mind with properties that do not inhere in them, upon an incitement from properties and qualities the existence of which is inherent and obvious. These processes of imagination are carried on either by conferring additional properties upon an object, or abstracting from it some of those which it actually possesses, and thus enabling it to react upon the mind which hath performed the process, like a new existence.

I pass from the Imagination acting upon an individual image to a consideration of the same faculty employed upon images in a conjunction by which they modify each other. The Reader has already had a fine instance before him in the passage quoted from Virgil, where the apparently perilous situation of the Goat, hanging upon the shaggy precipice, is contrasted with that of the Shepherd, contemplating it from the seclusion of the Cavern in which he lies stretched at ease and in security. Take these images separately, and how unaffecting the picture compared with that produced by their being thus connected with, and opposed to, each other!

> "As a huge Stone is sometimes seen to lie
> Couched on the bald top of an eminence,
> Wonder to all who do the same espy
> By what means it could thither come, and whence;
> So that it seems a thing endued with sense,
> Like a Sea-beast crawled forth, which on a shelf
> Of rock or sand reposeth, there to sun himself.

Such seemed this Man; not all alive or dead,
Nor all asleep, in his extreme old age.
Motionless as a cloud the old Man stood,
That heareth not the loud winds when they call,
And moveth altogether if it move at all."[19]

In these images, the conferring, the abstracting, and the modifying powers of the Imagination, immediately and mediately acting, are all brought into conjunction. The Stone is endowed with something of the power of life to approximate it to the Sea-beast; and the Sea-beast stripped of some of its vital qualities to assimilate it to the stone; which intermediate image is thus treated for the purpose of bringing the original image, that of the stone, to a nearer resemblance to the figure and condition of the aged Man; who is divested of so much of the indications of life and motion as to bring him to the point where the two objects unite and coalesce in just comparison. After what has been said, the image of the Cloud need not be commented upon.

Thus far of an endowing or modifying power: but the Imagination also shapes and *creates*; and how? By innumerable processes; and in none does it more delight than in that of consolidating numbers into unity, and dissolving and separating unity into number,— alternations proceeding from, and governed by, a sublime consciousness of the soul in her own mighty and almost divine powers. Recur to the passage already cited from Milton. When the compact Fleet, as one Person, has been introduced "Sailing from Bengala," "They," i.e. the "Merchants," representing the Fleet resolved into a Multitude of Ships, "ply" their voyage towards the extremities of the earth: "So" (referring to the word "As" in the commencement) "seemed the flying Fiend"; the image of his Person acting to recombine the multitude of Ships into one body,—the point from which the comparison set out. "So seemed," and to whom seemed? To the heavenly Muse who dictates the poem, to the eye of the Poet's mind, and to that of the Reader, present at one moment in the wide Ethiopian, and the next in the solitudes, then first broken in upon, of the infernal regions!

19. "Resolution and Independence," ll. 57–65, 75–77 (*Poetical Works*, II, 237). The second stanza is a composite of stanzas x and xi.

Modo me Thebis, modo ponit Athenis.[20]

Hear again this mighty Poet,—speaking of the Messiah going forth
to expel from Heaven the rebellious Angels,

> Attended by ten thousand, thousand Saints
> He onward came: far off his coming shone,—[21]

the retinue of Saints, and the Person of the Messiah himself, lost
almost and merged in the splendour of that indefinite abstraction,
"His coming!"

As I do not mean here to treat this subject further than to throw
some light upon the present Volumes, and especially upon one
division of them, I shall spare myself and the Reader the trouble of
considering the Imagination as it deals with thoughts and sentiments, as it regulates the composition of characters, and determines
the course of actions: I will not consider it (more than I have already
done by implication) as that power which, in the language of one
of my most esteemed Friends, "draws all things to one, which makes
things animate or inanimate, beings with their attributes, subjects
with their accessaries, take one colour and serve to one effect."[22]
The grand store-house of enthusiastic and meditative Imagination,
of poetical, as contradistinguished from human and dramatic
Imagination, is the prophetic and lyrical parts of the holy Scriptures,
and the works of Milton, to which I cannot forbear to add those of
Spenser. I select these writers in preference to those of ancient
Greece and Rome because the anthropomorphitism of the Pagan
religion subjected the minds of the greatest poets in those countries
too much to the bondage of definite form; from which the Hebrews
were preserved by their abhorrence of idolatry.[23] This abhorrence
was almost as strong in our great epic Poet, both from circumstances
of his life, and from the constitution of his mind. However imbued

20. "He lands me now in Thebes, now in Athens," Horace, *Epistles*, II, i.213,
praising a poet who "transports" him.

21. *Paradise Lost*, VI, 767–768.

22. [Charles Lamb upon the genius of Hogarth.—W.] "On the Genius of
Hogarth," *Works*, ed. E. V. Lucas [7 vols.; London: Methuen, 1903–1905], I, 73.

23. Cf. Coleridge's letter, September 10, 1802 (*Collected Letters*, ed. E. L. Griggs):
"In the Hebrew Poets each Thing has a Life of it's own, & yet they are all one
Life. In God they move & live & *have* their Being—not *had*, as the cold System of
Newtonian Theology represents / but *have*" (II, 866).

the surface might be with classical literature, he was a Hebrew in soul; and all things tended in him towards the sublime. Spenser, of a gentler nature, maintained his freedom by aid of his allegorical spirit, at one time inciting him to create persons out of abstractions; and at another, by a superior effort of genius, to give the universality and permanence of abstractions to his human beings, by means of attributes and emblems that belong to the highest moral truths and the purest sensations,[24]—of which his character of Una is a glorious example. Of the human and dramatic Imagination the works of Shakespear are an inexhaustible source.

> "I tax not you, ye Elements, with unkindness,
> I never gave you Kingdoms, called you Daughters."[25]

And if, bearing in mind the many Poets distinguished by this prime quality, whose names I omit to mention; yet justified by a recollection of the insults which the Ignorant, the Incapable, and the Presumptuous have heaped upon these and my other writings, I may be permitted to anticipate the judgment of posterity upon myself; I shall declare (censurable, I grant, if the notoriety of the fact above stated does not justify me) that I have given, in these unfavourable times, evidence of exertions of this faculty upon its worthiest objects, the external universe, the moral and religious sentiments of Man, his natural affections, and his acquired passions; which have the same ennobling tendency as the productions of men, in this kind, worthy to be holden in undying remembrance.

I dismiss this subject with observing—that, in the series of Poems placed under the head of Imagination, I have begun with one of the earliest processes of Nature in the development of this faculty.[26] Guided by one of my own primary consciousnesses, I have represented a commutation and transfer of internal feelings, co-operating with external accidents to plant, for immortality, images of sound

24. Cf. Thomas Warton, "Observations on the Faerie Queene" (1754): Spenser's imagination "bodies forth unsubstantial things, turns them to shape, and marks out the nature, powers, and effects of that which is ideal and abstracted, by visible and external symbols, as in his delineation of Fear, Despair, Fancy, Envy, and the like" (*Eighteenth Century Critical Essays*, ed. Scott Elledge, II, 773).

25. *King Lear*, III.ii.16–17.

26. "There Was a Boy" (*Poetical Works*, II, 206).

and sight, in the celestial soil of the Imagination. The Boy, there introduced, is listening, with something of a feverish and restless anxiety, for the recurrence of the riotous sounds which he had previously excited; and, at the moment when the intenseness of his mind is beginning to remit, he is surprised into a perception of the solemn and tranquillizing images which the Poem describes.—The Poems next in succession exhibit the faculty exerting itself upon various objects of the external universe; then follow others, where it is employed upon feelings, characters, and actions; and the Class is concluded with imaginative pictures of moral, political, and religious sentiments.

To the mode in which Fancy has already been characterized as the Power of evoking and combining, or, as my friend Mr. Coleridge has styled it, "the aggregative and associative Power,"[27] my objection is only that the definition is too general. To aggregate and to associate, to evoke and to combine, belong as well to the Imagination as to the Fancy; but either the materials evoked and combined are different; or they are brought together under a different law, and for a different purpose. Fancy does not require that the materials which she makes use of should be susceptible of change in their constitution, from her touch; and, where they admit of modification, it is enough for her purpose if it be slight, limited, and evanescent. Directly the reverse of these, are the desires and demands of the Imagination. She recoils from every thing but the plastic, the pliant, and the indefinite. She leaves it to Fancy to describe Queen Mab as coming,

> "In shape no bigger than an agate stone
> On the fore-finger of an Alderman."[28]

Having to speak of stature, she does not tell you that her gigantic Angel was as tall as Pompey's pillar; much less that he was twelve cubits, or twelve hundred cubits high; or that his dimensions

27. *Omniana* (2 vols.; London, 1812), II, 13. Coleridge replied in *Biographia Literaria* (ed. J. Shawcross), I, 194: "I am disposed to conjecture, that he has mistaken the copresence of fancy with imagination for the operation of the latter singly."

28. *Romeo and Juliet*, I.iv.55–56.

equalled those of Teneriffe or Atlas;—because these, and if they were a million times as high, it would be the same, are bounded: The expression is, "His stature reached the sky!"[29] the illimitable firmament!—When the Imagination frames a comparison, if it does not strike on the first presentation, a sense of the truth of the likeness, from the moment that it is perceived, grows—and continues to grow—upon the mind; the resemblance depending less upon outline of form and feature than upon expression and effect, less upon casual and outstanding, than upon inherent and internal, properties:—moreover, the images invariably modify each other.— The law under which the processes of Fancy are carried on is as capricious as the accidents of things, and the effects are surprizing, playful, ludicrous, amusing, tender, or pathetic, as the objects happen to be appositely produced or fortunately combined. Fancy depends upon the rapidity and profusion with which she scatters her thoughts and images, trusting that their number, and the felicity with which they are linked together, will make amends for the want of individual value: or she prides herself upon the curious subtilty and the successful elaboration with which she can detect their lurking affinities. If she can win you over to her purpose, and impart to you her feelings, she cares not how unstable or transitory may be her influence, knowing that it will not be out of her power to resume it upon an apt occasion. But the Imagination is conscious of an indestructible dominion;—the Soul may fall away from it, not being able to sustain its grandeur, but, if once felt and acknowledged, by no act of any other faculty of the mind can it be relaxed, impaired, or diminished.—Fancy is given to quicken and to beguile the temporal part of our Nature, Imagination to incite and to support the eternal.—Yet is it not the less true that Fancy, as she is an active, is also, under her own laws and in her own spirit, a creative faculty. In what manner Fancy ambitiously aims at a rivalship with the Imagination, and Imagination stoops to work with the materials of Fancy, might be illustrated from the compositions of all eloquent writers, whether in prose or verse; and chiefly from those of our own Country. Scarcely a page of the impassioned parts of Bishop Taylor's Works can be opened that shall not afford

29. *Paradise Lost*, IV, 988.

examples.[30]—Referring the Reader to those inestimable Volumes, I will content myself with placing a conceit (ascribed to Lord Chesterfield) in contrast with a passage from the Paradise Lost;

> "The dews of the evening most carefully shun,
> They are the tears of the sky for the loss of the Sun."[31]

After the transgression of Adam, Milton, with other appearances of sympathizing Nature, thus marks the immediate consequence,

> "Sky lowered, and muttering thunder, some sad drops
> Wept at completion of the mortal sin."[32]

The associating link is the same in each instance;—dew or rain, not distinguishable from the liquid substance of tears, are employed as indications of sorrow. A flash of surprize is the effect in the former case, a flash of surprize and nothing more; for the nature of things does not sustain the combination. In the latter, the effects of the act, of which there is this immediate consequence and visible sign, are so momentous that the mind acknowledges the justice and reasonableness of the sympathy in Nature so manifested; and the sky weeps drops of water as if with human eyes, as "Earth had, before, trembled from her entrails, and Nature given a second groan."[33]

Awe-stricken as I am by contemplating the operations of the mind of this truly divine Poet, I scarcely dare venture to add that "An address to an Infant,"[34] which the Reader will find under the Class of Fancy in the present Volumes, exhibits something of this communion and interchange of instruments and functions between the two powers; and is, accordingly, placed last in the class, as a preparation for that of Imagination which follows.

30. Coleridge called Jeremy Taylor "this Spenser of English prose" (*Coleridge on the Seventeenth Century*, ed. R. F. Brinkley [Durham: Duke University Press, 1955], p. 259); and Francis Jeffrey asserted that in his sermons was more of "the body and the soul of poetry, than in all the odes and the epics that have since been produced in Europe" (*Edinburgh Review*, XVIII [1811], 278).

31. "Advice to a Lady," ll. 25–26 (D. Nichol Smith, *Oxford Book of Eighteenth Century Verse* [Oxford: Clarendon Press, 1926], pp. 293–294).

32. IX, 1002–1003.   33. IX, 1000–1001.

34. "Address to My Infant Daughter, Dora" (*Poetical Works*, II, 174–176).

Finally, I will refer to Cotton's "Ode upon Winter," an admirable composition though stained with some peculiarities of the age in which he lived, for a general illustration of the characteristics of Fancy. The middle part of this ode contains a most lively description of the entrance of Winter, with his retinue, as "A palsied King," and yet a military Monarch,—advancing for conquest with his Army; the several bodies of which, and their arms and equipments, are described with a rapidity of detail, and a profusion of *fanciful* comparisons, which indicate on the part of the Poet extreme activity of intellect, and a correspondent hurry of delightful feeling. He retires from the Foe into his fortress, where

> "a magazine
> Of sovereign juice is cellared in.
> Liquor that will the siege maintain
> Should Phoebus ne'er return again."[35]

Though myself a water-drinker, I cannot resist the pleasure of transcribing what follows, as an instance still more happy of Fancy employed in the treatment of feeling than, in its preceding passages, the Poem supplies of her management of forms.

> 'Tis that, that gives the Poet rage,
> And thaws the gelly'd blood of Age;
> Matures the Young, restores the Old,
> And makes the fainting Coward bold.
>
> It lays the careful head to rest,
> Calms palpitations in the breast,
> Renders our lives' misfortune sweet;
> . . . .[36]
>
> Then let the chill Scirocco blow,
> And gird us round with hills of snow,
> Or else go whistle to the shore,
> And make the hollow mountains roar.

35. Lamb sent this poem to Wordsworth, March 5, 1803 (*Works*, ed. E. V. Lucas, VI, 262–265).
36. Wordsworth omits the last line of the stanza: "And Venus frolic in the sheet."

> Whilst we together jovial sit
> Careless, and crown'd with mirth and wit;
> Where, though bleak winds confine us home,
> Our fancies round the world shall roam.
>
> We'll think of all the Friends we know,
> And drink to all worth drinking to;
> When having drunk all thine and mine,
> We rather shall want healths than wine.
>
> But where Friends fail us, we'll supply
> Our friendships with our charity;
> Men that remote in sorrows live,
> Shall by our lusty Brimmers thrive.
>
> We'll drink the Wanting into Wealth,
> And those that languish into health,
> The Afflicted into joy; th' Opprest
> Into security and rest.
>
> The Worthy in disgrace shall find
> Favour return again more kind,
> And in restraint who stifled lie,
> Shall taste the air of liberty.
>
> The Brave shall triumph in success,
> The Lovers shall have Mistresses,
> Poor unregarded Virtue, praise,
> And the neglected Poet, Bays.
>
> Thus shall our healths do others good,
> Whilst we ourselves do all we would;
> For, freed from envy and from care,
> What would we be but what we are?"

It remains that I should express my regret at the necessity of separating my compositions from some beautiful Poems of Mr. Coleridge, with which they have been long associated in publication. The feelings, with which that joint publication was made, have been gratified; its end is answered, and the time is come when considerations of general propriety dictate the separation. Three short pieces (now first published) are the work of a Female Friend;[37] and the Reader, to whom they may be acceptable, is indebted to me for his pleasure; if any one regard them with dislike, or be disposed to condemn them, let the censure fall upon him, who, trusting in his own sense of their merit and their fitness for the place which they occupy, *extorted* them from the Authoress.

When I sate down to write this preface it was my intention to have made it more comprehensive; but as all that I deem necessary is expressed, I will here detain the reader no longer:—what I have further to remark shall be inserted, by way of interlude, at the close of this Volume.

Poems (2 vols.; London, 1815), I, [vii]–xlii.

37. Dorothy Wordsworth.

Essay, Supplementary to the Preface (1815)

By this time, I trust that the judicious Reader, who has now first become acquainted with these poems, is persuaded that a very senseless outcry has been raised against them and their Author.—Casually, and very rarely only, do I see any periodical publication, except a daily newspaper; but I am not wholly unacquainted with the spirit in which my most active and perserving Adversaries have maintained their hostility; nor with the impudent falsehoods and base artifices to which they have had recourse.[1] These, as implying a consciousness on their parts that attacks honestly and fairly conducted would be unavailing, could not but have been regarded by me with triumph; had they been accompanied with such display of talents and information as might give weight to the opinions of the Writers, whether favourable or unfavourable. But the ignorance of those who have chosen to stand forth as my enemies,[2] as far as I

1. An example of "base artifice" is in *The Satirist* for December, 1809 (V, 548–556): "The Bards of the Lake" describes a recitation by Wordsworth, Coleridge, Southey, and Lamb, surrounded by their womenfolk. Wordsworth recites "The Hermit and the Snail":

> A hermit walk'd forth from his cell one day,
> And he met a snail across his way,
> And thus to the snail did the hermit say,
> > "Silly snail!
> "Is it thy love thou goest to meet,
> To woo her in her green retreat?
> No—thou hast horns upon thy head,
> Thou art already married,
> > Silly snail!"

Mr. Satirist reported that "the ladies seemed not altogether to approve the indirect satire contained in it" (pp. 549–550).

2. Wordsworth had probably heard that Jeffrey had read only the first seventeen passages of *The Excursion* before writing the review beginning "This will never do!" See Elsie Smith, *Estimate of William Wordsworth* (Oxford: Blackwell, 1932), p. 173.

am acquainted with their enmity, has unfortunately been still more gross than their disingenuousness, and their incompetence more flagrant than their malice. The effect in the eyes of the discerning is indeed ludicrous: yet, contemptible as such men are, in return for the forced compliment paid me by their long-continued notice (which, as I have appeared so rarely before the public, no one can say has been solicited) I entreat them to spare themselves. The lash, which they are aiming at my productions, does, in fact, only fall on phantoms of their own brain; which, I grant, I am innocently instrumental in raising.—By what fatality the orb of my genius (for genius none of them seem to deny me)[3] acts upon these men like the moon upon a certain description of patients, it would be irksome to inquire; nor would it consist with the respect which I owe myself to take further notice of opponents whom I internally despise.

With the young, of both sexes, Poetry is, like love, a passion; but, for much the greater part of those who have been proud of its power over their minds, a necessity soon arises of breaking the pleasing bondage; or it relaxes of itself;—the thoughts being occupied in domestic cares, or the time engrossed by business. Poetry then becomes only an occasional recreation; while to those whose existence passes away in a course of fashionable pleasure it is a species of luxurious amusement.—In middle and declining age, a scattered number of serious persons resort to poetry, as to religion, for a protection against the pressure of trivial employments, and as a consolation for the afflictions of life. And lastly, there are many, who, having been enamoured of this art, in their youth, have found leisure, after youth was spent, to cultivate general literature; in which poetry has continued to be comprehended *as a study*.

Into the above Classes the Readers of poetry may be divided; Critics abound in them all; but from the last only can opinions be collected of absolute value, and worthy to be depended upon, as prophetic of the destiny of a new work. The young, who in nothing can escape delusion, are especially subject to it in their intercourse with poetry. The cause, not so obvious as the fact is unquestionable, is the same as that from which erroneous judgments in this art, in

3. Reviewing an edition of Ford's *Dramatic Works* in August, 1811, Jeffrey acknowledged that Wordsworth had "given great proofs of original genius" (*Edinburgh Review*, XVIII, 283).

the minds of men of all ages, chiefly proceed; but upon Youth it operates with peculiar force. The appropriate business of poetry (which, nevertheless, if genuine is as permanent as pure science) her appropriate employment, her privilege and her *duty*, is to treat of things not as they *are*, but as they *appear*; not as they exist in themselves, but as they *seem* to exist to the *senses* and to the *passions*.[4] What a world of delusion does this acknowledged principle prepare for the inexperienced! what temptations to go astray are here held forth for those whose thoughts have been little disciplined by the understanding, and whose feelings revolt from the sway of reason!—When a juvenile Reader is in the height of his rapture with some vicious passage, should experience throw in doubts, or common-sense suggest suspicions, a lurking consciousness that the realities of the Muse are but shows, and that her liveliest excitements are raised by transient shocks of conflicting feeling and successive assemblages of contradictory thoughts—is ever at hand to justify extravagance, and to sanction absurdity. But, it may be asked, as these illusions are unavoidable, and no doubt eminently useful to the mind as a process, what good can be gained by making observations the tendency of which is to diminish the confidence of youth in its feelings, and thus to abridge its innocent and even profitable pleasures? The reproach implied in the question could not be warded off, if Youth were incapable of being delighted with what is truly excellent; or if these errors always terminated of themselves in due season. But, with the majority, though their force be abated, they continue through life. Moreover, the fire of youth is too vivacious an element to be extinguished or damped by a philosophical remark; and, while there is no danger that what has been said will be injurious or painful to the ardent and the confident, it may prove beneficial to those who, being enthusiastic, are, at the

4. Cf. *Biographia Literaria* (ed. J. Shawcross [2 vols.; London: Oxford University Press, 1907]): "Images, however beautiful, though faithfully copied from nature, and as accurately represented in words, do not of themselves characterize the poet. They become proofs of original genius only as far as they are modified by a predominant passion, or by associated thoughts or images awakened by that passion; or when they have the effect of reducing multitude to unity, or succession to an instant; or lastly, when a human and intellectual life is transferred to them from the poet's own spirit . . ." (II, 16).

same time, modest and ingenuous. The intimation may unite with their own misgivings to regulate their sensibility, and to bring in, sooner than it would otherwise have arrived, a more discreet and sound judgment.

If it should excite wonder that men of ability, in later life, whose understandings have been rendered acute by practice in affairs, should be so easily and so far imposed upon when they happen to take up a new work in verse, this appears to be the cause;—that, having discontinued their attention to poetry, whatever progress may have been made in other departments of knowledge, they have not, as to this art, advanced in true discernment beyond the age of youth. If then a new poem falls in their way, whose attractions are of that kind which would have enraptured them during the heat of youth, the judgment not being improved to a degree that they shall be disgusted, they are dazzled; and prize and cherish the faults for having had power to make the present time vanish before them, and to throw the mind back, as by enchantment, into the happiest season of life. As they read, powers seem to be revived, passions are regenerated, and pleasures restored. The Book was probably taken up after an escape from the burthen of business, and with a wish to forget the world, and all its vexations and anxieties. Having obtained this wish, and so much more, it is natural that they should make report as they have felt.

If Men of mature age, through want of practice, be thus easily beguiled into admiration of absurdities, extravagances, and mis-placed ornaments, thinking it proper that their understandings should enjoy a holiday, while they are unbending their minds with verse, it may be expected that such Readers will resemble their former selves also in strength of prejudice, and an inaptitude to be moved by the unostentatious beauties of a pure style. In the higher poetry, an enlightened Critic chiefly looks for a reflexion of the wisdom of the heart and the grandeur of the imagination. Wherever these appear, simplicity accompanies them; Magnificence herself, when legitimate, depending upon a simplicity of her own, to regulate her ornaments. But it is a well known property of human nature that our estimates are ever governed by comparisons, of which we are conscious with various degrees of distinctness. Is it not, then, inevitable (confining these observations to the effects of style merely) that an eye, accustomed to the glaring hues of diction by which such Readers are caught and excited, will for the most part be rather repelled than attracted by an original Work the coloring of which is disposed according to a pure and refined scheme of harmony? It is in the fine arts as in the affairs of life, no man can *serve* (i.e. obey with zeal and fidelity) two Masters.

As Poetry is most just to its own divine origin when it administers the comforts and breathes the spirit of religion,[5] they who have learned to perceive this truth, and who betake themselves to reading verse for sacred purposes, must be preserved from numerous illusions to which the two Classes of Readers, whom we have been considering, are liable. But, as the mind grows serious from the weight of life, the range of its passions is contracted accordingly; and its sympathies become so exclusive that many species of high excellence wholly escape, or but languidly excite, its notice. Besides, Men who read from religious or moral inclinations, even when the subject is of that kind which they approve, are beset with misconceptions and mistakes peculiar to themselves. Attaching so much importance to the truths which interest them, they are prone to overrate the Authors by whom these truths are expressed and enforced. They come prepared to impart so much passion to the Poet's language, that they remain unconscious how little, in fact, they receive from it. And, on the other hand, religious faith is to him who holds it so momentous a thing, and error appears to be attended with such tremendous consequences, that, if opinions touching upon religion occur which the Reader condemns, he not only cannot sympathize with them however animated the expression, but there is, for the most part, an end put to all satisfaction and enjoyment. Love, if it before existed, is converted into dislike; and the heart of the Reader is set against the Author and his book.—To these excesses, they, who from their professions ought to be the most guarded against them, are perhaps the most liable; I mean those

5. Cf. John Dennis, "Grounds of Criticism in Poetry" (1704) (*Works*, ed. E. N. Hooker [2 vols.; Baltimore: Johns Hopkins Press, 1939–1943]): "Poetry is the natural language of Religion, and . . . Religion at first produced it, as a cause produces its Effect" (I, 364).

sects whose religion, being from the calculating understanding, is cold and formal.[6] For when Christianity, the religion of humility, is founded upon the proudest quality of our nature, what can be expected but contradictions? Accordingly, believers of this cast are at one time contemptuous; at another, being troubled as they are and must be with inward misgivings, they are jealous and suspicious; —and at all seasons, they are under temptation to supply, by the heat with which they defend their tenets, the animation which is wanting to the constitution of the religion itself.

Faith was given to man that his affections, detached from the treasures of time, might be inclined to settle upon those of eternity:— the elevation of his nature, which this habit produces on earth, being to him a presumptive evidence of a future state of existence; and giving him a title to partake of its holiness. The religious man values what he sees chiefly as an "imperfect shadowing forth"[7] of what he is incapable of seeing. The concerns of religion refer to indefinite objects, and are too weighty for the mind to support them without relieving itself by resting a great part of the burthen upon words and symbols. The commerce between Man and his Maker cannot be carried on but by a process where much is represented in little, and the infinite Being accommodates himself to a finite capacity.[8] In all this may be perceived the affinities between religion and poetry;—between religion—making up the deficiencies of reason by faith, and poetry—passionate for the instruction of reason; between religion—whose element is infinitude, and whose ultimate trust is the supreme of things, submitting herself to circumscription and reconciled to substitutions; and poetry— etherial and transcendant, yet incapable to sustain her existence without sensuous incarnation. In this community of nature may be perceived also the lurking incitements of kindred error;—so that

6. Cf. Wordsworth's comment on Patty Smith's criticism of *The Excursion*, above, p. 134.

7. Cf. Alexander Knox, *Remains*, ed. J. J. Hornby (4 vols.; London, 1834–1837), I, 15, speaking of every species of the sublime as being "a shadowing of Deity."

8. Cf. *Biographia Literaria* (ed. J. Shawcross) describing Coleridge's moving away from Unitarianism: "The *idea* of the Supreme Being appeared to me to be as necessarily implied in all particular modes of being as the idea of infinite space in all the geometrical figures by which space is limited" (I, 133).

we shall find that no poetry has been more subject to distortion, than that species the argument and scope of which is religious; and no lovers of the art have gone further astray than the pious and the devout.

Whither then shall we turn for that union of qualifications which must necessarily exist before the decisions of a critic can be of absolute value? For a mind at once poetical and philosophical; for a critic whose affections are as free and kindly as the spirit of society, and whose understanding is severe as that of dispassionate government? Where are we to look for that initiatory composure of mind which no selfishness can disturb? For a natural sensibility that has been tutored into correctness without losing any thing of its quickness; and for active faculties capable of answering the demands which an Author of original imagination shall make upon them,— associated with a judgment that cannot be duped into admiration by aught that is unworthy of it?—Among those and those only, who, never having suffered their youthful love of poetry to remit much of its force, have applied, to the consideration of the laws of this art, the best power of their understandings. At the same time it must be observed—that, as this Class comprehends the only judgments which are trust-worthy, so does it include the most erroneous and perverse. For to be mis-taught is worse than to be untaught; and no perverseness equals that which is supported by system, no errors are so difficult to root out as those which the understanding has pledged its credit to uphold. In this Class are contained Censors, who, if they be pleased with what is good, are pleased with it only by imperfect glimpses, and upon false principles; who, should they generalize rightly to a certain point, are sure to suffer for it in the end;—who, if they stumble upon a sound rule, are fettered by misapplying it, or by straining it too far; being incapable of perceiving when it ought to yield to one of higher order. In it are found Critics too petulant to be passive to a genuine Poet, and too feeble to grapple with him; Men, who take upon them to report of the course which *he* holds whom they are utterly unable to accompany,—confounded if he turn quick upon the wing, dismayed if he soar steadily into "the region";[9]—Men of palsied

9. *Paradise Lost*, III, 349.

imaginations and indurated hearts; in whose minds all healthy action is languid,—who, therefore, feed as the many direct them, or with the many, are greedy after vicious provocatives;—Judges, whose censure is auspicious, and whose praise ominous! In this Class meet together the two extremes of best and worst.

The observations presented in the foregoing series, are of too ungracious a nature to have been made without reluctance; and were it only on this account I would invite the Reader to try them by the test of comprehensive experience. If the number of judges who can be confidently relied upon be in reality so small, it ought to follow that partial notice only, or neglect, perhaps long continued, or attention wholly inadequate to their merits—must have been the fate of most works in the higher departments of poetry; and that, on the other hand, numerous productions have blazed into popularity, and have passed away, leaving scarcely a trace behind them:—it will be, further, found that when Authors have at length raised themselves into general admiration and maintained their ground, errors and prejudices have prevailed concerning their genius and their works, which the few who are conscious of those errors and prejudices would deplore; if they were not recompensed by perceiving that there are select Spirits for whom it is ordained that their fame shall be in the world an existence like that of Virtue, which owes its being to the struggles it makes, and its vigour to the enemies whom it provokes;—a vivacious quality ever doomed to meet with opposition, and still triumphing over it; and, from the nature of its dominion, incapable of being brought to the sad conclusion of Alexander, when he wept that there were no more worlds for him to conquer.

Let us take a hasty retrospect of the poetical literature of this Country for the greater part of the last two Centuries, and see if the facts correspond with these inferences.

Who is there that can now endure to read the "Creation" of Dubartas? Yet all Europe once resounded with his praise; he was caressed by Kings; and, when his Poem was translated into our language, the Faery Queen faded before it. The name of Spenser, whose genius is of a higher order than even that of Ariosto, is at this day scarcely known beyond the limits of the British Isles. And, if the value of his works is to be estimated from the attention now paid to them by his Countrymen, compared with that which they bestow on those of other writers, it must be pronounced small indeed.

> "The laurel, meed of mighty Conquerors
> And Poets *sage*"—10

are his own words; but his wisdom has, in this particular, been his worst enemy; while, its opposite, whether in the shape of folly or madness, has been their best friend. But he was a great power; and bears a high name: the laurel has been awarded to him.

A Dramatic Author, if he write for the Stage, must adapt himself to the taste of the Audience, or they will not endure him; accordingly the mighty genius of Shakespeare was listened to. The People were delighted; but I am not sufficiently versed in Stage antiquities to determine whether they did not flock as eagerly to the representation of many pieces of contemporary Authors, wholly undeserving to appear upon the same boards. Had there been a formal contest for superiority among dramatic Writers, that Shakespeare, like his predecessors Sophocles and Euripides, would have often been subject to the mortification of seeing the prize adjudged to sorry competitors, becomes too probable when we reflect that the Admirers of Settle and Shadwell were, in a later age, as numerous, and reckoned as respectable in point of talent as those of Dryden. At all events, that Shakespeare stooped to accommodate himself to the People, is sufficiently apparent; and one of the most striking proofs of his almost omnipotent genius, is, that he could turn to such glorious purpose those materials which the prepossessions of the age compelled him to make use of. Yet even this marvellous skill appears not to have been enough to prevent his rivals from having some advantage over him in public estimation; else how can we account for passages and scenes that exist in his works, unless upon a supposition that some of the grossest of them, a fact which in my own mind I have no doubt of, were foisted in by the Players, for the gratification of the many?

But that his Works, whatever might be their reception upon the

10. *Faerie Queene*, I, i.9.

stage, made little impression upon the ruling Intellects of the time, may be inferred from the fact that Lord Bacon, in his multifarious writings, no where either quotes or alludes to him.—[11] His dramatic excellence enabled him to resume possession of the stage after the Restoration; but Dryden tells us that in his time two of Beaumont's and Fletcher's Plays was acted for one of Shakespeare's.[12] And so faint and limited was the perception of the poetic beauties of his dramas in the time of Pope, that, in his Edition of the Plays, with a view of rendering to the general Reader a necessary service, he printed between inverted commas those passages which he thought most worthy of notice.

At this day, the French Critics have abated nothing of their aversion to this darling of our Nation: "the English with their Buffon de Shakespeare" is as familiar an expression among them as in the time of Voltaire.[13] Baron Grimm is the only French writer who seems to have perceived his infinite superiority to the first names of the French Theatre; an advantage which the Parisian Critic owed to his German blood and German education.[14] The most enlightened Italians, though well acquainted with our language, are wholly incompetent to measure the proportions of Shakespeare. The Germans only, of foreign nations, are approaching towards a knowledge and feeling of what he is. In some respects they have acquired a superiority over the fellow-countrymen of the Poet; for among us it is a current, I might say, an established opinion that Shakespeare is justly praised when he is pronounced to be "a wild irregular genius, in whom great faults are compensated by great

11. [The learned Hakewill (a 3d edition of whose book bears date 1635) writing to refute the error "touching Nature's perpetual and universal decay," cites triumphantly the names of Ariosto, Tasso, Bartas, and Spenser, as instances that poetic genius had not degenerated; but he makes no mention of Shakespeare.—W.] George Hakewill, *An Apologie or Declaration of the Power and Providence of God* (2 pts., 3rd ed.; Oxford, 1635), I, 290.

12. "Essay of Dramatic Poesy," *Essays of John Dryden*, ed. W. P. Ker (2 vols.; Oxford: Clarendon Press, 1926), I, 81.

13. Voltaire's letter to Walpole about the grand buffoon Shakespeare was published in the *Analytical Review* in 1789 (V, 567), eliciting a flurry of replies in Shakespeare's defense.

14. Baron Melchior von Grimm's *Correspondance Literaire* (1753–1790) appeared in 17 volumes, 1812–1814.

beauties."[15] How long may it be before this misconception passes away, and it becomes universally acknowledged that the judgment of Shakespeare in the selection of his materials, and in the manner in which he has made them, heterogeneous as they often are, constitute a unity of their own, and contribute all to one great end, is not less admirable than his imagination, his invention, and his intuitive knowledge of human Nature!

There is extant a small Volume of miscellaneous Poems in which Shakespeare expresses his own feelings in his own Person. It is not difficult to conceive that the Editor, George Stevens, should have been insensible to the beauties of one portion of that Volume, the Sonnets;[16] though there is not a part of the writings of this Poet where is found in an equal compass a greater number of exquisite feelings felicitously expressed. But, from regard to the Critic's own credit, he would not have ventured to talk of an[17] act of parliament not being strong enough to compel the perusal of these, or any production of Shakespeare, if he had not known that the people of England were ignorant of the treasures contained in those little pieces; and if he had not, moreover, shared the too common propensity of human nature to exult over a supposed fall into the mire of a genius whom he had been compelled to regard with admiration, as an inmate of the celestial regions,—"there sitting where he durst not soar."[18]

Nine years before the death of Shakespeare, Milton was born; and

15. Cf. *Coleridge's Shakespearean Criticism*, ed. T. M. Raysor (2 vols.; London: Constable and Company, 1930), I, 222: "Are the plays of Shakespeare works of rude uncultivated genius, in which the splendor of the parts compensates, if aught can compensate, for the barbarous shapelessness and irregularity of the whole? To which not only the French critics, but even his own English admirers, say [yes]."

16. George Steevens published Shakespeare's sonnets in 1766. The statement is in *English Poets*, ed. Alexander Chalmers (21 vols.; London, 1810), V, 15.

17. [This flippant insensibility was publickly reprehended by Mr. Coleridge in a course of Lectures upon Poetry given by him at the Royal Institution. For the various merits of thought and language in Shakespeare's Sonnets see Numbers 27, 29, 30, 32, 33, 54, 64, 66, 68, 73, 76, 86, 91, 92, 93, 97, 98, 105, 107, 108, 109, 111, 113, 114, 116, 117, 129, and many others.—W.] On this lecture, see *Collected Letters*, ed. E. L. Griggs (6 vols.; Oxford: Clarendon Press, 1956–1964), III, 362 n.

18. *English Poets*, ed. Alexander Chalmers, V, 15.

early in life he published several small poems, which, though on their first appearance they were praised by a few of the judicious, were afterwards neglected to that degree that Pope, in his youth, could pilfer from them without danger of detection.—Whether these poems are at this day justly appreciated I will not undertake to decide: nor would it imply a severe reflection upon the mass of Readers to suppose the contrary; seeing that a Man of the acknowledged genius of Voss, the German Poet, could suffer their spirit to evaporate; and could change their character, as is done in the translation made by him of the most popular of those pieces.[19] At all events it is certain that these Poems of Milton are now much read, and loudly praised; yet were they little heard of till more than 150 years after their publication; and of the Sonnets, Dr. Johnson, as appears from Boswell's Life of him, was in the habit of thinking and speaking as contemptuously as Stevens wrote upon those of Shakespeare.[20]

About the time when the Pindaric Odes of Cowley and his imitators, and the productions of that class of curious thinkers whom Dr. Johnson has strangely styled Metaphysical Poets, were beginning to lose something of that extravagant admiration which they had excited, the Paradise Lost made its appearance. "Fit audience find though few,"[21] was the petition addressed by the Poet to his inspiring Muse. I have said elsewhere that he gained more than he asked;[22] this I believe to be true; but Dr. Johnson has fallen into a gross mistake when he attempts to prove, by the sale of the work, that Milton's Countrymen were *"just* to it" upon its first appearance.[23] Thirteen hundred Copies were sold in two years; an uncommon example, he asserts, of the prevalence of genius in opposition to so much recent enmity as Milton's public conduct had excited. But be it remembered that, if Milton's political and religious opinions, and the manner in which he announced them,

19. J. H. Voss translated "L'Allegro" (1789) and "Il Penseroso" (1792).

20. Boswell, *Life,* ed. G. B. Hill and L. F. Powell (6 vols.; Oxford: Clarendon Press, 1934–1950), IV, 305.

21. *Paradise Lost,* VII, 31.

22. Preface to *The Excursion,* above, p. 129.

23. "Life of Milton," *Lives,* ed. G. B. Hill (3 vols.; Oxford: Clarendon Press, 1905), I, 143.

had raised him many enemies, they had procured him numerous friends; who, as all personal danger was passed away at the time of publication, would be eager to procure the master-work of a Man whom they revered, and whom they would be proud of praising. The demand did not immediately increase; "for," says Dr. Johnson, "many more Readers" (he means Persons in the habit of reading poetry) "than were supplied at first the Nation did not afford."[24] How careless must a writer be who can make this assertion in the face of so many existing title pages to belie it! Turning to my own shelves, I find the folio of Cowley, 7th Edition, 1681. A book near it is Flatman's Poems, 4th Edition, 1686; Waller, 5th Edition, same date. The Poems of Norris of Bemerton not long after went, I believe, through nine Editions. What further demand there might be for these works I do not know, but I well remember, that 25 Years ago, the Bookseller's stalls in London swarmed with the folios of Cowley. This is not mentioned in disparagement of that able writer and amiable Man; but merely to shew—that, if Milton's work was not more read, it was not because readers did not exist at the time. Only 3000 copies of the Paradise Lost sold in 11 Years; and the Nation, says Dr. Johnson, had been satisfied from 1623 to 1644, that is 41 Years, with only two Editions of the Works of Shakespeare; which probably did not together make 1000 Copies; facts adduced by the critic to prove the "paucity of Readers."— There were Readers in multitudes; but their money went for other purposes, as their admiration was fixed elsewhere. We are authorized, then, to affirm that the reception of the Paradise Lost, and the slow progress of its fame, are proofs as striking as can be desired that the positions which I am attempting to establish are not erroneous.—[25] How amusing to shape to one's self such a critique as a Wit of Charles's days, or a Lord of the Miscellanies, or trading Journalist, of King William's time, would have brought forth, if he had set his

24. *Ibid.*, I, 144.

25. [Hughes is express upon this subject; in his dedication of Spenser's Works to Lord Somers he writes thus. "It was your Lordship's encouraging a beautiful Edition of Paradise Lost that first brought that incomparable Poem to be generally known and esteemed."—W.] John Hughes (ed.), *Works of Mr Edmund Spenser* (6 vols.; London, 1715), I, v.

faculties industriously to work upon this Poem, every where impregnated with *original* excellence!

So strange indeed are the obliquities of admiration, that they whose opinions are much influenced by authority will often be tempted to think that there are no fixed principles in human nature for this art to rest upon.[26] I have been honoured by being permitted to peruse in MS. a tract composed between the period of the Revolution and the close of that Century.[27] It is the Work of an English Peer of high accomplishments, its object to form the character and direct the studies of his Son. Perhaps no where does a more beautiful treatise of the kind exist. The good sense and wisdom of the thoughts, the delicacy of the feelings, and the charm of the style, are, throughout, equally conspicuous. Yet the Author, selecting among the Poets of his own Country those whom he deems most worthy of his son's perusal, particularizes only Lord Rochester, Sir John Denham, and Cowley. Writing about the same time, Shaftesbury, an Author at present unjustly depreciated, describes the English Muses as only yet lisping in their Cradles.[28]

The arts by which Pope, soon afterwards, contrived to procure to himself a more general and a higher reputation than perhaps any English Poet ever attained during his life-time, are known to the judicious. And as well known is it to them, that the undue exertion of these arts, is the cause why Pope has for some time held a rank in literature, to which, if he had not been seduced by an over-love of immediate popularity, and had confided more in his native genius, he never could have descended. He bewitched the nation by his melody, and dazzled it by his polished style, and was himself blinded by his own success. Having wandered from humanity in

26. [This opinion seems actually to have been entertained by Adam Smith, the worst critic, David Hume not excepted, that Scotland, a soil to which this sort of weed seems natural, has produced.—W.] Smith was reported to have depreciated Percy's *Reliques* and some of Milton's minor poems. See F. W. Hirst *Adam Smith* (London: Macmillan, 1904), pp. 20–21; and above, p. 71.

27. It may be that Wordsworth refers to a lost manuscript of Sir William Temple's *Memoirs*, Part I of which was never published. See H. E. Woodbridge, *Sir William Temple* (New York: Modern Language Association, 1940), p. 113.

28. Shaftesbury, "Advice to an Author" (II, i), *Characteristicks* (6th ed.; London, 1737), I, 217.

his Eclogues with boyish inexperience, the praise, which these compositions obtained, tempted him into a belief that nature was not to be trusted, at least in pastoral Poetry. To prove this by example, he put his friend Gay upon writing those Eclogues which the Author intended to be burlesque. The Instigator of the work, and his Admirers, could perceive in them nothing but what was ridiculous. Nevertheless, though these Poems contain some odious and even detestable passages, the effect, as Dr. Johnson well observes, "of reality and truth became conspicuous even when the intention was to shew them grovelling and degrading."[29] These Pastorals, ludicrous to those who prided themselves upon their refinement, in spite of those disgusting passages "became popular, and were read with delight as just representations of rural manners and occupations."[30]

Something less than 60 years after the publication of the Paradise Lost appeared Thomson's Winter; which was speedily followed by his other Seasons. It is a work of inspiration; much of it is written from himself, and nobly from himself. How was it received? "It was no sooner read," says one of his contemporary Biographers,[31] "than universally admired: those only excepted who had not been used to feel, or to look for any thing in poetry, beyond a *point* of satirical or epigrammatic wit, a smart *antithesis* richly trimmed with rhyme, or the softness of an *elegiac* complaint. To such his manly classical spirit could not readily commend itself; till, after a more attentive perusal, they had got the better of their prejudices, and either acquired or affected a truer taste. A few others stood aloof, merely because they had long before fixed the articles of their poetical creed, and resigned themselves to an absolute despair of ever seeing any thing new and original. These were somewhat mortified to find their notions disturbed by the appearance of a poet, who seemed to owe nothing but to nature and his own genius. But, in a short time, the applause became unanimous; every one wondering how so many pictures, and pictures so familiar, should

29. "Life of Gay," *Lives*, ed. G. B. Hill, II, 269.

30. *Ibid.*

31. Patrick Murdoch (ed.), *Works of James Thomson* (3 vols.; London, 1788), I, xv–xvi.

have moved them but faintly to what they felt in his descriptions. His digressions too, the overflowings of a tender benevolent heart, charmed the reader no less; leaving him in doubt, whether he should more admire the Poet or love the Man."

This case appears to bear strongly against us:—but we must distinguish between wonder and legitimate admiration. The subject of the work is the changes produced in the appearances of nature by the revolution of the year: and, by undertaking to write in verse, Thomson pledged himself to treat his subject as became a Poet. Now it is remarkable that, excepting a passage or two in the Windsor Forest of Pope, and some delightful pictures in the Poems of Lady Winchelsea, the Poetry of the period intervening between the publication of the Paradise Lost and the Seasons does not contain a single new image of external nature; and scarcely presents a familiar one from which it can be inferred that the eye of the Poet had been steadily fixed upon his object, much less that his feelings had urged him to work upon it in the spirit of genuine imagination. To what a low state knowledge of the most obvious and important phenomena had sunk, is evident from the style in which Dryden has executed a description of Night in one of his Tragedies, and Pope his translation of the celebrated moon-light scene in the Iliad.[32] A blind man, in the habit of attending accurately to descriptions casually dropped from the lips of those around him, might easily depict these appearances with more truth. Dryden's lines are vague, bombastic, and sense-less,[33] those of Pope, though he had Homer to guide him, are

32.   As when the moon, refulgent lamp of night,
         O'er Heaven's clear azure spreads her sacred light,
         When not a breath disturbs the deep serene
         And not a cloud o'ercasts the solemn scene;
         Around her throne the vivid planets roll,
         And stars unnumber'd gild the glowing pole,
         O'er the dark trees a yellower verdur shed,
         And tip with silver ev'ry mountain's head;
         Then shine the vales, the rocks in prospect rise,
         A flood of glory bursts from all the skies.

                                                      (VIII, 687–695)

33.   [CORTES alone, in a night-gown.
         All things are hush'd as Nature's self lay dead:
         The mountains seem to nod their drowsy head:

throughout false and contradictory. The verses of Dryden, once highly celebrated, are forgotten; those of Pope still retain their hold upon public estimation,—nay, there is not a passage of descriptive poetry, which at this day finds so many and such ardent admirers. Strange to think of an Enthusiast, as may have been the case with thousands, reciting those verses under the cope of a moon-light sky, without having his raptures in the least disturbed by a suspicion of their absurdity.—If these two distinguished Writers could habitually think that the visible universe was of so little consequence to a Poet, that it was scarcely necessary for him to cast his eyes upon it, we may be assured that those passages of the elder Poets which faithfully and poetically describe the phenomena of nature, were not at that time holden in much estimation, and that there was little accurate attention paid to these appearances.

Wonder is the natural product of Ignorance; and as the soil was *in such good condition* at the time of the publication of the Seasons, the crop was doubtless abundant. Neither individuals nor nations become corrupt all at once, nor are they enlightened in a moment. Thomson was an inspired Poet, but he could not work miracles; in cases where the art of seeing had in some degree been learned, the teacher would further the proficiency of his pupils, but he could do little *more*, though so far does vanity assist men in acts of self-deception that many would often fancy they recognized a likeness when they knew nothing of the original. Having shewn that much of what his Biographer deemed genuine admiration must in fact have been blind wonderment,—how is the rest to be accounted for? —Thomson was fortunate in the very title of his Poem, which seemed to bring it home to the prepared sympathies of every one: in the next place, notwithstanding his high powers, he writes a vicious style; and his false ornaments are exactly of that kind which would be most likely to strike the undiscerning. He likewise

---

The little Birds in dreams their songs repeat,
And sleeping Flowers beneath the Night-dew sweat:
Even Lust and Envy sleep; yet Love denies
Rest to my soul, and slumber to my eyes.
Dryden's Indian Emperor—W.]
III.ii.1–6. Pope parodied the opening line in the *Dunciad*, II, 418.

abounds with sentimental common-places, that from the manner in which they were brought forward bore an imposing air of novelty. In any well-used Copy of the Seasons the Book generally opens of itself with the rhapsody on love,[34] or with one of the stories, (perhaps Damon and Musidora); these also are prominent in our Collections of Extracts; and are the parts of his Works which, after all, were probably most efficient in first recommending the Author to general notice. Pope, repaying praises which he had received, and wishing to extol him to the highest, only styles him "an elegant and philosophical Poet";[35] nor are we able to collect any unquestionable proofs that the true characteristics of Thomson's genius as an imaginative Poet were perceived, till the elder Warton, almost 40 Years after the publication of the Seasons, pointed them out by a note in his Essay on the life and writings of Pope.[36] In the Castle of Indolence (of which Gray speaks so coldly)[37] these characteristics were almost as conspicuously displayed, and in verse more harmonious and diction more pure. Yet that fine Poem was neglected on its appearance, and is at this day the delight only of a Few!

When Thomson died, Collins breathed his regrets into an Elegiac Poem, in which he pronounces a poetical curse upon *him* who should regard with insensibility the place where the Poet's remains were deposited.[38] The Poems of the mourner himself have now passed through innumerable Editions, and are universally known; but if, when Collins died, the same kind of imprecation had been pronounced by a surviving admirer, small is the number whom it would not have comprehended. The notice which his poems attained during his life-time was so small, and of course the sale so insignificant, that not long before his death he deemed it

34. "Spring," ll. 556–581, beginning "Hail, Source of Being, Universal Soul!"

35. The Preface to the *Dunciad* ("Testimonies of Authors") speaks of "his elegant and philosophical Poem of the Seasons" (*Works*, ed. W. L. Bowles [10 vols.; London, 1806], V, 39).

36. Joseph Warton, *An Essay on the Genius and Writings of Pope* (London, 1756), pp. 41–51.

37. *Correspondence*, ed. P. Toynbee and L. Whibley (3 vols.; Oxford: Clarendon Press, 1935), I, 307.

38. "Ode on the Death of Thomson," stanza 7 (*Poems*, ed. A. L. Poole [Oxford: Oxford University Press, 1937], p. 292).

right to repay to the Bookseller the sum which he had advanced for them, and threw the Edition into the fire.[39]

Next in importance to the Seasons of Thomson, though at considerable distance from that work in order of time, come the Reliques of Ancient English Poetry; collected, new-modelled, and in many instances (if such a contradiction in terms may be used) composed, by the editor, Dr. Percy. This Work did not steal silently into the world, as is evident from the number of legendary tales, which appeared not long after its publication; and which were modelled, as the Authors persuaded themselves, after the old Ballad. The Compilation was however ill-suited to the then existing taste of City society; and Dr. Johnson, mid the little senate to which he gave laws, was not sparing in his exertions to make it an object of contempt.[40] The Critic triumphed, the legendary imitators were deservedly disregarded, and, as undeservedly, their ill-imitated models sank, in this Country, into temporary neglect; while Burger, and other able Writers of Germany, were translating, or imitating, these Reliques, and composing, with the aid of inspiration thence derived, Poems, which are the delight of the German nation. Dr. Percy was so abashed by the ridicule flung upon his labours from the ignorance and insensibility of the Persons with whom he lived, that, though while he was writing under a mask he had not wanted resolution to follow his genius into the regions of true simplicity and genuine pathos, (as is evinced by the exquisite ballad of Sir Cauline and by many other pieces) yet, when he appeared in his own person and character as a poetical writer, he adopted, as in the tale of the Hermit of Warkworth, a diction scarcely in any one of its features distinguishable from the vague, the glossy, and unfeeling language of his day.[41] I mention this remarkable fact with regret,

39. Joseph Langhorne (ed.), *Poetical Works of Collins* (London, 1765), p. 31.

40. Dr. Johnson was reported to have mocked the ballads until Bishop Percy "cried for quarter" (*Johnsonian Miscellanies*, ed. G. B. Hill [2 vols.; Oxford, 1897], II, 314–315).

41. Perhaps, e.g., Part II, stanza 71:

> No more the slave of human pride,
> Vain hope, and sordid care;
> I meekly vowed to spend my life
> In penitence and prayer.

esteeming the genius of Dr. Percy in this kind of writing superior to that of any other man by whom, in modern times, it has been cultivated. That even Burger, (to whom Klopstock gave, in my hearing, a commendation which he denied to Goethe and Schiller, pronouncing him to be a genuine Poet, and one of the few among the Germans whose works would last) had not the fine sensibility of Percy, might be shewn from many passages, in which he has deserted his original only to go astray. For example,

> Now daye was gone, and night was come,
> And all were fast asleepe,
> All, save the Ladye Emmeline,
> Who sate in her bowre to weepe:
>
> And soone shee heard her true Love's voice
> Low whispering at the walle,
> Awake, awake, my deare Ladye,
> 'Tis I thy true-love call.[42]

Which is thus tricked out and dilated,

> Als nun die Nacht Gebirg' und Thal
> Vermummt in Rabenschatten,
> Und Hochburgs Lampen über-all
> Schon ausgeflimmert hatten,
> Und alles tief entschlafen war;
> Doch nur das Fraulein immerdar,
> Voll Fieberangst, noch wachte,
> Und seinen Ritter dachte:
> Da horch! Ein süsser Liebeston
> Kam leis empor geflogen.
> "Ho, Trudchen, ho! Da bin ich schon!
> Frisch auf! Dich angezogen!"[43]

42. "Childe of Elle," ll. 53–60, *Reliques*, ed. J. V. Prichard (2 vols.; London, 1892), I, 77.

43. From "Die Entfuehrung," the extract may be translated (without rhymes):

> And now the night vale and mountain
> Endrapes in raven shadows;
> The lights of Hochburg everywhere
> Had already flickered out
> And everyone was deep asleep

But from humble ballads we must ascend to heroics.

All hail Macpherson! hail to thee, Sire of Ossian! The Phantom was begotten by the snug embrace of an impudent Highlander upon a cloud of tradition—it travelled southward, where it was greeted with acclamation, and the thin Consistence took its course through Europe, upon the breath of popular applause. The Editor of the "Reliques" had indirectly preferred a claim to the praise of invention by not concealing that his supplementary labours were considerable: how selfish his conduct contrasted with that of the disinterested Gael, who, like Lear, gives his kingdom away, and is content to become a pensioner upon his own issue for a beggarly pittance!—Open this far-famed Book!—I have done so at random, and the beginning of the "Epic Poem Temora," in 8 Books, presents itself. "The blue waves of Ullin roll in light. The green hills are covered with day. Trees shake their dusky heads in the breeze. Grey torrents pour their noisy streams. Two green hills with aged oaks surround a narrow plain. The blue course of a stream is there. On its banks stood Cairbar of Atha. His spear supports the king; the red eyes of his fear are sad. Cormac rises on his soul with all his ghastly wounds."[44] Precious memorandums from the pocket-book of the blind Ossian!

If it be unbecoming, as I acknowledge that for the most part it is, to speak disrespectfully of Works that have enjoyed for a length of time a widely spread reputation, without at the same time producing irrefragable proofs of their unworthiness, let me be forgiven upon this occasion.—Having had the good fortune to be born and reared in a mountainous Country, from my very childhood I have felt the falsehood that pervades the volumes imposed upon the World under the name of Ossian. From what I saw with my own eyes, I knew that the imagery was spurious. In nature every thing is

---

> Save the young miss who, ever
> Feverishly anxious, still watched
> And thought of her cavalier—
> Then hark! sweet was the sound of love
> That wafted softly upwards:
> "Hey, Lizzie, hey! Here I am now!
> Up, up! Get your clothes on!"

44. *Temora* (London, 1763), pp. 3–4.

distinct, yet nothing defined into absolute independent singleness. In Macpherson's work it is exactly the reverse; every thing (that is not stolen) is in this manner defined, insulated, dislocated, deadened, —yet nothing distinct. It will always be so when words are substituted for things. To say that the characters never could exist, that the manners are impossible, and that a dream has more substance than the whole state of society, as there depicted, is doing nothing more than pronouncing a censure which Macpherson defied; when, with the steeps of Morven before his eyes, he could talk so familiarly of his Car-borne heroes;—Of Morven, which, if one may judge from its appearance at the distance of a few miles, contains scarcely an acre of ground sufficiently accommodating for a sledge to be trailed along its surface.—Mr. Malcolm Laing has ably shewn that the diction of this pretended translation is a motley assembly from all quarters; but he is so fond of making out parallel passages as to call poor Macpherson to account for his very "*ands*" and his "*buts!*" and he has weakened his argument by conducting it as if he thought that every striking resemblance was a *conscious* plagiarism.[45] It is enough that the coincidences are too remarkable for its being probable or possible that they could arise in different minds without communication between them. Now as the Translators of the Bible, Shakespeare, Milton, and Pope, could not be indebted to Macpherson, it follows that he must have owed his fine feathers to them; unless we are prepared gravely to assert, with Madame de Stael, that many of the characteristic beauties of our most celebrated English Poets, are derived from the ancient Fingallian;[46] in which case the modern translator would have been but giving back to Ossian his own.—It is consistent that Lucien Buonaparte, who could censure Milton for having surrounded Satan in the infernal regions with courtly and regal splendour, should pronounce the modern Ossian to be the glory of Scotland;—[47]a Country that has produced

45. "An Historical and Critical Dissertation on the Supposed Authenticity of Ossian's Poems," *History of Scotland* (2 vols.; London, 1800), II, 376–453.

46. *De la Literature considerée dans ses Rapports avec les Institutions Sociales* (London, 1812), p. 254.

47. Notes to *Charlemagne* (trans. S. Butler and F. Hodgson [2 vols.; Philadelphia, 1815]) call Ossian a "fine genius, the glory of Scotland" (I, 277) and complain that "Christian poets have given themselves up too much to the recollection of the pagan hell . . . have represented Satan, like Pluto, encircled by his court" (I, 278).

a Dunbar, a Buchanan, a Thomson, and a Burns! These opinions are of ill omen for the Epic ambition of him who has given them to the world.

Yet, much as these pretended treasures of antiquity have been admired, they have been wholly uninfluential upon the literature of the Country. No succeeding Writer appears to have caught from them a ray of inspiration; no Author in the least distinguished, has ventured formally to imitate them—except the Boy, Chatterton, on their first appearance. He had perceived, from the successful trials which he himself had made in literary forgery, how few critics were able to distinguish between a real ancient medal and a counterfeit of modern manufacture; and he set himself to the work of filling a Magazine with *Saxon poems*,—counterparts of those of Ossian, as like his as one of his misty stars is to another. This incapability to amalgamate with the literature of the Island, is, in my estimation, a decisive proof that the book is essentially unnatural; nor should I require any other to demonstrate it to be a forgery, audacious as worthless.—Contrast, in this respect, the effect of Macpherson's publication with the Reliques of Percy, so unassuming, so modest in their pretensions!—I have already stated how much Germany is indebted to this latter work; and for our own Country, its Poetry has been absolutely redeemed by it. I do not think that there is an able Writer in verse of the present day who would not be proud to acknowledge his obligations to the Reliques; I know that it is so with my friends; and, for myself, I am happy in this occasion to make a public avowal of my own.

Dr. Johnson, more fortunate in his contempt of the labours of Macpherson than those of his modest friend, was solicited not long after to furnish Prefaces biographical and critical for some of the most eminent English Poets. The Booksellers took upon themselves to make the collection; they referred probably to the most popular miscellanies, and, unquestionably, to their Books of accounts; and decided upon the claim of Authors to be admitted into a body of the most Eminent, from the familiarity of their names with the readers of that day, and by the profits, which, from the sale of his works, each had brought and was bringing to the Trade. The Editor was allowed a limited exercise of discretion, and the Authors whom he recommended are scarcely to be mentioned without a smile. We open the volume of Prefatory Lives, and to our astonishment the *first* name we find is that of Cowley!—What is become of the Morning-star of English Poetry?[48] Where is the bright Elizabethan Constellation? Or, if Names are more acceptable than images, where is the ever-to-be-honoured Chaucer? where is Spenser? where Sydney? and lastly where he, whose rights as a Poet, contradistinguished from those which he is universally allowed to possess as a Dramatist, we have vindicated, where Shakespeare?—These, and a multitude of others not unworthy to be placed near them, their contemporaries and successors, we have *not*. But in their stead, we have (could better be expected when precedence was to be settled by an abstract of reputation at any given period made as in the case before us?) we have Roscommon, and Stepney, and Phillips, and Walsh, and Smith, and Duke, and King, and Spratt—Halifax, Granville, Sheffield, Congreve, Broome, and other reputed Magnates; Writers in metre utterly worthless and useless, except for occasions like the present, when their productions are referred to as evidence what a small quantity of brain is necessary to procure a considerable stock of admiration, provided the aspirant will accommodate himself to the likings and fashions of his day.

As I do not mean to bring down this retrospect to our own times, it may with propriety be closed at the era of this distinguished event. From the literature of other ages and countries, proofs equally cogent might have been adduced that the opinions announced in the former part of this Essay are founded upon truth. It was not an agreeable office, not a prudent undertaking, to declare them, but their importance seemed to render it a duty. It may still be asked, where lies the particular relation of what has been said to these Volumes?—The question will be easily answered by the discerning Reader who is old enough to remember the taste that was prevalent when some of these Poems were first published, 17 years ago; who has also observed to what degree the Poetry of this Island has since that period been coloured by them; and who is further aware of the

48. "Old Chaucer, like the morning star, / To us discovers day from far," John Denham, "On Mr. Abraham Cowley's Death," *Works of the English Poets* (London, 1790), IX, 210.

unremitting hostility with which, upon some principle or other, they have each and all been opposed. A sketch of my own notion of the constitution of Fame, has been given; and, as far as concerns myself, I have cause to be satisfied. The love, the admiration, the indifference, the slight, the aversion, and even the contempt, with which these Poems have been received, knowing, as I do, the source within my own mind, from which they have proceeded, and the labour and pains, which, when labour and pains appeared needful, have been bestowed upon them,—must all, if I think consistently, be received as pledges and tokens, bearing the same general impression though widely different in value;—they are all proofs that for the present time I have not laboured in vain; and afford assurances, more or less authentic, that the products of my industry will endure.

If there be one conclusion more forcibly pressed upon us than another by the review which has been given of the fortunes and fate of Poetical Works, it is this,—that every Author, as far as he is great and at the same time *original*, has had the task of *creating* the taste by which he is to be enjoyed: so has it been, so will it continue to be. This remark was long since made to me by the philosophical Friend for the separation of whose Poems from my own I have previously expressed my regret. The predecessors of an original Genius of a high order will have smoothed the way for all that he has in common with them;—and much he will have in common; but, for what is peculiarly his own, he will be called upon to clear and often to shape his own road:—he will be in the condition of Hannibal among the Alps.

And where lies the real difficulty of creating that taste by which a truly original Poet is to be relished? Is it in breaking the bonds of custom, in overcoming the prejudices of false refinement, and displacing the aversions of inexperience? Or, if he labour for an object which here and elsewhere I have proposed to myself, does it consist in divesting the Reader of the pride that induces him to dwell upon those points wherein Men differ from each other, to the exclusion of those in which all Men are alike, or the same; and in making him ashamed of the vanity that renders him insensible of the appropriate excellence which civil arrangements, less unjust than might appear, and Nature illimitable in her bounty, have conferred on Men who stand below him in the scale of society? Finally, does it lie in establishing that dominion over the spirits of Readers by which they are to be humbled and humanized, in order that they may be purified and exalted?

If these ends are to be attained by the mere communication of *knowledge*, it does *not* lie here.—TASTE, I would remind the Reader, like IMAGINATION, is a word which has been forced to extend its services far beyond the point to which philosophy would have confined them. It is a metaphor, taken from a *passive* sense of the human body, and transferred to things which are in their essence *not* passive,—to intellectual *acts* and *operations*. The word, imagination, has been overstrained, from impulses honourable to mankind, to meet the demands of the faculty which is perhaps the noblest of our nature. In the instance of taste, the process has been reversed; and from the prevalence of dispositions at once injurious and discreditable,—being no other than that selfishness which is the child of apathy,—which, as Nations decline in productive and creative power, makes them value themselves upon a presumed refinement of judging. Poverty of language is the primary cause of the use which we make of the word, imagination; but the word, Taste, has been stretched to the sense which it bears in modern Europe by habits of self-conceit, inducing that inversion in the order of things whereby a passive faculty is made paramount among the faculties conversant with the fine arts. Proportion and congruity, the requisite knowledge being supposed, are subjects upon which taste may be trusted; it is competent to this office;—for in its intercourse with these the mind is *passive*, and is affected painfully or pleasurably as by an instinct. But the profound and the exquisite in feeling, the lofty and universal in thought and imagination; or in ordinary language the pathetic and the sublime;—are neither of them, accurately speaking, objects of a faculty which could ever without a sinking in the spirit of Nations have been designated by the metaphor—*Taste*. And why? Because without the exertion of a co-operating *power* in the mind of the Reader, there can be no adequate sympathy with either of these emotions: without this auxiliar impulse elevated or profound passion cannot exist.

Passion, it must be observed, is derived from a word which signifies, *suffering*; but the connection which suffering has with effort, with exertion, and *action*, is immediate and inseparable. How strikingly is this property of human nature exhibited by the fact, that, in popular language, to be in a passion, is to be angry!—But,

> "Anger in hasty *words* or *blows*
> Itself discharges on its foes."[49]

To be moved, then, by a passion, is to be excited, often to external, and always to internal, effort; whether for the continuance and strengthening of the passion, or for its suppression, accordingly as the course which it takes may be painful or pleasurable. If the latter, the soul must contribute to its support, or it never becomes vivid,— and soon languishes, and dies. And this brings us to the point. If every great Poet with whose writings men are familiar, in the highest exercise of his genius, before he can be thoroughly enjoyed, has to call forth and to communicate *power*, this service, in a still greater degree, falls upon an original Writer, at his first appearance in the world.—Of genius the only proof is, the act of doing well what is worthy to be done, and what was never done before: Of genius, in the fine arts, the only infallible sign is the widening the sphere of human sensibility, for the delight, honor, and benefit of human nature. Genius is the introduction of a new element into the intellectual universe: or, if that be not allowed, it is the application of powers to objects on which they had not before been exercised, or the employment of them in such a manner as to produce effects hitherto unknown. What is all this but an advance, or a conquest, made by the soul of the Poet? Is it to be supposed that the Reader can make progress of this kind, like an Indian Prince or General— stretched on his Palanquin, and borne by his Slaves? No, he is invigorated and inspirited by his Leader, in order that he may exert himself, for he cannot proceed in quiescence, he cannot be carried like a dead weight. Therefore to create taste is to call forth and bestow power, of which knowledge is the effect; and *there* lies the true difficulty.

49. Edmund Waller, "Of Love," *Works of the English Poets*, XVI, 79.

As the pathetic participates of an *animal* sensation, it might seem—that, if the springs of this emotion were genuine, all men, possessed of competent knowledge of the facts and circumstances, would be instantaneously affected. And, doubtless, in the works of every true Poet will be found passages of that species of excellence, which is proved by effects immediate and universal. But there are emotions of the pathetic that are simple and direct, and others— that are complex and revolutionary; some—to which the heart yields with gentleness, others,—against which it struggles with pride: these varieties are infinite as the combinations of circumstance and the constitutions of character. Remember, also, that the medium through which, in poetry, the heart is to be affected—is language; a thing subject to endless fluctuations and arbitrary associations. The genius of the Poet melts these down for his purpose; but they retain their shape and quality to him who is not capable of exerting, within his own mind, a corresponding energy. There is also a meditative, as well as a human, pathos; an enthusiastic, as well as an ordinary, sorrow; a sadness that has its seat in the depths of reason, to which the mind cannot sink gently of itself—but to which it must descend by treading the steps of thought. And for the sublime, —if we consider what are the cares that occupy the passing day, and how remote is the practice and the course of life from the sources of sublimity, in the soul of Man, can it be wondered that there is little existing preparation for a Poet charged with a new mission to extend its kingdom, and to augment and spread its enjoyments?

Away, then, with the senseless iteration of the word, *popular*, applied to new works in Poetry, as if there were no test of excellence in this first of the fine arts but that all Men should run after its productions, as if urged by an appetite, or constrained by a spell!— The qualities of writing best fitted for eager reception are either such as startle the world into attention by their audacity and extravagance; or they are chiefly of a superficial kind, lying upon the surfaces of manners; or arising out of a selection and arrange-ment of incidents, by which the mind is kept upon the stretch of curiosity, and the fancy amused without the trouble of thought.

But in every thing which is to send the soul into herself, to be admonished of her weakness or to be made conscious of her power;— wherever life and nature are described as operated upon by the creative or abstracting virtue of the imagination; wherever the instinctive wisdom of antiquity and her heroic passions uniting, in the heart of the Poet, with the meditative wisdom of later ages, have produced that accord of sublimated humanity, which is at once a history of the remote past and a prophetic annunciation of the remotest future, *there*, the Poet must reconcile himself for a season to few and scattered hearers.—Grand thoughts, (and Shakespeare must often have sighed over this truth) as they are most naturally and most fitly conceived in solitude, so can they not be brought forth in the midst of plaudits without some violation of their sanctity. Go to a silent exhibition of the productions of the Sister Art, and be convinced that the qualities which dazzle at first sight, and kindle the admiration of the multitude, are essentially different from those by which permanent influence is secured. Let us not shrink from following up these principles as far as they will carry us, and conclude with observing—that there never has been a period, and perhaps never will be, in which vicious poetry, of some kind or other, has not excited more zealous admiration, and been far more generally read, than good; but this advantage attends the good, that the *individual*, as well as the species, survives from age to age: whereas, of the depraved, though the species be immortal the individual quickly *perishes*; the object of present admiration vanishes, being supplanted by some other as easily produced; which, though no better, brings with it at least the irritation of novelty,—with adaptation, more or less skilful, to the changing humours of the majority of those who are most at leisure to regard poetical works when they first solicit their attention.

Is it the result of the whole that, in the opinion of the Writer, the judgment of the People is not to be respected? The thought is most injurious; and could the charge be brought against him, he would repel it with indignation. The People have already been justified, and their eulogium pronounced by implication, when it was said, above—that, of *good* Poetry, the *individual*, as well as the species, *survives*. And how does it survive but through the People? what preserves it but their intellect and their wisdom?

> "—Past and future, are the wings
> On whose support, harmoniously conjoined,
> Moves the great Spirit of human knowledge—"
>
> *MS.*[50]

The voice that issues from this Spirit, is that Vox populi which the Deity inspires. Foolish must he be who can mistake for this a local acclamation, or a transitory outcry—transitory though it be for years, local though from a Nation. Still more lamentable is his error, who can believe that there is any thing of divine infallibility in the clamour of that small though loud portion of the community, ever governed by factitious influence, which, under the name of the PUBLIC, passes itself, upon the unthinking, for the PEOPLE. Towards the Public, the Writer hopes that he feels as much deference as it is intitled to: but to the People, philosophically characterized, and to the embodied spirit of their knowledge, so far as it exists and moves, at the present, faithfully supported by its two wings, the past and the future, his devout respect, his reverence, is due. He offers it willingly and readily; and, this done, takes leave of his Readers, by assuring them—that, if he were not persuaded that the Contents of these Volumes, and the Work to which they are subsidiary, evinced something of the "Vision and the Faculty divine";[51] and that, both in words and things, they will operate in their degree, to extend the domain of sensibility for the delight, the honor, and the benefit of human nature, notwithstanding the many happy hours which he has employed in their composition, and the manifold comforts and enjoyments they have procured to him, he would not, if a wish could do it, save them from immediate destruction;—from becoming at this moment, to the world, as a thing that had never been.

Poems (2 vols.; London, 1815), I, [341]–375.

50. *Prelude*, VI, 448–450.
51. *The Excursion*, I, 79 (*Poetical Works*, V, 10).

A Letter to a Friend of
Robert Burns (1816)

Wordsworth's pamphlet appeared in April, 1816, an open letter to James Gray, who had asked advice on behalf of Gilbert Burns about a new edition of his brother's works. The first edition (4 vols., Liverpool, 1800), edited by Dr. James Currie, had included a "Life" emphasizing that Burns had died a chronic alcoholic. Dr. Currie died in 1805, his copyright expired in 1814, and in 1815 his "Life of Burns" was reissued by Alexander Peterkin, an Edinburgh attorney with literary ambitions. Peterkin, trying to salvage Burns's character, prefaced the "Life" with ninety-eight pages of testimony gleaned from reviews, memoirs, and correspondence in rebuttal to Dr. Currie's charges. The "authorized" publishers asked Gilbert Burns to prepare a new edition of Currie's work to counter Peterkin's. They stipulated, however, that he do nothing to suggest that Dr. Currie had been inaccurate. Thus when his edition appeared in 1820, it did nothing to revise the popular image of his brother created by Dr. Currie, and Wordsworth's efforts on this score were pointless. But the pamphlet did offer him the chance to say a few public words about Francis Jeffrey. Jeffrey had reviewed Burns's poems in 1809, concluding with an invidious comparison between Wordsworth and Burns. This review had been reprinted by Peterkin and is quoted by Wordsworth in his own pamphlet. More recently, Jeffrey, reviewing Wordsworth's White Doe of Rylstone, *had said that the poem displayed the author as a drunkard or an imbecile.[1] The* Letter to a Friend of Robert Burns *offered the occasion to reply in Jeffrey's own manner after fourteen years of silent sufferance.*

I have carefully perused the Review of the Life of your friend Robert Burns[2] which you kindly transmitted to me; the author has rendered a substantial service to the poet's memory; and the

1. *Edinburgh Review*, XXV (October 1815), 355.
2. [A Review of the Life of Robert Burns, and of various criticisms on his character and writings, by Alexander Peterkin, 1814.—W.]

annexed letters are all important to the subject. After having expressed this opinion, I shall not trouble you by commenting upon the publication; but will confine myself to the request of Mr. Gilbert Burns, that I would furnish him with my notions upon the best mode of conducting the defence of his brother's injured reputation; a favourable opportunity being now afforded him to convey his sentiments to the world, along with a republication of Dr. Currie's book, which he is about to superintend. From the respect which I have long felt for the character of the person who has thus honoured me, and from the gratitude which, as a lover of poetry, I owe to the genius of his departed relative, I should most gladly comply with this wish; if I could hope that any suggestions of mine would be of service to the cause. But, really, I feel it a thing of much delicacy, to give advice upon this occasion, as it appears to me, mainly, not a question of opinion, or of taste, but a matter of conscience. Mr. Gilbert Burns must know, if any man living does, what his brother was; and no one will deny that he, who possesses this knowledge, is a man of unimpeachable veracity. He has already spoken to the world in contradiction of the injurious assertions that have been made, and has told why he forbore to do this on their first appearance. If it be deemed adviseable to reprint Dr. Currie's narrative, without striking out such passages as the author, if he were now alive, would probably be happy to efface, let there be notes attached to the most obnoxious of them, in which the misrepresentations may be corrected, and the exaggerations exposed. I recommend this course, if Dr. Currie's Life is to be republished, as it now stands, in connexion with the poems and letters, and especially if prefixed to them; but, in my judgment, it would be best to copy the example which Mason has given in his second edition of Gray's works. There, inverting the order which had been properly adopted, when the Life and Letters were new matter, the poems are placed first; and the rest takes it place as subsidiary to them. If this were done in the intended edition of Burns's works, I should strenuously recommend, that a concise life of the poet be prefixed, from the pen of Gilbert Burns, who has already given public proof how well qualified he is for the undertaking.[3] I know no better model as to

3. To Currie's edition, Gilbert Burns had contributed notes on his brother's early life (I, 130 n.–135 n.) and on his poems (III, Appendix A, pp. 1–16).

proportion, and the degree of detail required, nor, indeed, as to the general execution, than the life of Milton by Fenton, prefixed to many editions of the Paradise Lost. But a more copious narrative would be expected from a brother; and some allowance ought to be made, in this and other respects, for an expectation so natural.

In this prefatory memoir, when the author has prepared himself by reflecting, that fraternal partiality may have rendered him, in some points, not so trust-worthy as others less favoured by opportunity, it will be incumbent upon him to proceed candidly and openly, as far as such a procedure will tend to restore to his brother that portion of public estimation, of which he appears to have been unjustly deprived. Nay, when we recal to mind the black things which have been written of this great man, and the frightful ones that have been insinuated against him; and, as far as the public knew, till lately, without complaint, remonstrance, or disavowal, from his nearest relatives; I am not sure that it would not be best, at this day, explicitly to declare to what degree Robert Burns had given way to pernicious habits, and, as nearly as may be, to fix the point to which his moral character had been degraded. It is a disgraceful feature of the times that this measure should be necessary; most painful to think that a *brother* should have such an office to perform. But, if Gilbert Burns be conscious that the subject will bear to be so treated, he has no choice; the duty has been imposed upon him by the errors into which the former biographer has fallen, in respect to the very principles upon which his work ought to have been conducted.

I well remember the acute sorrow with which, by my own fireside, I first perused Dr. Currie's Narrative, and some of the letters, particularly of those composed in the latter part of the poet's life. If my pity for Burns was extreme, this pity did not preclude a strong indignation, of which he was not the object. If, said I, it were in the power of a biographer to relate the truth, the *whole* truth, and nothing *but* the truth, the friends and surviving kindred of the deceased, for the sake of general benefit to mankind, might endure that such heart-rending communication should be made to the world. But in no case is this possible; and, in the present, the opportunities of directly acquiring other than superficial knowledge have been most scanty; for the writer has barely seen the person who is the subject of his tale; nor did his avocations allow him to take the pains necessary for ascertaining what portion of the information conveyed to him was authentic. So much for facts and actions; and to what purpose relate them even were they true, if the narrative cannot be heard without extreme pain; unless they are placed in such a light, and brought forward in such order, that they shall explain their own laws, and leave the reader in as little uncertainty as the mysteries of our nature will allow, respecting the spirit from which they derived their existence, and which governed the agent? But hear on this pathetic and awful subject, the poet himself, pleading for those who have transgressed!

> "One point must still be greatly dark,
> The moving *why* they do it,
> And just as lamely can ye mark
> How far, perhaps, they rue it.

> Who made the heart, 'tis *he* alone
> Decidedly can try us;
> He knows each chord—its various tone,
> Each spring, its various bias.

> Then at the balance let's be mute,
> We never can adjust it;
> What's done we partly may compute,
> But know not what's *resisted*."[4]

How happened it that the recollection of this affecting passage did not check so amiable a man as Dr. Currie, while he was revealing to the world the infirmities of its author? He must have known enough of human nature to be assured that men would be eager to sit in judgment, and pronounce *decidedly* upon the guilt or innocence of Burns by his testimony; nay, that there were multitudes whose main interest in the allegations would be derived from the incitements which they found therein to undertake this presumptuous office. And where lies the collateral benefit, or what ultimate advantage can be expected, to counteract the injury that the many are thus tempted to do to their own minds; and to compensate the sorrow which must be fixed in the hearts of the considerate few, by

4. "Address to the Unco Guid," ll. 53–64.

language that proclaims so much, and provokes conjectures as unfavourable as imagination can furnish? Here, said I, being moved beyond what it would become me to express, here is a revolting account of a man of exquisite genius, and confessedly of many high moral qualities, sunk into the lowest depths of vice and misery! But the painful story, notwithstanding its minuteness, is incomplete,—in essentials it is deficient; so that the most attentive and sagacious reader cannot explain how a mind, so well established by knowledge, fell—and continued to fall, without power to prevent or retard its own ruin.

Would a bosom friend of the author, his counsellor and confessor, have told such things, if true, as this book contains? and who, but one possessed of the intimate knowledge which none but a bosom friend can acquire, could have been justified in making these avowals? Such a one, himself a pure spirit, having accompanied, as it were, upon wings, the pilgrim along the sorrowful road which he trod on foot; such a one, neither hurried down by its slippery descents, nor entangled among its thorns, nor perplexed by its windings, -nor discomfited by its founderous passages—for the instruction of others—might have delineated, almost as in a map, the way which the afflicted pilgrim had pursued till the sad close of his diversified journey. In this manner the venerable spirit of Isaac Walton was qualified to have retraced the unsteady course of a highly-gifted man, who, in this lamentable point, and in versatility of genius, bore no unobvious resemblance to the Scottish bard; I mean his friend COTTON—whom, notwithstanding all that the sage must have disapproved in his life, he honoured with the title of son.[5] Nothing like this, however, has the biographer of Burns accomplished; and, with his means of information, copious as in some respects they were, it would have been absurd to attempt it. The only motive, therefore, which could authorize the writing and publishing matter so distressing to read—is wanting!

Nor is Dr. Currie's performance censurable from these considera-

5. Cotton contributed a second part to Walton's *Compleat Angler* (1676), addressing it to "my most worthy Father and Friend." Warton's response, printed at the end of the second part, concludes: "Your most affectionate Father and Friend."

tions alone; for information, which would have been of absolute worth if in his capacity of biographer and editor he had known when to stop short, is rendered unsatisfactory and inefficacious through the absence of this reserve, and from being coupled with statements of improbable and irreconcileable facts. We have the author's letters discharged upon us in showers; but how few readers will take the trouble of comparing those letters with each other, and with the other documents of the publication, in order to come at a genuine knowledge of the writer's character!—The life of Johnson by Boswell had broken through many pre-existing delicacies, and afforded the British public an opportunity of acquiring experience, which before it had happily wanted; nevertheless, at the time when the ill-selected medley of Burns's correspondence first appeared, little progress had been made (nor is it likely that, by the mass of mankind, much ever will be made) in determining what portion of these confidential communications escapes the pen in courteous, yet often innocent, compliance—to gratify the several tastes of correspondents; and as little towards distinguishing opinions and sentiments uttered for the momentary amusement merely of the writer's own fancy, from those which his judgment deliberately approves, and his heart faithfully cherishes. But the subject of this book was a man of extraordinary genius; whose birth, education, and employments had placed and kept him in a situation far below that in which the writers and readers of expensive volumes are usually found. Critics upon works of fiction have laid it down as a rule that remoteness of place, in fixing the choice of a subject, and in prescribing the mode of treating it, is equal in effect to distance of time;—restraints may be thrown off accordingly. Judge then of the delusions which artificial distinctions impose, when to a man like Doctor Currie, writing with views so honourable, the *social condition* of the individual of whom he was treating, could seem to place him at such a distance from the exalted reader, that ceremony might be discarded with him, and his memory sacrificed, as it were, almost without compunction. The poet was laid where these injuries could not reach him; but he had a parent, I understand, an admirable woman, still surviving; a brother like Gilbert Burns!—a widow estimable for her virtues; and children, at that time infants, with the world before them, which they must face to obtain a maintenance; who remembered their father probably with the tenderest affection; —and whose opening minds, as their years advanced, would become conscious of so many reasons for admiring him.—Ill-fated child of nature, too frequently thine own enemy,—unhappy favourite of genius, too often misguided,—this is indeed to be "crushed beneath the furrow's weight!"[6]

Why, sir, do I write to you at this length, when all that I had to express in direct answer to the request, which occasioned this letter, lay in such narrow compass?—Because having entered upon the subject, I am unable to quit it!—Your feelings, I trust, go along with mine; and, rising from this individual case to a general view of the subject, you will probably agree with me in opinion that biography, though differing in some essentials from works of fiction, is nevertheless, like them, an *art*,—an art, the laws of which are determined by the imperfections of our nature, and the constitution of society. Truth is not here, as in the sciences, and in natural philosophy, to be sought without scruple, and promulgated for its own sake, upon the mere chance of its being serviceable; but only for obviously justifying purposes, moral or intellectual.

Silence is a privilege of the grave, a right of the departed: let him, therefore, who infringes that right, by speaking publicly of, for, or against, those who cannot speak for themselves, take heed that he opens not his mouth without a sufficient sanction. De mortuis nil nisi bonum, is a rule in which these sentiments have been pushed to an extreme that proves how deeply humanity is interested in maintaining them. And it was wise to announce the precept thus absolutely; both because there exist in that same nature, by which it has been dictated, so many temptations to disregard it,— and because there are powers and influences, within and without us, that will prevent its being literally fulfilled—to the suppression of profitable truth. Penalties of law, conventions of manners, and personal fear, protect the reputation of the living; and something of this protection is extended to the recently dead,—who survive, to a certain degree, in their kindred and friends. Few are so insensible as not to feel this, and not to be actuated by the feeling. But only

6. "To a Mountain Daisy," l. 53.

to philosophy enlightened by the affections does it belong justly to estimate the claims of the deceased on the one hand, and of the present age and future generations, on the other; and to strike a balance between them.—Such a philosophy runs a risk of becoming extinct among us, if the coarse intrusions into the recesses, the gross breaches upon the sanctities, of domestic life, to which we have lately been more and more accustomed, are to be regarded as indications of a vigorous state of public feeling—favourable to the maintenance of the liberties of our country.—Intelligent lovers of freedom are from necessity bold and hardy lovers of truth; but, according to the measure in which their love is intelligent, is it attended with a finer discrimination, and a more sensitive delicacy. The wise and good (and all others being lovers of licence rather than of liberty are in fact slaves) respect, as one of the noblest characteristics of Englishmen, that jealousy of familiar approach, which, while it contributes to the maintenance of private dignity, is one of the most efficacious guardians of rational public freedom.

The general obligation upon which I have insisted, is especially binding upon those who undertake the biography of *authors*. Assuredly, there is no cause why the lives of that class of men should be pried into with the same diligent curiosity, and laid open with the same disregard of reserve, which may sometimes be expedient in composing the history of men who have borne an active part in the world. Such thorough knowledge of the good and bad qualities of these latter, as can only be obtained by a scrutiny of their private lives, conduces to explain not only their own public conduct, but that of those with whom they have acted. Nothing of this applies to authors, considered merely as authors. Our business is with their books,—to understand and to enjoy them. And, of poets more especially, it is true—that, if their works be good, they contain within themselves all that is necessary to their being comprehended and relished. It should seem that the ancients thought in this manner; for of the eminent Greek and Roman poets, few and scanty memorials were, I believe, ever prepared; and fewer still are preserved. It is delightful to read what, in the happy exercise of his own genius, Horace chooses to communicate of himself and his friends; but I confess I am not so much a lover of knowledge, independent of its quality, as to make it likely that it would much rejoice me, were I to hear that records of the Sabine poet and his contemporaries, composed upon the Boswellian plan, had been unearthed among the ruins of Herculaneum. You will interpret what I am writing, *liberally*. With respect to the light which such a discovery might throw upon Roman manners, there would be reasons to desire it: but I should dread to disfigure the beautiful ideal of the memories of those illustrious persons with incongruous features, and to sully the imaginative purity of their classical works with gross and trivial recollections. The least weighty objection to heterogeneous details, is that they are mainly superfluous, and therefore an incumbrance.

But you will perhaps accuse me of refining too much; and it is, I own, comparatively of little importance, while we are engaged in reading the Iliad, the Eneid, the tragedies of Othello and King Lear, whether the authors of these poems were good or bad men; whether they lived happily or miserably. Should a thought of the kind cross our minds, there would be no doubt, if irresistible external evidence did not decide the question unfavourably, that men of such transcendant genius were both good and happy: and if, unfortunately, it had been on record that they were otherwise, sympathy with the fate of their fictitious personages would banish the unwelcome truth whenever it obtruded itself, so that it would but slightly disturb our pleasure. Far otherwise is it with that class of poets, the principal charm of whose writings depends upon the familiar knowledge which they convey of the personal feelings of their authors. This is eminently the case with the effusions of Burns; —in the small quantity of narrative that he has given, he himself bears no inconsiderable part; and he has produced no drama. Neither the subjects of his poems, nor his manner of handling them, allow us long to forget their author. On the basis of his human character he has reared a poetic one, which with more or less distinctness presents itself to view in almost every part of his earlier, and, in my estimation, his most valuable verses. This poetic fabric, dug out of the quarry of genuine humanity, is airy and spiritual:— and though the materials, in some parts, are coarse, and the disposition is often fantastic and irregular, yet the whole is agreeable and strikingly attractive. Plague, then, upon your remorseless hunters after matter of fact (who, after all, rank among the blindest of human beings) when they would convince you that the foundations of this admirable edifice are hollow; and that its frame is unsound! Granting that all which has been raked up to the prejudice of Burns were literally true; and that it added, which it does not, to our better understanding of human nature and human life (for that genius is not incompatible with vice, and that vice leads to misery—the more acute from the sensibilities which are the elements of genius—we needed not those communications to inform us) how poor would have been the compensation for the deduction made, by this extrinsic knowledge, from the intrinsic efficacy of his poetry—to please, and to instruct!

In illustration of this sentiment, permit me to remind you that it is the privilege of poetic genius to catch, under certain restrictions of which perhaps at the time of its being exerted it is but dimly conscious, a spirit of pleasure wherever it can be found,—in the walks of nature, and in the business of men.—The poet, trusting to primary instincts, luxuriates among the felicities of love and wine, and is enraptured while he describes the fairer aspects of war: nor does he shrink from the company of the passion of love though immoderate—from convivial pleasure though intemperate—nor from the presence of war though savage, and recognized as the hand-maid of desolation. Frequently and admirably has Burns given way to these impulses of nature; both with reference to himself and in describing the condition of others. Who, but some impenetrable dunce or narrow-minded puritan in works of art, ever read without delight the picture which he has drawn of the convivial exaltation of the rustic adventurer, Tam o'Shanter? The poet fears not to tell the reader in the outset that his hero was a desperate and sottish drunkard, whose excesses were frequent as his opportunities. This reprobate sits down to his cups, while the storm is roaring, and heaven and earth are in confusion;—the night is driven on by song and tumultuous noise—laughter and jest thicken as the beverage improves upon the palate—conjugal fidelity archly bends to the service of general benevolence—selfishness is not absent, but wearing the mask of social cordiality—and, while these various elements of humanity are blended into one proud and happy composition of elated spirits, the anger of the tempest without doors only heightens and sets off the enjoyment within.—I pity him who cannot perceive that, in all this, though there was no moral purpose, there is a moral effect.

> "Kings may be blest, but Tam was glorious,
> O'er a' the *ills* of life victorious."[7]

What a lesson do these words convey of charitable indulgence for the vicious habits of the principal actor in this scene, and of those who resemble him!—Men who to the rigidly virtuous are objects almost of loathing, and whom therefore they cannot serve! The poet, penetrating the unsightly and disgusting surfaces of things, has unveiled with exquisite skill the finer ties of imagination and feeling, that often bind these beings to practices productive of so much unhappiness to themselves, and to those whom it is their duty to cherish;—and, as far as he puts the reader into possession of this intelligent sympathy, he qualifies him for exercising a salutary influence over the minds of those who are thus deplorably enslaved.

Not less successfully does Burns avail himself of his own character and situation in society, to construct out of them a poetic self,—introduced as a dramatic personage—for the purpose of inspiriting his incidents, diversifying his pictures, recommending his opinions, and giving point to his sentiments. His brother can set me right if I am mistaken when I express a belief that, at the time when he wrote his story of "Death and Dr. Hornbook," he had very rarely been intoxicated, or perhaps even much exhilarated by liquor. Yet how happily does he lead his reader into that track of sensations! and with what lively humour does he describe the disorder of his senses and the confusion of his understanding, put to test by a deliberate attempt to count the horns of the moon!

> "But whether she had three or four
> He could na' tell."[8]

Behold a sudden apparition that disperses this disorder, and in a moment chills him into possession of himself! Coming upon no more

7. "Tam o'Shanter," ll. 57–58.
8. "Death and Dr. Hornbook," ll. 23–24.

important mission than the grisly phantom was charged with, what mode of introduction could have been more efficient or appropriate?

But, in those early poems, through the veil of assumed habits and pretended qualities, enough of the real man appears to shew that he was conscious of sufficient cause to dread his own passions, and to bewail his errors! We have rejected as false sometimes in the letter, and of necessity as false in the spirit, many of the testimonies that others have borne against him:—but, by his own hand—in words the import of which cannot be mistaken—it has been recorded that the order of his life but faintly corresponded with the clearness of his views. It is probable that he would have proved a still greater poet if, by strength of reason, he could have controlled the propensities which his sensibility engendered; but he would have been a poet of a different class: and certain it is, had that desirable restraint been early established, many peculiar beauties which enrich his verses could never have existed, and many accessary influences, which contribute greatly to their effect, would have been wanting. For instance, the momentous truth of the passage already quoted, "One point must still be greatly dark," &c.[9] could not possibly have been conveyed with such pathetic force by any poet that ever lived, speaking in his own voice; unless it were felt that, like Burns, he was a man who preached from the text of his own errors; and whose wisdom, beautiful as a flower that might have risen from seed sown from above, was in fact a scion from the root of personal suffering. Whom did the poet intend should be thought of as occupying that grave over which, after modestly setting forth the moral discernment and warm affections of its "poor inhabitant," it is supposed to be inscribed that

> "—Thoughtless follies laid him low,
> "And stained his name."[10]

Who but himself,—himself anticipating the too probable termination of his own course? Here is a sincere and solemn avowal—a public declaration *from his own will*—a confession at once devout, poetical, and human—a history in the shape of a prophecy! What

9. See above, p. 191.
10. "A Bard's Epitaph," ll. 23–24.

more was required of the biographer than to have put his seal to the writing, testifying that the foreboding had been realized, and that the record was authentic?—Lastingly is it to be regretted in respect to this memorable being, that inconsiderate intrusion has not left us at liberty to enjoy his mirth, or his love; his wisdom or his wit; without an admixture of useless, irksome, and painful details, that take from his poems so much of that right—which, with all his carelessness, and frequent breaches of self-respect, he was not negligent to maintain for them—the right of imparting solid instruction through the medium of unalloyed pleasure.

You will have noticed that my observations have hitherto been confined to Dr. Currie's book: if, by fraternal piety, the poison can be sucked out of this wound, those inflicted by meaner hands may be safely left to heal of themselves. Of the other writers who have given their names,[11] only one lays claim to even a slight acquaintance with the author, whose moral character they take upon them publicly to anatomize. The Edinburgh reviewer—and him I single out because the author of the vindication of Burns has treated his offences with comparative indulgence, to which he has no claim, and which, from whatever cause it might arise, has interfered with the dispensation of justice—the Edinburgh reviewer thus writes:[12] "The *leading vice* in Burns's character, and the *cardinal deformity*, indeed, of ALL his productions, was his contempt, or affectation of contempt, for prudence, decency, and regularity, and his admiration of thoughtlessness, oddity, and vehement sensibility: his belief, in short, in the dispensing power of genius and social feeling in all matters of morality and common sense," adding, that these vices and erroneous notions "have communicated to a great part of his productions a character of immorality at once contemptible and hateful." We are afterwards told, that he is *perpetually* making a parade of his thoughtlessness, inflammability, and imprudence; and,

11. I.e., to the prefatory matter in Peterkin's book. James Gray was the writer among them who knew Burns intimately.

12. [From Mr. Peterkin's pamphlet, who vouches for the accuracy of his citations; omitting, however, to apologize for their length.—W.] Peterkin reprints from the *Edinburgh Review*, XVIII (1809), 249–276; statements quoted by Wordsworth are from pp. 253–254.

in the next paragraph, that he is *perpetually* doing something else; i.e. "boasting of his own independence."—Marvellous address in the commission of faults! not less than Caesar shewed in the management of business; who, it is said, could dictate to three secretaries upon three several affairs, at one and the same moment! But, to be serious. When a man, self-elected into the office of a public judge of the literature and life of his contemporaries, can have the audacity to go these lengths in framing a summary of the contents of volumes that are scattered over every quarter of the globe, and extant in almost every cottage of Scotland, to give the lie to his labours; we must not wonder if, in the plenitude of his concern for the interests of abstract morality, the infatuated slanderer should have found no obstacle to prevent him from insinuating that the poet, whose writings are to this degree stained and disfigured, was "one of the sons of fancy and of song, who spend in vain superfluities the money that belongs of right to the pale industrious tradesman and his famishing infants; and who rave about friendship and philosophy in a tavern, while their wives' hearts." &c. &c.

It is notorious that this persevering Aristarch;[13] as often as a work of original genius comes before him, avails himself of that opportunity to re-proclaim to the world the narrow range of his own comprehension. The happy self-complacency, the unsuspecting vain-glory, and the cordial *bonhommie*, with which this part of his duty is performed, do not leave him free to complain of being hardly dealt with if any one should declare the truth, by pronouncing much of the foregoing attack upon the intellectual and moral character of Burns, to be the trespass (for reasons that will shortly appear, it cannot be called the venial trespass) of a mind obtuse, superficial, and inept. What portion of malignity such a mind is susceptible of, the judicious admirers of the poet, and the discerning friends of the man, will not trouble themselves to enquire; but they will wish that

13. [A friend, who chances to be present while the author is correcting the proof sheets, observes that Aristarchus is libelled by this application of his name, and advises that "Zoilus" should be substituted. The question lies between spite and presumption; and it is not easy to decide upon a case where the claims of each party are so strong: but the name of Aristarch, who, simple man! would allow no verse to pass for Homer's which he did not approve of, is retained, for reasons that will be deemed cogent.—W.]

this evil principle had possessed more sway than they are at liberty to assign to it; the offender's condition would not then have been so hopeless. For malignity *selects* its diet; but where is to be found the nourishment from which vanity will revolt? Malignity may be appeased by triumphs real or supposed, and will then sleep, or yield its place to a repentance producing dispositions of good will, and desires to make amends for past injury; but vanity is restless, reckless, intractable, unappeasable, insatiable. Fortunate is it for the world when this spirit incites only to actions that meet with an adequate punishment in derision; such, as in a scheme of poetical justice, would be aptly requited by assigning to the agents, when they quit this lower world, a station in that not uncomfortable limbo—the Paradise of Fools! But, assuredly, we shall have here another proof that ridicule is not the test of truth, if it prevent us from perceiving, that *depravity* has no ally more active, more inveterate, nor, from the difficulty of divining to what kind and degree of extravagance it may prompt, more pernicious than self-conceit. Where this alliance is too obvious to be disputed, the culprit ought not to be allowed the benefit of contempt—as a shelter from detestation; much less should he be permitted to plead, in excuse for his transgressions, that especial malevolence had little or no part in them. It is not recorded, that the ancient, who set fire to the temple of Diana, had a particular dislike to the goddess of chastity, or held idolatry in abhorrence: he was a fool, an egregious fool, but not the less, on that account, a most odious monster. The tyrant who is described as having rattled his chariot along a bridge of brass over the heads of his subjects, was, no doubt, inwardly laughed at; but what if this mock Jupiter, not satisfied with an empty noise of his own making, had amused himself with throwing fire-brands upon the housetops, as a substitute for lightning; and, from his elevation, had hurled stones upon the heads of his people, to shew that he was a master of the destructive bolt, as well as of the harmless voice of the thunder!—The lovers of all that is honourable to humanity have recently had occasion to rejoice over the downfal of an intoxicated despot,[14] whose vagaries furnish more solid materials by which the philosopher will exemplify how strict is the

14. Napoleon.

connection between the ludicrously, and the terribly fantastic. We know, also, that Robespierre was one of the vainest men that the most vain country upon earth has produced;—and from this passion, and from that cowardice which naturally connects itself with it, flowed the horrors of his administration. It is a descent, which I fear you will scarcely pardon, to compare these redoubtable enemies of mankind with the anonymous conductor of a perishable publication. But the moving spirit is the same in them all; and, as far as difference of circumstances, and disparity of powers, will allow, manifests itself in the same way; by professions of reverence for truth, and concern for duty—carried to the giddiest heights of ostentation, while practice seems to have no other reliance than on the omnipotence of falshood.

The transition from a vindication of Robert Burns to these hints for a picture of the intellectual deformity of one who has grossly outraged his memory, is too natural to require an apology: but I feel, sir, that I stand in need of indulgence for having detained you so long. Let me beg that you would impart to any judicious friends of the poet as much of the contents of these pages as you think will be serviceable to the cause; but do not give publicity to any *portion* of them, unless it be thought probable that an open circulation of the whole may be useful.[15] The subject is delicate, and some of the opinions are of a kind, which, if torn away from the trunk that supports them, will be apt to wither, and, in that state, to contract poisonous qualities; like the branches of the yew, which, while united by a living spirit to their native tree, are neither noxious, nor without beauty; but, being dissevered and cast upon the ground, become deadly to the cattle that incautiously feed upon them.

To Mr. Gilbert Burns, especially, let my sentiments be conveyed, with my sincere respects, and best wishes for the success of his praiseworthy enterprize. And if, through modest apprehension, he should doubt of his own ability to do justice to his brother's memory, let him take encouragement from the assurance that the most odious part of the charges owed its credit to the silence of those who were deemed best entitled to speak; and who, it was thought, would not

15. [It was deemed that it would be so, and the letter is published accordingly. —W.]

have been mute, had they believed that they could speak beneficially. Moreover, it may be relied on as a general truth, which will not escape his recollection, that tasks of this kind are not so arduous as, to those who are tenderly concerned in their issue, they may at first appear to be; for, if the many be hasty to condemn, there is a re-action of generosity which stimulates them—when forcibly summoned—to redress the wrong; and, for the sensible part of mankind, *they* are neither dull to understand, nor slow to make allowance for, the aberrations of men, whose intellectual powers do honour to their species.

A Letter to a Friend of Robert Burns (London, 1816).

Selected Books about Wordsworth's Literary Criticism

ABRAMS, M. H. *The Mirror and the Lamp*. New York: Oxford University Press, 1953.

BATE, W. J. *From Classic to Romantic: Premises of Taste in Eighteenth Century England*. Cambridge: Harvard University Press, 1946.

BEATTY, ARTHUR. *William Wordsworth: His Doctrine and Art in Their Historical Relations*. Rev. ed. Madison: University of Wisconsin Press, 1960.

BERNBAUM, E., AND LOGAN, J. V. "Wordsworth" in *English Romantic Poets: A Review of Research*. Ed. T. M. Raysor. Rev. ed. New York: Modern Language Association, 1956.

ELLEDGE, SCOTT (ed.). *Eighteenth Century Critical Essays*. 2 vols. Ithaca: Cornell University Press, 1961.

FAIRCHILD, H. N. *Religious Trends in English Poetry*. 5 vols. New York: Columbia University Press, 1939–1962. Vol. III.

FRYE, NORTHROP (ed.). *Romanticism Reconsidered*. New York: Columbia University Press, 1963.

HAVENS, R. D. *The Mind of a Poet*. Baltimore: Johns Hopkins University Press, 1941.

LOGAN, J. V. *Wordsworthian Criticism, a Guide and Bibliography*. Columbus: Ohio State University Press, 1947. Continued by David Stamm and E. F. Henley (New York: New York Public Library, 1960).

MEYER, G. W. *Wordsworth's Formative Years*. Ann Arbor: University of Michigan Press, 1943.

NOYES, RUSSELL. *Wordsworth and Jeffrey in Controversy*. Bloomington: University of Indiana Press, 1941.

OWEN, W. J. B. *Wordsworth's Preface to the Lyrical Ballads. Anglistica IX*. Copenhagen: Rosenkilde and Bagger, 1957.

PEACOCK, M. L. *The Critical Opinions of William Wordsworth*. Baltimore: Johns Hopkins University Press, 1950.

SMITH, ELSIE. *Estimate of William Wordsworth*. Oxford: Blackwell, 1932.

WELLEK, RENÉ. *A History of Modern Criticism, 1750–1950: "The Romantic Age"*. New Haven: Yale University Press, 1955.

Acknowledgments

The Penrose Fund of the American Philosophical Society aided the preparation of this edition. Of immeasurable assistance were Dr. Lucyle Werkmeister, Elisabeth Zall, and Anne Hyder of the Huntington Library.

PAUL M. ZALL

Index